JACKIE'S FAMILY FOOD FAVORITES

by Jackie Olden

THE KNAPP PRESS
LOS ANGELES

Library of Congress Cataloging-in-Publication Data

Olden, Jackie, 1934-
Jackie's Family Food Favorites.

1. Cookery. I. Title.
TX715.0447 1987 641.5 87-4008
ISBN 0-89535-191-9

table of contents

appetizers

HOLIDAY SAUSAGE DIP FOR A GANG

2 pounds hot bulk sausage
2 pounds processed American cheese
1 (16-ounce) can evaporated milk
Tabasco to taste
1 package dry garlic salad dressing mix
1 jar pimientos, minced
Fresh tortilla chips

In a skillet crumble and cook sausage until well-done. Drain grease. In a double boiler or a microwave melt cheese. Add evaporated milk. Stir in sausage, seasonings and pimientos. Heat thoroughly. Serve in a chafing dish with tortilla chips.

Serves 15 to 20

EASY WESTERN DIP

½ pound pork, ground
½ pound beef, ground
1 teaspoon salt
¼ teaspoon pepper
4 medium tomatoes, peeled and diced
3 cloves garlic, minced
3 green onions, chopped
1 (6-ounce) can tomato paste
2 jalapeno peppers, rinsed, seeded and diced
Dash of oregano
¾ cup pimiento, chopped
¾ cup seedless raisins
¾ cup whole blanched almonds

In a saucepan, crumble and brown beef and pork. Add salt and pepper and enough water to cover meat. Bring to a boil, reduce heat and simmer 30 minutes. Drain and add remaining ingredients. Bring to a boil and simmer for 45 minutes or until mixture is very thick. Serve hot with tortilla chips.

Serves a big bunch and is very different for that favorite Mexican-flavored appetizer.

Makes 6 cups

POT LUCK DIP FOR THE FAMILY

1 loaf French bread (round loaf)
1 loaf French bread (rectangular loaf) cut into pieces for dipping
1 cup mayonnaise
1 cup sour cream
1 package Knorr's leek soup
2 green onions, chopped
½ can water chestnuts, diced (or use jicama)

Cut top from round loaf. Scoop out bread, leaving ½-inch inside. Combine remaining ingredients, except bread in a bowl. Cover and chill. When ready to serve, put dip mixture inside the round loaf in the center of a tray. Serve with pieces of cut-up French bread around the loaf. As the dip is eaten, crust may be broken off and eaten also. Marvelous!

Serves 6 to 8

CURRY DIP

1 cup mayonnaise
1 teaspoon onion, grated
1 teaspoon horseradish
1 teaspoon tarragon vinegar
¼ teaspoon curry powder

Combine all ingredients. Blend well. Chill. Serve with crisp caulifloweretś, broccoli or celery.

Makes 1 cup

BRIE EN CROUTE

3 small rounds Brie cheese
1 package frozen patty shells
1 egg yolk, beaten

Roll out 2 patty shells for each Brie. Place Brie on top of one round of pastry and fold up sides. Cut circle in second pastry round with empty Brie container. Place this round on top of the Brie. Now cut 2 strips of pastry 3x⅓-inches. Use this to wrap around the top edges and crimp to join crust at fold up sides. Brush with egg yolk. Cheese can be frozen at this point. Bake at 450 degrees for 10 minutes, then reduce heat to 350 degrees and bake 20 minutes more or until crust is lightly browned. Cut into wedges and serve with crackers or fruit.

A super make ahead appetizer and so easy.

Serves 6 to 8

BRIE ALMONDINE

4 to 8-ounces Brie
1 tablespoon butter
⅓ to ½ cup slivered almonds

Select the dish in which to bake and serve. Trim off top crust of Brie and cut cheese to fit dish in a single layer. If you need to piece it, trim crust off sides of cheese as well. Otherwise, when the Brie is heated, the crust remains firm and the cheese will be lumpy and difficult to serve. Saute the almonds in butter until lightly browned. Drain and sprinkle on top of the cheese. (Can make ahead to this point.) Bake at 350 degrees for about 10 minutes. Serve with crackers or small toasted slices of French bread.

Serves 6 to 8

MIKE ROY'S CHEESE FONDUE

1 pound Swiss cheese, diced
1 cup dry white wine
1½ tablespoons potato flour
Nutmeg, freshly grated
Salt and pepper (freshly ground)
2 tablespoons Kirsch
1 loaf French bread, cubed; crackers or toast

Rub the inside of an earthenware casserole or chafing dish with a clove of garlic. Place the casserole in bottom pan of the chafing dish, adding just enough water to cover the bottom of the pan in order to protect it. Pour wine in the casserole or chafing dish and heat. When the wine is heated, add the cheese which has been dredged in the potato flour (this is the secret). Bring to a slow simmer, stirring with a French wire whisk until the cheese is melted and well-blended with the wine. Season with freshly grated nutmeg, salt and freshly ground pepper to taste. When ready to serve, add kirsch. Serve with toast, crackers or French bread to be dipped into the fondue.

Serve 6 to 8

CHICKEN LIVER AND MUSHROOM PATE

¼ pound butter
1 pound chicken livers
1 medium onion, chopped
3 shallots, chopped
½ teaspoon thyme
½ teaspoon rosemary
1 bay leaf
12 large fresh mushrooms, chopped
¼ cup brandy
½ teaspoon salt
⅛ teaspoon pepper

In a large skillet melt the butter. Add chicken livers, onions and shallots. Stir over medium heat about 10 minutes. Add spices and mushrooms. Stir frequently while cooking for 5 minutes. Discard bay leaf and pour mixture into blender. Pour in brandy, salt and pepper. Blend 2 minutes, then pour into a 2-cup souffle dish. Chill. Garnish with parsley. Serve with melba toast rounds.

Makes 1 pint

NOTE: Dish may be covered with plastic wrap and kept in the refrigerator for 1 week.

DOWN HOME PATE

1 pound chicken livers or calves liver
1 tablespoon chicken fat or cooking oil
1 small onion, chopped
2 hard-cooked eggs, chopped
Salt and pepper
1 tablespoon sherry or brandy

Bake liver until nearly done (20 minutes at 325 degrees). Put liver pieces through a meat grinder twice or use a blender to make a paste. Saute onion in fat or oil until lightly browned. Stir in liver along with remaining ingredients. Press liver mixture into a buttered rectangular dish or mold and refrigerate. When chilled, turn out on a plate and serve with parsley or watercress garnish.

Serves 6

MAGIC MEATBALLS

1 pound lean ground beef
2 cups white bread, torn into small pieces
1 package dry onion soup mix
1 egg, lightly beaten
1 tablespoon parsley flakes

Mix all ingredients for meatballs well. Shape into 1-inch balls and arrange in a baking dish.

SAUCE

1 cup catsup
⅓ cup lemon juice
⅓ cup grape jelly

Blend ingredients for sauce and pour over meatballs. Bake at 350 degrees for 45 minutes. If necessary, spoon off any excess fat. Transfer to a chafing dish.

This is so easy and good and everyone needs one meatball recipe.

Serves 10 to 12

MEATBALLS WITH GRAPE JELLY

1 pound of ground meat made into your own recipe, cooked
1 (10-ounce) jar grape jelly
1 bottle chili sauce (Heinz, Del Monte whatever)

Heat the jelly and chili sauce till thoroughly mixed. Drop meatballs into the mixture and simmer till done.

Serves 6 to 8

STEAK TARTARE

1 pound fat-free raw tenderloin steak, chopped
1 egg yolk
1 teaspoon capers
1 teaspoon Dijon mustard
½ teaspoon coarse ground pepper
2 tablespoons onion or scallion, chopped
1 teaspoon Worcestershire sauce
Salt to taste

On a chilled plate, form a wide patty of meat. Make a depression in the top and drop in egg yolk. Sprinkle remaining ingredients over top except the salt. Mix together with a spoon and fork. Taste, season with salt if necessary. Serve chilled with parsley or watercress garnish and with thin-sliced black bread.

NOTE: Seasonings may vary to taste. A dash of Tabasco is popular, as is a tablespoon of burgundy wine.

Serves 4

HOLIDAY HAM PUFFS

1 (8-ounce) package cream cheese, softened
1 egg yolk
1 teaspoon baking powder
Dash salt
10 to 15 slices thin bread (I adore rye)
Mayonnaise
1 (4½ ounce) can deviled ham
Paprika

Combine cream cheese with egg yolk, baking powder, salt and deviled ham. Mix until well-blended. Spread each slice of bread with mayonnaise and then a generous amount of ham mixture. Sprinkle with paprika. Cut each bread slice into 4 triangles. This much can be done ahead and appetizers frozen. To serve, place in a 375 degree oven for 12 to 15 minutes or until puffed and brown.

The only trouble with this appetizer is that the fellows eat them like peanuts.

Serves 12

EASY ONION PIZZAS

1 (13¾ ounce) package hot roll mix
1 cup mayonnaise
4 cups Cheddar cheese, shredded
½ cup green onions or chives, minced
¼ cup green stuffed olives, chopped
1 tablespoon capers
2 tablespoons Parmesan cheese, grated

Prepare hot roll mix as directed on package adding chives or onion. Cover and let rise in warm place until doubled in bulk 30 to 45 minutes. Roll out or pat into a greased 14-inch pan. Combine mayonnaise, cheese, onions, olives and capers. Spread mayonnaise mixture over dough in pan to within 1-inch of the edge. Sprinkle top with Parmesan cheese. Bake at 375 degrees for 30 to 40 minutes or until bubbly and golden brown.

Makes 36 appetizers
Serves 6 as main course

SAUERKRAUT LOAF

1 (29-ounce) can sauerkraut
2 cups sharp Cheddar cheese, grated
2 tablespoons onion, chopped
2 tablespoons pimiento, chopped
3 tablespoons green pepper, chopped
1 hard-cooked egg, chopped
¼ cup mayonnaise
½ teaspoon salt
½ cup bread crumbs
1 tablespoon sugar
1 (8-ounce) package cream cheese, softened
Stuffed green olives and pimiento, sliced

Drain sauerkraut and squeeze as dry as possible. Mix all ingredients except cream cheese and shape into a loaf. Chill overnight. Spread loaf with cream cheese. Garnish with olives and pimiento. Serve with your favorite rye bread wedges or party crackers.

Serves 6 to 8

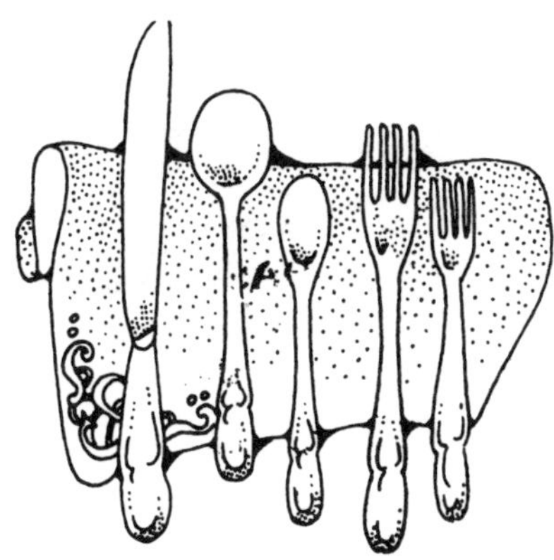

MUSHROOMS STUFFED WITH SMOKED OYSTERS

1 tin smoked oysters
24 large mushroom caps
¼ cup butter
¼ cup sherry
Salt and pepper
¼ cup chives, chopped
2 (3-ounce) packages cream cheese
¼ pound salted cashew nuts, chopped

Saute mushrooms in butter until just cooked and heated through. Add sherry and cook another 3 minutes. Remove mushrooms from pan and saute chives and cashews for a minute; blend into cream cheese. Fill the mushroom caps with the cheese mixture. Top with smoked oysters. Serve warm with salt and pepper to taste.

Makes 24 appetizers

EARLY CALIFORNIA SPREAD

½ pound ground beef
¼ cup onions, chopped
¼ cup catsup
Few drops Tabasco sauce (my family uses several)
1½ teaspoons chili powder
½ teaspoon salt
1 (8-ounce) can kidney beans, undrained
½ cup sharp Cheddar cheese, shredded
½ cup onion, chopped
¼ cup stuffed green olives, chopped

Brown beef and ¼ cup onion in a skillet. Stir in catsup, Tabasco, chili powder and salt. Add beans with liquid and mash to mix thoroughly with other ingredients. Heat and garnish with shredded cheese, ½ cup onion and olives. Serve with corn chips.

Makes 3 cups

SWISS SPINACH BALLS

2 (10-ounce) packages frozen chopped spinach, thawed
2 cups seasoned bread crumbs
4 eggs
¾ cup butter or margarine, melted
1 onion, finely chopped
½ cup Swiss cheese, grated
¼ cup Parmesan cheese, grated
2 cloves garlic, minced

Squeeze spinach dry of liquid. Combine remaining ingredients and refrigerate overnight. Roll into 1-inch balls. Place on a lightly greased baking sheet and bake in a preheated oven 350 degrees for 15 minutes.

For parties you can make these balls ahead of time and just wrap them and freeze them. Just remove a few at a time from freezer before you bake them.

Makes 50 wonderful appetizers

EGG-SPINACH MOLD

1 dozen hard-cooked eggs, peeled
1 bunch fresh spinach
1 small onion, chopped
½ cup mayonnaise
Salt and pepper to taste

Combine eggs, spinach and onion in your food processor. Process on and off a few times or until finely chopped . Season with mayonnaise, salt and pepper. Place mixture into a greased 4-cup mold. Refrigerate overnight. Unmold on a bed of greens. Decorate with cherry tomatoes, cucumber and carrot curls. Serve with sliced rye or pumpernickle.

Easy and light for the holidays.

Serves 12

CRAB MOLD

2 (8-ounce) packages cream cheese
½ pound sharp Cheddar cheese, grated
1 (3-ounce) package Roquefort cheese
1 teaspoon garlic salt
½ teaspoon curry powder
2 tablespoons Worcestershire sauce
1 teaspoon paprika
1 tablespoon mayonnaise
1 tablespoon lemon juice
1 (6½ ounce) can crab meat, drained

Mix together all ingredients with an electric mixer. Turn into a buttered 1-quart mold. Chill several hours or overnight. Unmold and garnish with chopped parsley. Serve with crackers.

Serves 6 to 8

SEVICHE DE PESCADO

Marinated Fish

1 pound boneless fish, uncooked
Lime juice, enough to cover
3 bay leaves
1 clove garlic, finely minced
4 tablespoons white vinegar
Salt to taste
1 large sweet onion, thinly sliced
2 small dry red peppers, chopped
2 lemons, sliced
4 sprigs of watercress

Cut the filets of uncooked fish into small thin strips. Use any white meat fish, such as red snapper, corbina, fresh tuna or sea bass. Place in porcelain container. Add the bay leaves, salt to taste and enough lime juice to cover. Lift the fish so that the lime juice will cover all sides and place in refrigerator to marinate overnight. Then add the minced garlic, onion and red peppers that have all been soaked in the vinegar. Decorate with slices of lemon and sprigs of watercress. Chill well and serve as an appetizer.

Serves 4 to 6

SHRIMP BAYOU

½ pound cocktail (bay) shrimp
2 tablespoons oil
1 tablespoon prepared mustard
2 tablespoons lemon juice or vinegar
2 green onions with tops, minced
Salt and pepper to taste

Mix all ingredients thoroughly and refrigerate at least 2 hours. Serve with thin wheat-flavored crackers or your choice of cocktail crackers. I serve this before a heavy meal. Invariably everyone says this is terrific, what's in it? Great and easy . . .

Serves 4

PICKLED EGGS (SIMPLE)

16 hard-boiled eggs, peeled
½ ounce black peppercorns
½ ounce whole ginger
½ ounce allspice
1 quart vinegar

Pack eggs in wide-mouthed jar. Boil spices in vinegar 10 minutes, then pour over eggs. Cool and seal.

PICKLED EGGS (NO. TWO)

18 hard-boiled eggs, peeled
2 cups white vinegar
1 ½ quarts water
2 teaspoons salt

Spice bag
1 small dry red pepper
1 tablespoon mixed pickling spices

Make pickling solution from vinegar, water and salt and when boiling add eggs and bring to a boil again. Pack in hot sterilized jars. Cover completely with pickling solution and seal immediately. May be pickled with beets for color.

EGG ROLLS

¾ cup celery, finely chopped
1 cup cabbage, shredded
½ cup water
Peanut oil
½ cup cooked shrimp, diced
½ cup cooked pork, ham, veal, beef or chicken, diced
¾ cup water chestnuts, finely chopped
4 green onions, finely chopped with tops included
8 wonton skins for egg rolls
1 tablespoon flour
2 tablespoons chicken broth

In a small saucepan combine celery, cabbage and water. Bring to a boil. Drain well. Heat 2 tablespoons oil in skillet. Add shrimp and meat. Stir over medium heat for 3 minutes. Add celery mixture, water chestnuts and scallions. Cook over medium heat, stirring constantly, until delicately brown. Remove from heat. Cool. Place about 4 tablespoons filling on each egg roll skin. In a small bowl, blend flour and broth to a paste and use to brush edges of skins. Fold in 2 sides of skins, roll up, press lightly to seal. Heat sufficient oil in a large skillet to come 1-inch up the side. Fry egg rolls, turning frequently, until golden on all sides. Drain on absorbent paper. Serve at once.

Makes 8

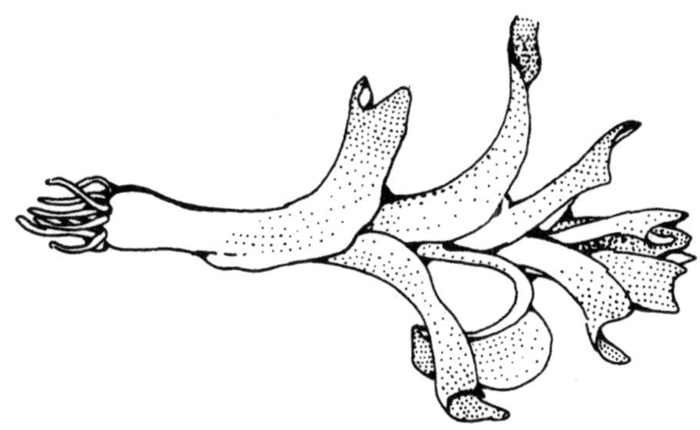

beverages

MOCHA SHAKE

1 cup cold coffee
⅓ cup nonfat dry milk
1–2 teaspoons granulated sugar replacement, or to taste
1 teaspoon unsweetened cocoa
4 ice cubes

Combine all ingredients except ice cubes in blender container and process until smooth. Add ice cube, one at a time, and process until smooth and frothy.

Serves 1

STRAWBERRY SHAKE

½ cup chilled evaporated skimmed milk
½ cup strawberry-flavored dietetic soda
4 ice cubes

Combine all ingredients except ice cubes in blender container and process until smooth. Ad ice cubes, one at a time, and process until smooth and frothy.

Serves 1

CHERRY THICK SHAKE

½ cup frozen cherries, no sugar added, reserve 1 cherry
½ cup plain unflavored yogurt
1–2 teaspoons granulated sugar replacement, or to taste
1 teaspoon vanilla extract

Combine all ingredients except reserved cherry in a blender container and process until smooth. Serve at once with reserved cherry on top.

Serves 1

BANANA SHAKE

1 cup skim milk
½ medium banana, sliced
1 to 2 teaspoons granulated sugar replacement, or to taste
½ teaspoon each vanilla extract and banana extract
4 ice cubes

Combine all ingredients except ice cubes in blender container and process until smooth. Add ice cubes, one at a time, and process until smooth and frothy.

Serves 1

CHOCOLATE MILKSHAKE

1 cup skim milk
2 teaspoons granulated sugar replacement or to taste
1 teaspoon chocolate extract
2–3 drops brown food coloring, optional
4 ice cubes

Combine all ingredients except ice cubes in blender container and process until smooth. Add ice cubes, one at a time, and process until smooth and frothy. Serve at once.

Serves 1

STRAWBERRY LEMONADE

4 cups strawberries, hulled and coarsly chopped
1½ cups sugar
3 cups water
1½ cups lemon juice
Crushed ice
Whole strawberries

Place strawberries in a blender, puree. In a saucepan, combine sugar and water. Heat slowly until sugar dissolves. Mix with strawberry puree. Add lemon juice. Chill to serve. Fill tall glass with crushed ice, pour in mixture and garnish with whole strawberries.

This is a wonderful drink for a brunch or a shower or any type of luncheon.

Serves 6 to 8

HOT GOBLINS BREW

2 cups sugar
2 quarts water
20 whole cloves
S.Dash of allspice
1 stick cinnamon
1 (46-ounce) can orange juice
1 (46-ounce) can grapefruit and orange juice blend
3 quarts apple juice or cider

Combine sugar, water and spices. Boil mixture for 30 minutes. Remove cloves and cinnamon. Add remaining juices and reheat when ready to serve.

Serves 30

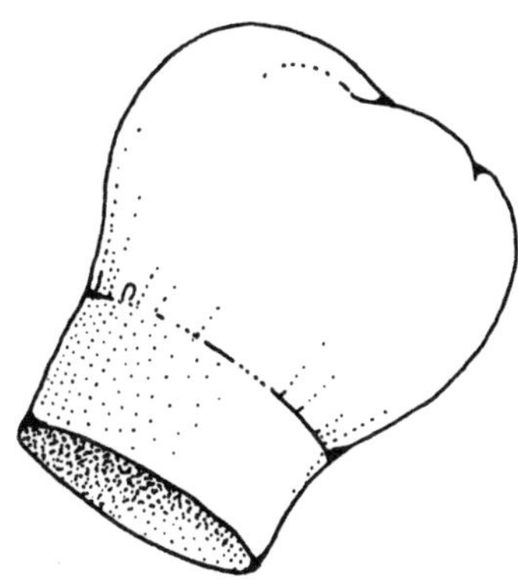

MULLED CIDER

1 cup brown sugar
2 teaspoons whole allspice
2 teaspoons whole cloves
⅓ teaspoon salt
Dash nutmeg
1 (3-inch) pieces of cinnamon sticks
1 gallon cider
1 orange cut into wedges, each stuck with a whole clove for garnish

Place allspice and the cloves into a metal tea caddy. Add remaining ingredients except oranges. Slowly bring to a boil. Cover and simmer for 20 minutes. Remove spices and serve in warmed mugs with orange wedge in each.

This is a wonderful fall punch . . . always make this when the family is going skiing or after a football game.

Serves 12 to 16

NON-ALCOHOLIC HOLIDAY CHEER

1 cup sugar
½ cup water
12 whole cloves
2 (2-inch) pieces cinnamon stick
6 cups grapefruit juice
3 cups orange juice
1 quart apple cider

In a saucepan combine the first 4 ingredients and simmer 20 minutes. In a punch bowl combine fruit juices then stir in sugar syrup. This whole punch can be served hot or cold. It can be made up to 2 weeks in advance.

Serves 25

CHILLED TOMATO & CUCUMBER PICK ME UP

1 teaspoon Worcestershire sauce
½ teaspoon curry powder
1 (10½ ounce) can cream of tomato soup
2 cups buttermilk
1 medium cucumber, chopped
Cracked black pepper

Combine all ingredients except black pepper, thoroughly. Chill. Serve in mugs with black pepper sprinkled on top of each serving.

Serves 6 to 8

KIWI FRUIT DAIQUIRI

1 kiwi fruit, peeled
1 ounce light rum
1 ounce sweet and sour
1 teaspoon sugar or equivalent sugar substitute
1 scoop ice

Mix with blender. Garnish with slices of kiwi fruit.

Serves 1

CRANBERRY SLUSH FOR THANKSGIVING

2 pints cranberry juice
2 tablespoons lemon juice
1 (6-ounce) can orange juice
1 quart lemon-lime carbonated beverage
2 quarts pineapple sherbert

Combine juice and freeze in a tray until mushy. Put in punch bowl and add carbonated beverage. Mix in sherbert. Delightful non-alcoholic punch for the whole family.

Makes 30 punch cups full

PAT'S WEDDING PUNCH

3 cups water
3 cups sugar
1 quart cranberry juice
1 quart apricot nectar
3 cups lemon juice
2 cups orange juice
1 cup pineapple
2 quarts chilled ginger ale

Combine water and sugar in a saucepan. Bring water to a boil over low heat, stirring until sugar is dissolved. Boil over medium heat for 5 minutes. Remove from heat, pour into a large bowl. Add fruit juices, mix well, refrigerate until serving time. Just before serving, pour mixture into punch bowl, stir in ginger ale.

Serves 50

PINK WEDDING PUNCH

2 fifths pink champagne (well chilled)
1 cup Mai Tai mix (non-alcoholic)
2 quarts lemon-lime soda
2 fifths sauterne (well chilled)
1 cup brandy or vodka
1 (3-pound) block of ice
Fresh fruit such as strawberries, orange slices or cherries for garnish

Place ice block into punch bowl. Pour on sauterne, Mai Tai mix and brandy. Stir. Add lemon-lime soda. Stir. Add champagne last and stir gently. A 3-pound block of ice is about the size of a half-gallon milk container. (You may also freeze orange blossoms, etc. in the ice block.) If making your own, be sure to use distilled water so that you will have clear ice.

Makes 50 (3-ounce) servings

HAWAIIAN WEDDING PUNCH

8 cups water
4 cups sugar
2 quarts pineapple juice
4 (6-ounce) can frozen orange juice, diluted with 12 cans water
½ cup lemon juice
5 large bananas, pureed in blender
2 quarts ginger ale

Combine water and sugar. Boil 15 minutes. Cool. Add all other ingredients except ginger ale. Mix and freeze. Take out of freezer 2 hours before serving. Add ginger ale at serving time. No extra ice needed.

Serves 50

WINE PUNCH

3 quarts sauterne
1 pint brandy
1 (6-ounce) can frozen pineapple juice
1 (6-ounce) can frozen lemon juice
3 (28-ounce) bottles sparking water, chilled
For garnish: whole strawberries, pineapple slices, melon balls or sliced peaches

Combine wine, brandy and fruit juice concentrates. Chill thoroughly. Just before serving, add sparkling water. If desired, float fresh or canned fruits in punch bowl, such as those suggested.

This is easy and can be doubled very easily. This will be a great punch for those on a budget.

Makes 50 (4-ounce) servings

ORANGE BLOSSOM PUNCH

3 cups sugar
3 cups water
6 cups grapefruit juice
6 cups orange juice
1½ cups lime juice
1 quart ginger ale

Combine sugar and water, stir until sugar is dissolved. Bring to a boil, let boil 5 minutes without stirring. Chill. Add juices and ginger ale and pour over ice.

Serves 50

HOT BUTTERED CRANBERRY PUNCH

1 (16-ounce) can jellied cranberry sauce
⅓ cup light brown sugar, firmly packed
¼ teaspoon cinnamon
¼ teaspoon allspice
⅛ teaspoon cloves
⅛ teaspoon nutmeg
⅛ teaspoon salt
2 cups water
2 cups unsweetened pineapple juice
Butter pats

Crush cranberry sauce with a fork. Mix with sugar, cinnamon, allspice, cloves, nutmeg and salt. Add water and pineapple juice. Cover and simmer 2 hours. Ladle into mugs and float a pat of butter on each serving.

Yields 50 ounces

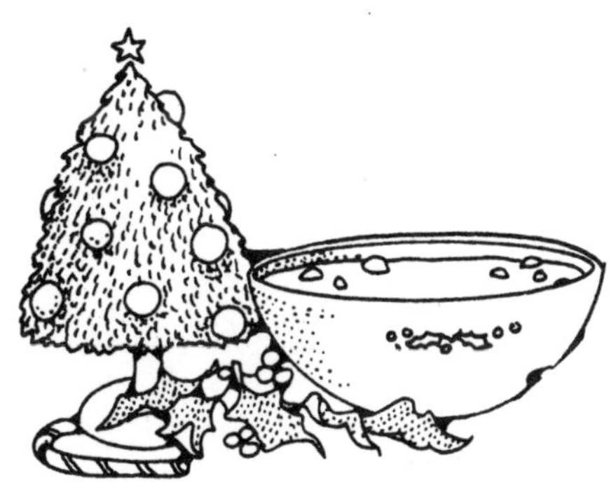

casseroles

EASY BOSTON BAKED BEANS

2 cups dried large navy beans, soaked overnight
1 medium onion, finely chopped
¼ pound salt pork
4 tablespoons brown sugar
½ cup molasses
½ teaspoon salt
⅛ teaspoon pepper
1 teaspoon dry mustard
Hot water to cover

Cook beans, using water beans were soaked in, until skins split when blown on. In bean pot, layer beans with mixture of remaining ingredients. Cook covered, at low temperature, approximately 250 degrees, for 5 to 6 hours. Check occasionally and add hot water if necessary—always keeping beans covered. Remove cover during last hour of cooking to allow browning.

Serves 8

BOSTON BAKED BEANS

6 cups pea or navy beans
1 pound salt pork
1 tablespoon dry mustard
1 tablespoon salt
1 teaspoon black pepper
1 cup molasses
1 small onion (optional)

Pick over beans, cover with cold water and soak overnight. In the morning drain, cover with fresh water, bring to a boil very slowly, then simmer until the skins burst. Drain beans. Scald the salt pork by letting it stand in boiling water 5 to 10 minutes. Cut off two thin slices, one to placed in bottom of pot, the other to be cut into bits. Score rind of the remaining piece with a sharp knife. Mix dry mustard, salt, black pepper and molasses. Alternate the layers of beans in the pot with the molasses mixture and the bits of pork. If you use an onion, bury it in the middle. When the bean pot is full, push the large piece of pork down into the beans with the rind sticking up. Add boiling water to cover, put the lid on and bake all day (a minimum of 6 to 8 hours) in a 250 degree oven. Check from time to time and add boiling water if needed. Uncover pot during last hour of baking so the rind can brown and crisp. To this day many old-timers believe the rich brown goodness of Boston Baked Beans is largely due to the earthenware bean pot, with its narrow throat and big, bulging sides. Lacking one of these pots, you can successfully use any deep earthenware caserole that has a cover.

Serves 10 to 12

3 BEAN BAKE

1 (1-pound) can cut green beans, drained
1 (1-pound) can red kidney beans, drained
1 (1-pound) can garbanzo beans, drained
1 package Lawry's chile seasoning mix
1 (14½ ounce) can stewed tomatoes
1 cup Cheddar cheese, grated
Corn chips

Combine all ingredients except the cheese and corn chips in a 1½ quart casserole. Bake, uncovered, in 350 degree oven 30 minutes. Sprinkle with cheese. Bake 5 minutes or until cheese melts. Serve over corn chips.

Serves 6

PORK PIE

1 pound lean ground pork
1 teaspoon salt
½ teaspoon pepper
¼ teaspoon ground nutmeg
¼ teaspoon ground mace
2 tablespoons corn starch
1 cup water
Pastry for 2 crust 8-inch pie (unbaked)

Combine all ingredients except pastry. Blend together thoroughly. Simmer, covered, for 30 minutes, stirring frequently. Roll out pastry and use half to line an 8-inch pan. Pour meat mixture into pan. Cover meat with remaining pastry and seal edges with water. Prick with a fork to allow steam to escape during baking. Bake at 425 degrees for 10 minutes. Reduce heat to 350 degrees and bake 35 minutes longer or until top is browned.

Serves 6

BROCCOLI AND CAULIFLOWER CASSEROLE FOR THE FAMILY

2 packages frozen broccoli
2 packages frozen cauliflower
1 can cream of mushroom soup
½ cup milk
1 small onion, minced
3 tablespoons Cheddar cheese, grated
Cracker crumbs or crushed potato chips

Cook vegetables according to package instructions. Arrange vegetables in a baking dish. Blend soup and milk in a saucepan, add onion and cheese. Stir over low heat until cheese is melted and mixture is heated through. Pour over vegetables and top with crumbs. Bake at 350 degrees for 20 to 25 minutes.

Great dish for the holiday buffet.

Serves 14

RICE AND BROCCOLI CASSEROLE

2 (10-ounce) packages chopped broccoli, thawed
2 cans mushroom soup or 1 can mushroom soup and 1 can cream of celery soup
2 cups minute rice
¾ cups celery, chopped
⅓ cup green onions with tops, chopped
1 cube butter or margarine, softened
1 (8-ounce) jar processed cheese spread

Combine all ingredients in a 2 or 3-quart baking dish. Bake at 325 degrees for 1 hour. Wonderful!

This is a great casserole when you are entertaining a large group. It is a do-ahead and tastes terrific.

Serves 8

GREEN CHILE BURRITOS

1 pound lean pork, diced
3 (10½ ounce) cans chicken broth
2 (7-ounce) cans chopped mild green chiles, chopped
1 (16-ounce) can tomatoes, chopped
12 flour tortillas
2 (16 ounce) cans refried beans
Flour
2 cups Cheddar cheese, grated
3 cups lettuce, shredded
3 tomatoes, chopped

Simmer pork in broth until tender and thoroughly cooked. Add chiles and canned tomatoes. Simmer 15 to 20 minutes longer. Spread each tortilla with refried beans. Using a slotted spoon, put some pork mixture on each tortilla, reserving liquid to serve as sauce. Roll each tortilla and place in a shallow greased baking dish. Bake at 350 degrees for 15 minutes or until hot. Thicken sauce with a little flour and spoon over burritos. Serve topped with cheese, lettuce and tomato.

Serves 6 healthy appetites

CHEESE ENCHILADAS

2 (10-ounce) cans Spanish red chile sauce
1 dozen tortillas
4 hard-cooked eggs, finely chopped
4 cups sharp Cheddar cheese, shredded
1 large onion, finely chopped
1 (4½ ounce) can pitted ripe olives, drained

Heat chile sauce in a large frying pan. Bring to a boil and simmer for five minutes. Dip each tortilla in hot sauce and lay on a plate. Spread across the tortilla center a spoonful each of eggs, cheese and onion. Top with 2 or 3 pitted olives. Roll tortilla and secure with a toothpick. Arrange stuffed tortillas in a baking dish. Pour over any remaining sauce. Sprinkle remaining cheese over top and garnish with rest of olives. Bake in a 350 degree oven for 15 minutes or until cheese melts and the sauce is bubbly.

Makes 6 servings

ENCHILADAS ROJAS

3 tablespoons flour
3 tablespoons bacon drippings
2 beef bouillon cubes
1 teaspoon salt
½ teaspoon garlic powder
½ teaspoon ground comino
2 tablespoons red chile powder
1 — 2 cups boiling water
½ cup oil
1 dozen corn tortillas
1 onion, chopped
1 to 3 cups Cheddar cheese, grated

Preheat oven to 350 degrees. Brown flour in bacon drippings until almost burned. Remove from heat. Add next 5 ingredients. Mix well and return to heat. Slowly add water, stirring to a smooth red sauce. Simmer gently while preparing other ingredients, adding more water if the sauce becomes to thick. In another skillet heat oil. Quickly dip the tortillas, one at a time, into the hot oil and then into the enchilada sauce. (Note: The tortillas must be dipped into the oil and removed very rapidly in order to prevent them from becoming rubbery.) Fill each tortilla with 2 tablespoons cheese and 1 teaspoon onion. Roll and place side by side in a 9 x 12-inch baking dish. Pour remaining sauce over enchiladas. Sprinkle with remaining cheese and onion. Cover and bake for 20 minutes. Enchiladas must be covered tightly to prevent the edges of the tortillas from becoming hard. Do not overcook.

Makes 12

CHILE RELLENOS

2 tablespoons butter
2 (4 ounce) cans Ortegas green chiles
½ pound Monterey Jack cheese
6 eggs, separated
2 tablespoons flour
1 teaspoon baking powder
Salt and pepper to taste

Preheat oven to 500 degrees. Melt butter in 10x15-inch baking pan. Remove seeds and veins from chiles. Cut cheese in strips 2″ long and ½″ wide and wrap in chiles. Arrange chiles on bottom of baking dish. Beat egg yolks until yellow and creamy and blend in flour, baking powder, salt and pepper. Beat the egg whites and fold into the egg yolk mixture. Pour over the chiles and bake about 45 minutes or until eggs are set.

Serves 4

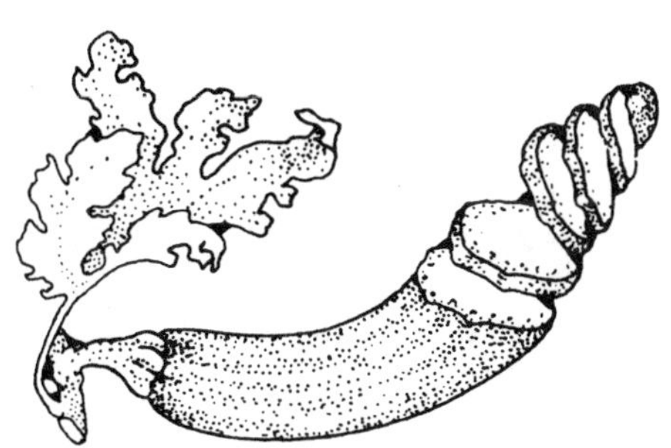

TAMALE PIE

1 pound lean ground beef
1 (8-ounce) can cream style corn
1 green pepper, chopped
1 teaspoon chile powder
1 (12-ounce) can tomatoes
1 cup pitted ripe olives
½ cup corn meal
1 cup milk

Brown beef in skillet, drain fat. Add corn, peppers, chile powder, tomatoes and olives. Mix together cornmeal and milk, stirring to blend into meat mixture. Bake at 375 degrees for 1 hour.

Serves 6

TORTILLA FLATS

1½ pounds ground beef
1 package spaghetti sauce mix
1 teaspoon salt
1 clove garlic, crushed
1 (1-pound) can tomatoes, cut up
1 (8-ounce) can tomato sauce
½ cup red wine
1 (4-ounce) can diced green chiles
1 pound Ricotta cheese
2 eggs, lightly beaten
8 corn tortillas
1 pound Monterey Jack cheese, grated

Preheat oven to 350 degrees. Brown beef in a heavy skillet,add spaghetti sauce mix, salt, tomatoes, tomato sauce, garlic, wine and chilies. Blend thoroughly and simmer 10 minutes. In a bowl combine the Ricotta cheese with the eggs. In a 8x12-inch baking dish place about 1 cup of the meat mixture. Place 2 tortillas over the meat, side by side and spoon some of the Ricotta mixture on top of each. Then layer with more meat and sprinkle with grated cheese. Repeat until each of the 2 stacks has 4 tortillas, ending with the grated cheese. Bake for 30 minutes. Let stand 5 minutes before cutting into pie shaped wedges.

This is so easy to prepare and so good. Great for supper or luncheon.

Serves 8

BAKED POTATOES WITH CRAB AND CREAM

4 large Russett potatoes
⅓ cup butter
½ cup cream
Salt to taste
Dash of cayenne
2 tablespoons green onion, chopped
1 cup sharp Cheddar cheese, grated
1 cup cooked crab meat

Bake the potatoes in a 400 degree oven until tender, about 1 hour. Carefully slit the top of potatoes, scoop out and mash. Beat in butter, cream, seasonings, onion and cheese. Fold in crab meat. Pile back into potato shells. May refrigerate until ready to serve or wrap air tight and freeze. To serve, reheat in a 450 degree oven for 12 to 15 minutes or until heated through.

Serves 4

BAKED CRAB CASSEROLE

1 pound crab meat, flaked
1 (4-ounce) can pimientos, drained and chopped
3 tablespoons green pepper, finely chopped
2 tablespoons prepared mustard
1 teaspoon Worcestershire sauce
1 teaspoon salt
1 egg, lightly beaten
¼ cup cracker crumbs
2 tablespoons milk
1 cup mayonnaise
2 egg yolks

Preheat oven to 425 degrees. Grease a 1½ quart casserole. In mixing bowl combine all ingredients except mayonnaise and egg yolks. Mix well. Turn into casserole. In a small bowl blend mayonnaise and egg yolks. Spread on crab mixture. Bake for 15 minutes or until golden brown.

Serves 4

OLD FASHIONED GRITS CASSEROLE

1 cup quick cooking grits
1 (6-ounce) stick of garlic cheese
½ cup melted butter or margarine
2 eggs (break eggs into a cup, beat with a fork and add enough milk to make 1 full cup)
Grated sharp Cheddar cheese for topping
Paprika

Follow directions on grits box (stiff, not soupy). Cut cheese into small pieces and add to grits along with butter and egg mixture. Bake for 45 minutes at 400 degrees in a buttered casserole dish. Remove, cover with grated cheese and generous dashes of paprika. Bake 10 minutes longer. Can stay in oven on warm until ready to serve.

Serves 6 to 8

GRANDMA'S KUBA (BARLEY WITH MUSHROOMS)

1 cup pearl barley
1 (6-ounce) can mushrooms, finely chopped (including liquid)
3 small onions
1 tablespoon lard
1 tablespoon salt
½ teaspoon pepper
⅛ teaspoon ginger
⅛ teaspoon allspice
1 tablespoon marjoram
Butter

Cover barley with water and soak overnight. Next morning drain off water. Place in a large saucepan and cover with boiling water and cook slowly until barley is plump. Stir often to prevent scorching. Fry the onion until tender but do not brown. Combine all ingredients and put into a baking dish. Spread about 2 tablespoons of the butter over the top and bake in in a 300 degree oven for 1 to 2 hours . . . SO DOBRE

Serves 4 to 6

PEAS AND PEANUTS

3 tablespoons butter
1 tablespoon flour
½ teaspoon salt
½ teaspoon pepper
1½ cups milk
¾ cups peanuts
¼ cup bread crumbs
2 cups frozen peas

Mix all ingredients and place in a casserole. Bake at 400 degrees for 20 minutes.

Serves 4 to 6

SWISS CHARD CUSTARD

2 cups cooked Swiss chard, drained and chopped
2 tablespoons butter, melted
2 eggs, beaten
1 cup milk
¼ teaspoon sugar
½ teaspoon onion juice
¼ teaspoon nutmeg
Salt and pepper

Combine all ingredients and put in a buttered casserole. Bake 25 to 30 minutes at 300 degrees or until center has set.

SWISS CHARD SOUFFLE: Follow above instructions, except
separate the eggs. Add yolks to custard mixture. Beat egg whites and fold them in last.

Serves 4

POTATO KUGEL

5 pounds potatoes, peeled
1 large onion
1 medium carrot
9 eggs, beaten
1 cup of oil
Salt and pepper to taste

Grate first three ingredients. Add remaining ingredients. Pour into a greased 9x13-inch pan. Bake at 400 degrees 1 hour.

Serves 6

CREAMED POTATO CASSEROLE

6 large white rose potatoes
¼ cup butter, melted
1 can cream of chicken soup
1 pint sour cream
¼ cup green onion, finely chopped
1 cup sharp Cheddar cheese, grated
2 cups corn flakes
3 tablespoons butter, melted

Parboil potatoes, cool. Remove skins. Grate potatoes and add salt to taste. Mix together the ¼ cup butter, chicken soup, sour cream, green onion and cheese. Pour sauce over the potatoes and toss lightly. Spoon into a buttered 9x13-inch baking dish. Top with the corn flakes that have been mixed with the 3 tablespoons melted butter. Bake 30 to 40 minutes in a 350 degree oven.

Serves 10

SWEET POTATO AND ORANGE CASSEROLE

10 large sweet potatoes, boiled, peeled and sliced
1 cup brown sugar
½ cup butter
3 oranges, unpeeled and thinly sliced
½ cup honey
1 cup orange juice
½ cup fresh bread crumbs

Preheat oven to 350 degrees. Grease a 3-quart casserole. Arrange half the potatoes in casserole. Sprinkle with ⅓ cup of the sugar. Dot with 2 tablespoons of the butter, arrange half the orange slices on the top. Cover with remaining potatoes. Sprinkle with ⅓ cup sugar and dot with two tablespoons butter. Top with remaining oranges. Blend orange juice and honey in a small bowl and pour into casserole. Combine remaining sugar and crumbs, sprinkle on top. Dot with remaining butter. Cover and bake for 45 minutes. Remove cover and bake for 15 minutes longer.

Serves 12

YAM AND APPLE CASSEROLE

6 to 8 yams (may use canned)
2 to 3 oranges
5 to 6 cooking apples
Maraschino cherries
2 cups boiling water
1 cup sugar
4 tablespoons corn starch
1 teaspoon salt
¼ pound butter

Parboil yams, cool, peel and slice. Peel and core apples. Slice. Peel and slice oranges. Layer yams, apples and oranges in a buttered baking dish. Arrange cherries on top to add color. Prepare sauce by pouring boiling water over the dry ingredients. Stir. Add butter. Cook until sauce thickens. Pour sauce over the yams and bake in a 350 degree oven for 35 to 45 minutes.

Serves 6 to 8

MEXICAN CHEESE SOUFFLE

3½ cups Jack cheese, grated
3½ cups sharp Cheddar cheese, grated
1 large can green chiles, chopped
2 medium-sized tomatoes, chopped
1 can black olives, sliced (size depends on your taste)
½ cup flour
6 eggs, separated
1 small can evaporated milk
½ teaspoon salt
½ teaspoon oregano
¼ teaspoon ground cumin
¼ teaspoon pepper
¼ teaspoon cream of tartar

Stir together the cheeses, chiles, tomatoes, olives and 2 table spoons of the flour. Place in a well-greased casserole. Beat egg yolks in a small bowl. Add remaining flour and milk. Beat until smooth. Stir in salt, oregano, cumin and pepper. Beat in a large bowl the egg whites with the cream of tartar until they are stiff but not dry. Fold into yolk mixture. Spoon egg mixture over cheese mixture in casserole. Bake in a 300 degree oven for 1 hour or until golden brown and firm to the touch. Let stand 10 minutes before serving.

Serves 12

JACKIE'S FABULOUS HAM AND CHEESE SOUFFLE

16 slices white bread, without crusts and cubed
1 pound ham, cubed (can use more if you like)
1 pound sharp Cheddar cheese, grated
1½ cups Swiss cheese, cut into small pieces
6 eggs
3 cups milk
½ teaspoon onion salt
½ teaspoon dry mustard
3 cups cornflakes, crushed
½ cup butter, melted

Grease a 9x13-inch baking pan. Spread half the bread cubes evenly in dish. Add ham and both the cheeses. Cover with remaining bread cubes. Mix eggs, milk, onion salt and mustard. Pour evenly over bread cubes and refrigerate overnight. Combine cornflakes and butter and spread on top. Bake at 375 degrees for 40 minutes.

This is so fabulous and easy to entertain with that everyone will want this recipe. You can double, triple or even quadruple this . . . wonderful.

Serves 10

CHEESE STRATA

8 slices day old bread
8-ounces process American cheese, sliced
4 eggs
2½ cups milk
½ teaspoon prepared mustard
1 tablespoon onion, chopped
1½ teaspoons salt
Dash pepper

Trim crusts from 5 slices of bread, cut in half diagonally. Use trimmings and remaining 3 slices of untrimmed bread to cover bottom of 8 or 9-inch square baking dish. Top with the slices of cheese. Arrange the 10 trimmed triangles in 2 rows atop the cheese (point should overlap bases of preceding triangles). Beat eggs. Blend in milk, mustard, onion, salt and pepper. Pour over bread and cheese. Cover with wax paper. Let stand 1 hour at room temperature or several hours in refrigerator. Bake in 325 degree oven for 1 hour or till knife comes out clean. Let stand 5 minutes before serving to firm.

Serves 6

SCHOOL CAFETERIA MACARONI AND CHEESE

1 (8-ounce) package macaroni
4 tablespoons butter
2¼ cups cheese, grated
1 cup milk
1 teaspoon salt
Pepper to taste
Buttered crumbs or crumbled potato chips

Preheat oven to 300 degrees. Cook macaroni in salted water 8 minutes, until just tender, drain. Stir butter into macaroni. Add two cups cheese, milk, salt and pepper and pour into a 2-quart casserole. Bake 30 minutes until cheese is well set. Sprinkle on remaining ¼ cup cheese and crumbs or chips and broil 1 minute or until brown on top.

Serves 4 to 6

CREAMY MACARONI AND CHEESE

8-ounces elbow macaroni
4 tablespoons butter or margarine
¼ cup flour
½ teaspoon dry mustard
1 teaspoon salt
½ teaspoon pepper
¾ teaspoon Worcestershire sauce
3 cups milk
1 teaspoon instant minced onion
¾ pound sharp Cheddar cheese, shredded
(reserve some for topping)

Cook macaroni, drain. Melt butter or margarine and blend in flour, seasonings and Worcestershire sauce. Add milk and onion. Cook until thickened, stirring constantly. Add cheese. Mix with cooked macaroni. Place in a 2½ quart casserole. Bake in a 375 degree oven approximately 40 minutes. (You may want to spray casserole with Pam.)

Makes 4 to 6 servings

CHICKEN NOODLE CASSEROLE

2 (2½ pound) chickens, cut up
1 medium onion, quartered
1 medium carrot, cut up
1 stalk celery
3 quarts water
2 (10-ounce) packages frozen chopped spinach
1 pound broad noodles
6 tablespoons butter, melted
2 tablespoons butter
4 tablespoons flour
1 teaspoon oregano
1 clove garlic, crushed
1½ cups white wine
6 egg yolks
½ cup Parmesan cheese, grated

In a large pot combine chickens, carrot, onion, celery and water. Simmer, uncovered, 45 minutes. Skim top. Remove chicken and set aside. Strain broth. Return broth to pot and boil rapidly until liquid is reduced to about 3 cups. Bone cooled cooked chicken, discarding skin and bones. Cut chicken into bite-sized pieces. Set aside. Cook the spinach and noodles separately according to package directions. Drain well. Cover the bottom of a large shallow baking dish with the cooked noodles mixed with the melted butter. Spread the cooked chicken pieces on the noodles. In a small saucepan, melt the butter. Add flour and blend well to make a roux. Stir in oregano, garlic and chicken broth. Stir and simmer slowly 3 to 5 minutes or until thickened. Fold in spinach and pour mixture over the chicken. (If preparing a day ahead, refrigerate at this point.) Boil the wine until reduced to 1 cup. Beat in egg yolks and cheese. Pour over top of chicken dish, spreading smooth. Bake at 400 degrees for 25 minutes or until top is golden. Cool for 5 minutes.

Serves 8

BEEF AND NOODLES FOR THE GANG

1 pound small egg noodles
2 pounds lean ground beef
2 (6-ounce) cans tomato sauce
1 tablespoon Worcestershire sauce
Salt to taste
1 cup cream style cottage cheese
1 (8-ounce) package cream cheese, softened
1 cup sour cream
1 bunch green onions, chopped with some of the green
2 tablespoons butter, melted

Cook noodles, rinse under hot water. Brown meat well. Add tomato sauce, Worcestershire and salt. Mix together the cottage cheese, cream cheese, sour cream and onions. Grease two 2-quart casserole dishes. Place ¼ of the noodles in each, pour a little melted butter over the noodles and add half the cheese mixture to each casserole. Add remaining noodles, more butter and top with meat mixture. Bake at 350 degrees 30 to 45 minutes. Can be frozen.

Serves 8 to 10

$10,000 CASSEROLE

½ pound fine noodles
2—3 tablespoons shortening
(may use ½ butter, ½ olive oil)
2 cups onion, chopped
2 pounds ground chuck
1 (4-ounce) can mushrooms
l can cream of chicken soup
½ cup milk
½ teaspoon salt
¼ teaspoon pepper
1 cup soy sauce
1 teaspoon Worcestershire sauce
½ pound Cheddar cheese, grated
¼ pound mixed salted nuts
1 (8½ ounce) can Chinese chow mein noodles

Cook and drain noodles. Saute onion in large skillet in shortening until golden. Add meat, cook until browned. Combine mushrooms, soup and milk and add to meat mixture. Blend in spices, soy sauce and Worcestershire. Mix well and heat thoroughly. Butter a 3-quart casserole and spread cooked noodles over bottom. Cover with meat mixture. Top with cheese. Heat well in 350 degree oven for 15 minutes until cheese bubbles. Remove and top with nuts and crisp noodles. Return to oven for 10 more minutes cooking time.

Serves 10

HAMBURGER PUDDING

½ pound ground beef
½ teaspoon salt
2 teaspoons Worcestershire sauce
1 package onion gravy mix
2 cups biscuit mix
½ cup plus 1 tablespoon milk
2 packages brown gravy mix
2 cups hot water

Cook the ground beef in a skillet, stirring to crumble and drain well. Add the salt and Worcestershire sauce. Place biscuit mix in medium-size bowl and add the onion gravy mix (dry), the cooked hamburger and milk. (The dough should be stiff.) Spread dough over bottom of well-greased or oiled 9x9x2 glass pan. Press down firmly to all the edges. Sprinkle the dry brown gravy mix over the top, then add the hot water. Bake at 375 degrees for 25 to 30 minutes. Cut in squares and serve with bottom up so the gravy is on top.

Serves 4

BEEF AND NOODLES

1 (8-ounce) package noodles, cooked and drained
1½ pounds lean ground beef
2 small onions, chopped
1 cup celery, chopped
1 small green pepper, seeded and chopped
1 (16 ounces) can peas, undrained
1 can tomato soup, undiluted
¼ teaspoon Worcestershire sauce
½ cup Cheddar cheese, grated

Brown meat in a skillet. Add onions, celery and pepper. Cook until limp. Add peas. Season with salt and pepper. In a greased casserole, alternate noodles with meat mixture. Combine tomato soup with Worcestershire and pour over casserole. Top with grated cheese. Bake at 350 degrees for 45 minutes.

Serves 4 to 6

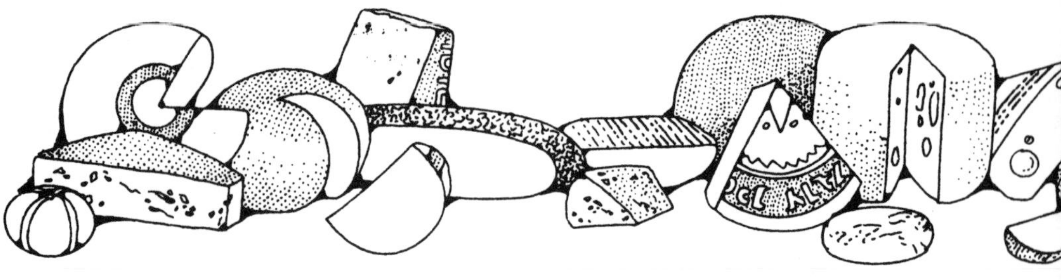

HOLIDAY SPINACH AND CHEESE CASSEROLE

1 (10-ounce) package frozen chopped spinach, thawed
1 (6-ounce) jar marinated artichoke hearts
1 tablespoon butter or margarine
1 medium onion, chopped
¼ teaspoon nutmeg
¾ teaspoon oregano
1 (10-ounce) can cream of celery soup
4 eggs, beaten
1 (8-ounce) package cream cheese
⅓ cup milk
⅓ cup Parmesan cheese

Squeeze moisture from thawed spinach, drain artichokes, saving 2 tablespoons of the marinade. Heat the marinade and margarine or butter in a skillet. Cook onion in this until tender. Combine all ingredients except cheeses and milk. Spread in shallow 2-quart buttered baking dish. Smooth top. Beat cream cheese, milk and parmesan. Spread evenly over the spinach. Bake at 350 degrees for 40 minutes or until firm. This can be doubled with no problems, just increase baking time to 50 or 60 minutes.

Serves 5

BAKED ZUCCHINI CASSEROLE

2 pounds zucchini
½ teaspoon salt
2 medium-sized onions, minced
1 clove garlic
1 tablespoon butter
3 slices French bread, cut in small pieces
2 tablespoons parsley, minced
1 cup Cheddar cheese, grated
4 eggs
Dash Tabasco sauce
Dash Worcestershire sauce

Cook zucchini in small amount of water and salt until tender, drain and mash. Saute onions and garlic in butter. Add to bread cubes with parsley and cheese. Beat eggs well and add Tabasco and Worcestershire. Mix everything together and spoon into well buttered baking dish. Set in pan of hot water and bake at 350 degrees until well set—about 30 minutes.

Serves 6

CASSOULET

2 bacon slices, minced
½ pound boneless pork, cut into ½-inch cubes
1 onion
6 cloves
½ pound boneless lamb, cut into ½-inch cubes
1 clove garlic, crushed
2 Italian sausages, cut into ¼-inch slices
1 teaspoon salt
¼ teaspoon pepper
¼ teaspoon dried thyme
2 (16-ounce) cans white beans, undrained
1 (16-ounce) can tomato sauce

In a large skillet saute bacon and pork until pork is tender. Cut onion into six wedges, insert a clove into each onion wedge. Add onion wedges, lamb, garlic and sausages to pork mixture. Saute until the lamb is tender. Add seasonings, beans and tomato sauce. Cover and simmer 15 minutes.

An easy and quick version of a classic dish from southern France.

Serves 4

SAUSAGE CANTONESE

2 pounds bulk pork sausage
2 medium green peppers, diced
2 large onions, diced
2 cups celery, diced
2 cups raw rice
9 cups water
3 packages chicken noodle soup
1 cup blanched sliced almonds

Brown sausage, peppers, onion and celery in a skillet, drain off grease. Add rice and mix well. Put in a large roaster and add dry soup mix and water. Mix thoroughly and add almonds. Bake at 375 degrees for 1 hour. May be divided into smaller casseroles for baking. Add more water if necessary. Garnish with pepper or pimiento rings and almonds.

Serves 14 to 16

HOLIDAY SCALLOPED POTATOES AND HAM

6 cups potatoes, thinly sliced
1½ cups onions, thinly sliced
8 slices boiled or baked ham, cut into cubes
2 cans celery soup
1 cup sour cream
½ cup parsley, chopped
¼ teaspoon marjoram
½ teaspoon sage
Almonds, sliced

Layer potatoes, onions and ham in a 9x13-inch casserole dish. Blend soup, sour cream, parsley and spices. Pour over layers and bake, covered, at 375 degrees for 1 hour. Uncover and top with sliced almonds. Bake uncovered 15 minutes or until lightly browned.

Serves 12

JACKIE'S PAELLA

¼ cup oil
2 (9-inch) pepperoni, sliced thick
8 boned chicken breasts, cut into halves
1 large onion, chopped
2 cloves garlic, minced
2 (7-ounce) cans clams, drained (save juice)
1½ pounds shrimp, shelled and deveined
2 cups raw, converted rice
1 teaspoon freshly ground pepper
Salt to taste
¼ teaspoon powdered saffron
4 cups chicken broth

In a large skillet or paella pan, heat oil until hot and brown pepperoni slices. Remove pepperoni with a slotted spoon and drain. Add the chicken breasts and brown in the same oil. Set aside. Add the onion and garlic and saute until translucent. Remove. Stir in the clams and shrimp. Saute until shrimp are almost done and set aside. In remaining oil (you may have to add a little more) add rice, pepper, salt and saffron and brown slightly. Stir in chicken broth and clam juice, cover pan tightly and simmer 10 minutes. Uncover pan and add the pepperoni, chicken breasts and seafood. This can be prepared ahead up to this point. You may have to add a little more liquid. Bake, uncovered, at 400 degrees for 20 to 30 minutes or until rice is done. Garnish with clam shells, pimiento, black olives, peas and asparagus. Serve with a crusty bread and butter.

Serves 6 to 8

soups & sandwiches

ASPARAGUS-LEEK SOUP

2 packages frozen asparagus
1 ½ cups boiling water
2 envelopes leek soup mix
6 cups milk
½ teaspoon pepper
Salt to taste
Sour cream
Chives

Cook the frozen asparagus in the boiling water until it is tender. Pour the cooked asparagus, including the water into the blender and whirl until smooth. Add leek soup mix, 3 cups milk and the pepper. Blend. Pour into a pan and refrigerate. When ready to serve, add rest of the milk (3 cups) and heat. Add salt. Pour soup into a soup tureen and serve with a dollop of sour cream and chives on top. Terrific with bread sticks.

Serves 6 to 8

CHILLED AVOCADO-YOGURT SOUP

2 avocados, seeded and peeled
2 teaspoons lemon juice
2 cups chicken broth
1 clove garlic, crushed
Salt and pepper to taste
1 (16-ounce) carton plain low-fat yogurt
¼ cup sherry
1 tablespoon chives, chopped

Place all the ingredients in a blender and blend until smooth. Chill soup thoroughly. Garnish each serving with an extra dollop of yogurt and chives.

Serve 4 to 6

QUICK BEAN SOUP

Place half a 1-pound can (do not drain) of northern beans into a blender and puree on high speed till very smooth — about 1 minute. Add to the other half of the canned beans and heat gently in a 1 ½ quart saucepan with 10-ounces chicken broth, 2 scissor-snipped green onions, ½ teaspoon sugar, 2 tablespoons bacon drippings or butter, ¼ teaspoon pepper and 1 tablespoon catsup — stirring completely. When piping hot, and never close to a boil please — divide it up between 4 reasonable bowls.

Serves 4

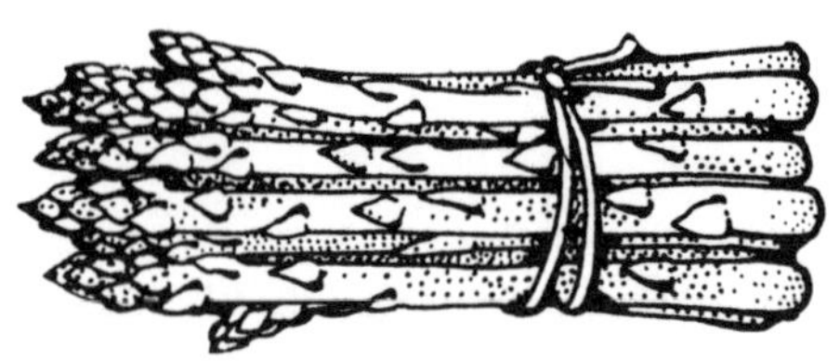

SAUSAGE BEAN CHOWDER

1 pound bulk pork sausage
2 (16-ounce) cans kidney beans, drained
1 (1-pound 13-ounce) can tomatoes, broken up
1 quart water
1 large onion, chopped
1 bay leaf
1 ½ teaspoons seasoned salt
½ teaspoon garlic salt
½ teaspoon thyme
⅛ teaspoon pepper
1 cup potatoes, diced
½ green pepper, chopped

In a skillet cook sausage until brown. Pour off drippings. In a large kettle combine beans, tomatoes, water, onion, bay leaf, seasoned salt, garlic salt, thyme and pepper. Add sausage and simmer covered for 1 hour. Add potatoes and green pepper. Cook covered 15 to 20 minutes until potatoes are tender. Remove bay leaf.

This is a wonderful old standby one dish meal that comes from the archives of my Cornhuskers background. Serve with a big piece of cornbread . . . Yumm

Serves 8

CHICKEN LEMON SOUP

3 (10 ½ ounce) cans chicken soup with rice
2 eggs
¼ cup lemon juice
½ lemon, sliced
2 tablespoons parsley, chopped

Heat soup with water as directed on can. Beat eggs well, stir in lemon juice slowly. Gradually add about 2 cups hot broth from the soup. Stir the mixture into rest of the soup. Garnish with thin slices of lemon sprinkled with parsley.

Serves 8

EASY FIRST DOWN CHILI

2 pounds ground beef
2 or 3 (15½ ounce) cans kidney beans, drained
1 (32-ounce) can tomato juice
1 package dry onion soup mix
3 tablespoons chili powder
2 to 3 cloves garlic, minced
Salt and pepper to taste

Cook beef until lightly browned. Drain off grease. Combine all ingredients in a crock cooker. Cover and cook on LOW power 10 hours or on HIGH 5 hours.

Serves 6

NEW YEAR'S EVE CHILI

4 large onions, chopped
2 cloves garlic, minced
3 pounds ground beef, separated
1 (28-ounce) can tomatoes, mashed
4 tablespoons chili powder
2 (7-ounce) cans Ortega chiles, chopped
1 bunch fresh cilantro, minced
Salt to taste
Pepper to taste
5 (15½-ounce) cans small red beans
Sour cream
Chopped chives or green onions to sprinkle

Combine onions, garlic and beef. Brown slightly in a large kettle. Add everything else except the sour cream and chives. Simmer very slowly 6 hours, stirring often to avoid burning. If need be may be thickened with flour and wine. Serve with a dollop of sour cream and a sprinkling of chives. Fried flour tortillas that have been lightly salted are a dynamite accompaniment. Great party fare, just right for New Year's Eve or all the bowl games.

Serves 18

JACKIE'S PARTY CHILI

½ pound dried pinto beans
5 cups canned tomatoes, drained
4 peppers, chopped
6 teaspoons oil
1½ pounds onions, chopped
2 cloves garlic, minced (I usually add more . . . I love garlic.)
½ cup parsley, chopped
½ cup butter or margarine
2½ pounds ground beef
1 pound lean ground pork
⅓ cup chili powder
2 tablespoons salt
1½ teaspoons cumin
1 tablespoon cocoa

Wash beans and soak overnight in water to cover. Next day simmer beans in the same water for 2 hours. Add tomatoes and simmer 6 minutes more. In a skillet saute the green peppers in the oil for 5 minutes, add onions and cook until tender, stirring constantly. Add garlic and parsley and continue to cook for 5 minutes. In a separate skillet add butter and melt, add meat and cook 15 minutes or until crumbly. Add meats to the onion mixture and stir in the chili powder and cook for 10 minutes. Add this to the beans with the remaining ingredients. Stir well. Simmer covered over very low heat for 1 hour. Now, uncover and cook 30 minutes longer. Refrigerate overnight. To serve, remove excess fat from the top of the chili and reheat on the top of the stove over very low heat.

This takes a couple of days to make, but it is well worth the effort. It seems to take 2 days for all the ingredients to get to know one another. Also they freeze beautifully.

I am never quite sure how many this will serve the way everyone at my house eats it. I will take a stab and say 10.

CREAM OF CORN SOUP

Heat together 1 (10-ounce) can cream of celery soup, 1 (10-ounce) can of cream of chicken soup, 1 soup can of milk and 1 (12-ounce) can of cream style corn, a fleck or 2 of nutmeg, a pinch of sugar and 2 or 3 tablespoons of butter or margarine. Heat gently without letting it boil and serve it promptly.

Serves 3 to 4

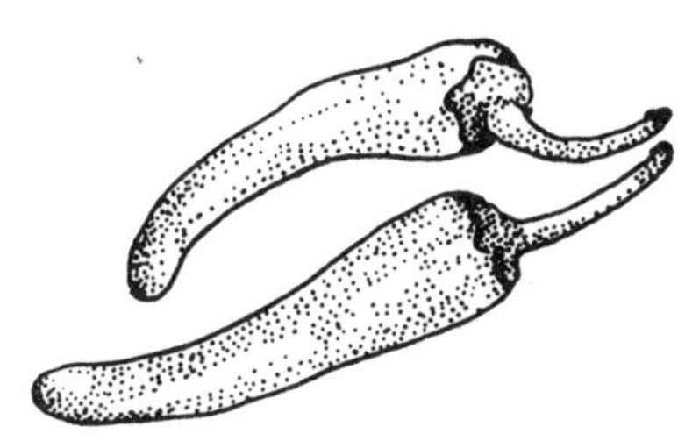

CORN CHOWDER

4 cups potatoes, peeled and diced
2 cups water
2 tablespoons salt pork, diced
3 tablespoons onion, chopped
2 cups corn kernels, fresh or canned
2 cups milk
2 teaspoons salt
½ teaspoon pepper

Cook potatoes in water for 15 minutes. In a skillet cook the salt pork and onions until browned. Add to undrained potatoes with remaining ingredients. Heat but do not boil.

Serves 6

OLD FASHIONED MUSHROOM SOUP

1 pound fresh mushrooms
1 quart rich chicken broth
3 tablespoons butter
2 tablespoons flour
½ teaspoon salt
⅛ teaspoon pepper
⅛ teaspoon ginger
¼ cup dry sherry
½ cup cream

Remove stems from mushrooms and set caps aside. Chop stems and add to broth. Simmer 20 minutes, strain out stems and discard. Slice caps and saute in butter until browned. Remove from pan leaving remaining butter and mushroom broth. Stir in flour and seasonings and cook over low heat until a smooth paste is formed. Pour this mixture into the broth and heat until smooth and thickened. Add mushrooms and sherry. Blend in cream and reduce heat to very low. Serve in bowls garnished with pepper and paprika.

Serves 4 to 6

PANTRY MUSHROOM SOUP

Drain 2 (8-ounce) cans mushrooms, reserving the liquid in a 2-quart sauce-pan. Set it aside. Melt ¼ cup butter or margarine with 1 tablespoon oil in a 10-inch skillet and saute mushrooms till golden. Turn mushrooms and drippings into sauce-pan with their reserved liquid and add 2 cups water, 1 (10-ounce) can Franco American Mushroom Gravy ands 1 (10-ounce) can beef broth. Heat gently to piping hot. Leftovers should be covered and refrigerated to be rewarmed within 3 or 4 days. Do NOT freeze.

Serve 6

SATURDAY NIGHT'S ONION SOUP

1 (10-ounce) can beef gravy
1 (10-ounce) can beef broth
2 tablespoons butter or margarine
¼ cup dry chopped onion
2 (½-inch thick each) slices French bread
4 tablespoons grated Parmesan cheese
4 tablespoons mayonnaise
¼ cup dry sherry

Combine first 4 ingredients in teflon lined 2-quart saucepan over medium heat, just till piping hot and onion flakes are tender. Do not let it boil. Cut slices of bread in pieces to fit top of oven-proof soup bowls. Ladle soup into 4 oven-proof soup bowls and add 2 tablespoons of the sherry to each. Combine Parmesan with mayonnaise to make a paste. Divide between 4 slices of French bread. Float these pieces of bread atop each of the servings of soup and place them 4-inches from broiler heat, just for half a minute or so to let cheese mixture bubble and turn golden. Serve at once.

Serves 4

PEACH SOUP

1 cup water
¼ cup sugar
1 teaspoon whole cloves
1 cinnamon stick
1½ tablespoons arrowroot dissolved in
2 cups dry white wine
2½ pounds frozen peaches, defrosted, undrained and pureed

Combine first 4 ingredients in medium saucepan and bring to boil over medium-high heat. Reduce heat, cover and simmer 30 minutes. Strain and return to pan. Dissolve arrowroot in wine and blend thoroughly into syrup. Bring to boil, stirring occasionally. Let cool, then add pureed peaches. Chill well. Ladle into bowls and serve.

Serves 6 to 8

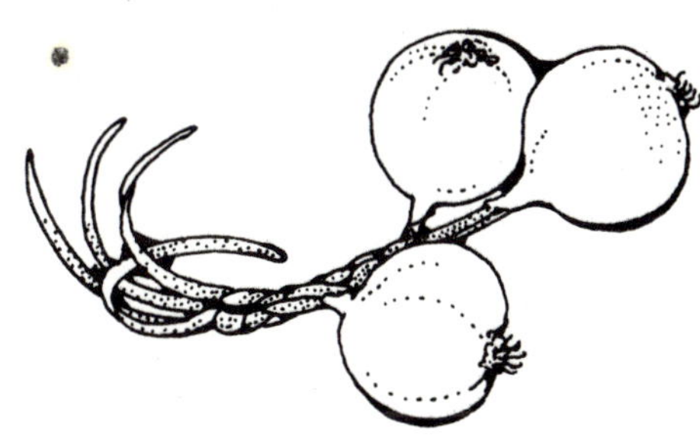

PARTY RASPBERRY SOUP

1½ tablespoons unflavored gelatin
⅓ cup cold water
¾ cup hot water
3 (10-ounce) packages frozen raspberries, thawed
3½ cups sour cream
1⅓ cups pineapple juice
1⅓ cups light cream
1⅓ cups dry sherry
⅓ cup grenadine
2 tablespoons lemon juice
Garnish with mint and whole raspberries

Soak gelatin in cold water for 5 minutes. Stir in hot water and dissolve over low heat. Push raspberries through a strainer to remove seeds then puree. Combine all ingredients and place in a glass bowl. Cover and refrigerate overnight. Garnish with mint and whole raspberries.

This is a great first course party soup. If you have any leftovers, you can freeze for a yogurt-like snack.

Serves 12

EASY SAUSAGE CHOWDER

1 pound bulk sausage
1 onion, firmly chopped
1 large can kidney beans, drained
1 large can tomatoes, chopped
1 quart water or stock
Salt and pepper to taste
¼ teaspoon thyme
1 bay leaf
2 large potatoes, cut into small cubes
¼ cup green pepper, chopped

Crumble sausage and brown, drain off fat. Add remaining ingredients. Bring to a boil, then simmer 1 hour. Serve with sourdough bread.

Serves 8

CLEAR TOMATO CONSOMME

1 (1-pound 14-ounce) can tomatoes
2 (10½ ounce) cans beef bouillon
2 cups water
3 tablespoons onions, chopped
1 bay leaf
1 stalk celery
6 cloves
Salt and pepper to taste

Combine all the ingredients and simmer uncovered for 30 minutes. Strain and taste to adjust seasoning. This is better if prepared the day before so all the flavors have a chance to get acquainted.

Serves 6 to 8

TORTILLA SOUP

Everytime I go to Texas I come back with a fabulous recipe. This time a lady rancher from El Paso shared her cousin's tortilla soup with me... so naturally I have to share it with you. It will be a real hit every time you serve it.

1 small onion, chopped
1 (4-ounce) can green chiles, chopped
2 cloves garlic, crushed
2 tablespoons oil
1 cup tomatoes, peeled and chopped
1 (10½ ounce) can beef bouillon
1 (10½ ounce) can chicken broth
1½ cups water
1½ cups tomato juice
1 teaspoon ground cumin
1 teaspoon chili powder
1 teaspoon salt
⅛ teaspoon pepper
2 teaspoons Worcestershire sauce
1 tablespoon steak sauce
3 tortillas, cut into ½-inch strips
¼ cup Cheddar cheese, shredded

Saute onion, chiles and garlic in oil until soft. Add the tomatoes, bouillon, chicken broth, water, tomato juice, cumin, chili powder, salt, pepper, Worcestershire and steak sauce. Bring this to a boil. Lower the heat. Cover the pan and simmer for 1 hour. Add tortillas and the cheese and simmer 10 minutes longer.

My husband could make this his whole meal. However, this recipe is supposed to serve 6.

VICHYSSOISE IN MUGS

2 leeks
2 tablespoons butter
1½ cups potatoes, thinly sliced
1 can chicken broth
2 teaspoons sugar
½ teaspoon salt
¼ teaspoon pepper
1 cup milk
1 cup heavy cream

Remove the green tops from leeks and slice the white part into thin slices. Saute the leek in the butter for 5 minutes, add potatoes and chicken broth. Cook uncovered over low to medium heat until the potatoes are tender. Put half the mixture in the blender and blend. Repeat with other half of mixture. Add remaining ingredients and stir well. May serve this warmed as well as chilled in a mug with a sprinkling of chives.

Serves 6

CHILLED ZUCCHINI SOUP

4 medium zucchini, quartered and sliced
2 (15-ounce) cans chicken broth
1 bunch green onions, chopped
1 teaspoon salt
1 teaspoon pepper
Dill to taste
2 (8-ounce) packages cream cheese
1 cup sour cream
Chopped chives or paprika for garnish

In a saucepan combine the zucchini, chicken broth, green onions, salt, pepper and dill to taste. Simmer about 20 minutes. Blend the cream cheese and sour cream until smooth. Then blend in zucchini mixture a small portion at a time until smooth. Cool and then chill overnight. Serve very cold, garnished with chives or paprika.

Serves 6 to 8

GRILLED CHEESERS FOR GOBLINS

24 slices white bread, trimmed of crusts
12 slices Swiss cheese
12 thin slices baked or broiled ham
½ cup butter

Place a slice of cheese and a slice of ham on each of 12 slices. Cover with remaining bread and press firmly together. Melt butter in a skillet. Dip both sides of each sandwich in the butter. Lay sandwiches on a cookie sheet and bake in a 300 degree oven 5 to 10 minutes, or until cheese melts. Cut diagonally. Serve hot. Big kids and little kids love these. We serve these with mugs of tomato soup. Great fun.

CLASSIC HAM AND CHEESE

12 slices firm white bread
½ cup butter, softened
1 tablespoon Dijon mustard
6 slices boiled ham
6 slices Fontina cheese
3 eggs
½ teaspoon salt
1 cup milk
Butter for frying

Spread one side of the bread with ½ cup butter mixed with mustard. Top 6 of the slices, butter side up, with ham and cheese, and another slice of bread butter side down. In a shallow dish beat eggs with salt and milk. Melt butter in a frying pan. Soak each sandwich in the egg mixture and brown slowly in the butter on both sides. Drain on paper towels and cut into 4 squares. Keep warm until ready to serve.

A miniature version of the grilled ham and cheese sandwich you will find in French cafes. C'est magnifique—

Serves 6

MORNAY SAUCE

2 tablespoons butter
1 tablespoon onion, minced
2 tablespoons flour
1 cup hot milk
Salt to taste
¼ cup Jarlsberg or Gruyere cheese, shredded

Melt butter in a saucepan and in it saute onion, until it is soft. Stir in flour and cook over low heat for 3 minutes, stirring constantly. Remove pan from heat and add salt and milk, stirring with a wire whisk. Simmer over medium heat for 10 minutes, stirring occassionally. Add cheese and remove from heat as soon as the cheese is melted.

SANDWICH

4 slices dark pumpernickle bread (from round loaf)
2 avocados, peeled and sliced
8 slices poached chicken breasts (3 half breasts of chicken)
8 mushrooms, sliced
4 to 8 slices Jarlsberg or Gruyere cheese

Heat broiler. Put slices of bread on the broiler pan. Cover with avocado slices then chicken slices. Put sliced mushrooms on chicken and cover with Mornay sauce. Top with cheese. Put sandwiches under broiler until the cheese melts.

This is so fabulous you'll make it again and again.

Serves 4

APPLESAUCE NUT BURGER

2 pounds lean ground beef
1 onion, finely chopped
⅔ cup applesauce
1 egg
Salt and pepper to taste
8 hamburger buns, toasted and buttered
½ cup butter or margarine
1 cup nuts, chopped
Salt to taste

Combine beef, onion, applesauce, eggs and seasonings. Shape into 8 patties. Place on grill and cook over medium coals 4 minutes per side or until done. While burgers are cooking, saute nuts in butter or margarine and season to taste. When meat is done, place in buns and spoon nut mixture over each patty. Serve immediately.

Scrumptious

Serves 6 to 8

BEEF BURGERS

1½ pounds lean ground beef
Salt and pepper to taste
1 can French fried onion rings, chopped
¼ cup beer

Lightly mix all ingredients and shape into 6 patties. Place on grill. Cook over medium coals 4 minutes per side or until done. Serve on toasted Kaiser roll with all your favorite goodies.

Serves 4 to 6

BARBECUE BURGERS FOR THE GANG

1 medium onion, chopped
1½ pounds hamburger
2 tablespoons cooking oil
2 tablespoons vinegar
2 tablespoons brown sugar
¼ cup lemon juice
3 tablespoons Worcestershire sauce
½ tablespoon mustard
1 cup catsup
1 cup water
½ cup celery, chopped
Pinch of salt

Brown hamburger and onion in oil in a skillet, add remaining ingredients and simmer for 30 minutes. Serve in hamburger buns or pita halves.

This is a great family burger.

Serves 12 to 14

ORIENTAL BURGERS

1½ pounds lean ground beef
Pepper to taste
¼ tablespoon mushrooms, chopped
¼ teaspoon ground ginger
1 teaspoon soy sauce
1 teaspoon sugar

Lightly mix all ingredients and shape into 6 patties. Place on grill and cook 4 minutes per side or until done. Serve with hot rice and oriental stir fried vegetables.

Serves 4 to 6

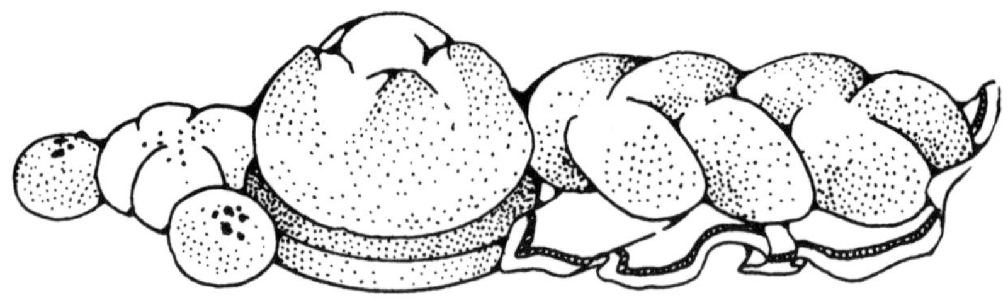

PATRIOTIC BURGERS FOR THE FOURTH

¾ cup onion, chopped
1 tablespoon cooking oil
½ (10-ounce) package frozen chopped spinach
1 egg
Salt and pepper to taste
½ teaspoon oregano
1½ pounds ground chuck
Toasted French rolls or sesame hamburger buns

Cook onion slowly in oil until transparent. Add spinach, heat until thawed and liquid evaporates. Cool. Beat egg with seasonings. Mix in beef and egg with spinach mixture. Shape into 6 patties. Grill over hot coals to desired degree of doneness. Serve on toasted rolls.

Serves 6

SLOPPY JOES

1 pound ground beef
½ cup catsup
1 tablespoon vinegar
1 teaspoon sugar
1 tablespoon prepared mustard
1 tablespoon Worcestershire sauce
½ cup onion, chopped
Salt and pepper to taste
English muffins or hamburger buns

Combine all the ingredients except the buns and cook over medium heat for 20 minutes. Serve over hot buns or muffins.

Serves 4

AVOCADO PITAS

1 avocado, peeled, seeded and chopped
½ cup cucumber, chopped
½ cup carrot, chopped
½ cup cauliflower, chopped
½ cup mushrooms, sliced
½ cup tomatoes, sliced
½ cup Monterey jack cheese, cubed
½ cup chicken or turkey, chopped and cubed
½ cup bottled Italian dressing
1 teaspoon lemon juice
4 pita breads

Combine all ingredients, except bread. Slit the pita in half and fill each pocket with ¼ of the mixture.

Serves 4

EASY PITA POCKETS

1 pound ground beef
½ cup barbecue sauce
2 tablespoons parsley, chopped
1 teaspoon salt
½ teaspoon mint flakes
1 medium green pepper, diced
1 medium onion, chopped
3 pita rounds, cut in half
1 small carton sour cream or plain yogurt

Brown ground beef and drain off fat. Add remaining ingredients except pita and sour cream. Cover and simmer for 5 minutes. Warm pita bread and fill with meat mixture. Serve with a dab of sour cream or plain yogurt on top.

Serves 4 to 6

LEMON-TUNA SANDWICH SPREAD

1 can tuna
3 tablespoons soft butter
3 tablespoons lemon juice
⅛ teaspoon celery seed
2 tablespoons sweet pickle relish

Mix all ingredients well. Best on rye or pumpernickel bread.

Makes 1 cup

eggs, cheese & pancakes

BREAKFAST APPLE CHEESE BAKE

½ pound bacon
8 slices white bread, crusts removed
2 cups applesauce
2 cups Cheddar cheese, grated
6 eggs
2 cups milk
1 teaspoon celery salt
½ teaspoon dry mustard
Dash pepper
Additional bacon for garnish, if desired

Cook bacon until crisp, drain and crumble. Place half the bread slices in the bottom of a greased baking dish. Cover bread with applesauce, cheese and bacon. Top with remaining bread slices. Beat eggs, stir in milk, celery salt, mustard and pepper. Pour egg mixture over ingredients in baking dish. Let stand in refrigerator 1 hour or overnight. Bake in a 325 degree oven for 50 to 55 minutes or until top is puffy and golden. If desired, garnish with additional crisp bacon strips. Serve immediately.

Wonderful!

Serves 6

SUNDAY EGGS A LA CAPERS

1 dozen hard-boiled eggs, halved
1 jalapeno pepper with the juice, minced
2 cups mayonnaise
1 cup sour cream
1 (2¼ ounce) bottle capers, undrained
Dash Tabasco
¼ cup chives, fresh or frozen
2 teaspoons dill weed
2 teaspoons fresh parsley, chopped
½ medium onion, finely chopped
Seasoned salt and pepper to taste

Arrange egg halves in a 9x13-inch baking dish. Top each with jalapeno pepper and a little juice. Mix remaining ingredients and pour over eggs. Bake in a 200 degree oven for 30 minutes. Serve with your favorite quick bread and honey dew melon wedges with fresh lime juice and a pitcher of bloody marys.

Fabulous!

Serves 12

EGGS EL PASO FOR BRUNCH

Olive oil
6 cloves garlic
Oregano
Salt
Parsley
6 eggs

Pour enough olive oil into large muffin tins to cover the bottom. To each tin, add 1 clove garlic, dash of oregano, salt and parsley. Put in preheated 400 degree oven When container is spittin' oil, remove from the oven and remove garlic. Drop an egg into each container. The eggs cook without returning to the oven. Cover with the chili sauce and serve.

CHILI SAUCE

1 tomato, chopped
1 jalapeno pepper, chopped and seeded
1 small onion, chopped
Salt and pepper to taste
Chopped fresh cilantro to taste

Mix all ingredients together. Cover eggs with sauce to serve. Sauce may be covered in the refrigerator.

Wonderful with hot corn bread and sliced fruit. My family also likes it served with buttered hot flour tortillas. Serve along side a margarita or Mexican coffee.

Serves 3

HAWAIIAN EGGS

½ cup butter
2 slices ham, 1-inch thick
1 pineapple, skinned and sliced
3 bananas, skinned and quartered
4 tablespoons honey or ⅓ cup brown sugar
6 eggs, beaten

Melt butter in a large skillet. Add ham. Fry until brown on both sides. Remove ham from skillet and cut each piece in half. Keep on warm platter. Put sliced pineapple and quartered bananas in skillet with the honey or the brown sugar. Fry until they are barely soft, not mushy. Remove fruit from skillet. Scramble the beaten eggs in the skillet. Be sure that each guest gets a little of the pineapple, bananas and scrambled eggs with their piece of ham. This is wonderful with baking powder biscuits. Start the brunch with gin fizzes.

MARVELOUS!

Serves 4

LONDON EGGS AND ONIONS

2 large sweet Bermuda onions
3 slices white bread
1 cup Jack cheese, grated (you can use more if you like)
Softened butter
3 eggs
1 cup milk
Salt
3 tablespoons butter

Peel onions and place in a saucepan. Cover with water, bring to a boil and cook 5 minutes. Drain well, cool. Cut onions into ½-inch slices and set aside. Toast bread, butter and cut in half diagonally. Place buttered side down in the bottom of a 9x13-inch pan. Place onion slices over toast and then sprinkle with the cheese. Beat together eggs, milk and salt to taste. Pour over onions. Dot with 3 tablespoons butter. Bake at 350 degrees for 30 minutes or until firm.

Serves 6 to 8

MUSHROOM STUFFED EGGS

8 hard-cooked eggs
1 cup fresh mushrooms, finely chopped
1 tablespoon butter or margarine
3 tablespoons mayonnaise
1 tablespoon chili sauce
¼ teaspoon lemon juice
Salt and pepper to taste

Lightly saute mushrooms in butter or margarine and cool. Slice eggs lengthwise and remove yolks. Blend crumbled yolks with mushroom mixture and other ingredients. Refill egg halves and chill before serving.

Serves 4

MAKE AHEAD SCRAMBLED EGGS AND MUSHROOMS

1 dozen eggs
½ cup light cream
1 teaspoon salt
¼ teaspoon pepper
1½ tablespoons butter

SAUCE

2 tablespoons butter
2 tablespoons flour
¼ teaspoon salt
⅛ teaspoon pepper
1 cup milk
Parsley
1 (3 to 4-ounce) can mushrooms, drained

Crack eggs into a bowl and add light cream, salt and pepper. Beat until blended. Melt butter in a large frying pan and pour in the egg mixture. Cook slowly, stirring occasionally until the eggs are almost set. Fold sauce into eggs while they are still creamy. Keep the mixture warm over hot water in chafing dish, in slow oven or low heat in an electric skillet. Sprinkle with parsley.

SAUCE

Melt butter over low heat in a saucepan, blend in flour and seasonings. Cook over low heat stirring until mixture is smooth and bubbly. Remove from heat. Stir in milk and mushrooms. Return to heat and bring to a boil, stirring constantly. Boil 1 minute.

These wonderful eggs can be made a little in advance and kept warm over boiling water, in a chafing dish or in a 200 degree oven. Now you can have fun at your own brunch.

Serves 6

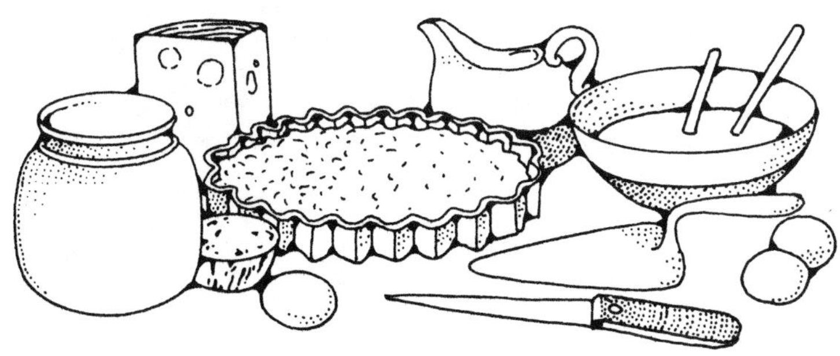

HAM AND POTATO OMELET FOR TWO

1 potato, cooked and thinly sliced
½ onion, thinly sliced
5 tablespoons butter
Salt and pepper to taste
½ cup cooked ham, diced
4 eggs, beaten
Parsley

Saute potato and onion with 4 tablespoons hot butter until cooked. Salt and pepper to taste. Stir in ham and quickly cook until crisp. In an omelet pan, melt 1 tablespoon butter and add eggs. As mixture begins to thicken add ham, onion and the potato. Place omelet pan under the broiler. Broil, watching closely until it is well-done and brown on the top. Serve hot on warmed plate. Sprinkle with parsley.

I serve this dish with thick beefsteak tomatoes, homemade toasted bread and steamy hot coffee in mugs with a cinnamon stick for the stirrer.

Serves 2

SAUSAGE STRATA

For lunch, brunch or a midnight supper here is a casserole that is popular with both men and women.

Lightly brown 1½ pounds bulk sausage, stirring it to make it crumble. Pour off fat. Add 2 tablespoons minced green onions, ¼ cup chopped pimiento and 1 cup petite peas. Season to taste with salt and pepper. Blend in 1 teaspoon dry mustard and set aside. Line the bottom of a greased 8x12-inch baking pan with 6 slices of white or wheat bread that have had the crusts removed. If there are any spaces, fill with bread strips. Spoon sausage mixture over bread slices and cover with 6 more slices of bread with crusts removed. Over the top pour 6 beaten eggs with 3 cups of milk, ½ teaspoon salt and 2 teaspoons Worcestershire sauce. Chill overnight in the fridge. Next day place casserole in pan of hot water and bake at 325 degrees for 1 hour and 15 minutes. Cut into 6 to 8 squares for serving. Garnish each square with pimiento strips and sliced olives.

Serves 6

DOLPHINS SUPER BOWL PANCAKE

2 tablespoons butter or margarine
3 eggs
½ teaspoon salt
½ cup flour
½ cup milk
1 large apple, cored and sliced
½ cup butter
¾ cup powdered sugar
1 lemon

Preheat oven to 450 degrees. Place butter in a 10-inch oven proof skillet. Put in oven and melt. Beat eggs. Add salt, flour and milk. Beat until smooth. Place apple slices into melted butter in pan. Pour batter over all. Reduce heat to 350 degrees and bake until crisp and golden. Serve in wedges with butter, powdered sugar and lemon juice.

Serves 3

pasta, dressings, dumplings & rice

CANNELLONI

¼ pound veal, cut in ½-inch cubes
½ pound beef, cut in ½-inch cubes
¼ cup onion, chopped
1 garlic clove, minced
½ teaspoon lemon peel
2 tablespoons butter or margarine
1 (10-ounce) package chopped spinach, cooked and drained
Dash thyme
Dash pepper
½ teaspoon salt
2 eggs, beaten
16 pieces crepes, cooked
1½ cups spaghetti sauce
½ cup Parmesan cheese

Cook first 6 ingredients together for 20 minutes. Add spinach and put mixture through the fine blade of a meat grinder. Season with thyme, pepper and salt. Add eggs and mix well. Put mixture in a pastry bag and fill each crepe. Arrange side by side in a 10x6x1½-inch baking dish. Cover with spaghetti sauce. Bake in 350 degree oven for 10 minutes. Sprinkle with cheese and brown under broiler for 2 minutes.

Serves 8

CREPES ENSENADA

12 flour tortillas
1 pound Jack cheese, grated
12 ham slices
White sauce
Avocado slices for garnish

WHITE SAUCE

1 quart milk
8 tablespoons butter
8 tablespoons flour
1 teaspoon salt
Dash pepper
Chopped green chiles (optional)
¾ cup Cheddar cheese, grated

To make sauce, melt butter over low heat, blend in flour and seasonings. Add milk all at once and cook stirring constantly, until thickened. Remove from heat and add chiles and cheese. On each tortilla place a slice of ham and sprinkle some Jack cheese over ham. Roll up and place seam side down in a 9x13-inch baking pan. Pour white sauce over all. Bake at 350 degrees for 35 to 45 minutes or until hot. Garnish with avocado slices. Serve with a fruit salad.

Serves 6

MOM'S CORN BREAD DRESSING

2 quarts crumbled corn bread (packaged mix can be used)
3 slices loaf bread or cold biscuits
2 cups celery, chopped
1 cup onion, chopped
2 teaspoons poultry seasoning
1 tablespoon sugar (if package mix is not used for corn bread)
2 cups turkey stock
1 (10¾ ounce) can chicken broth
4 eggs, well-beaten

Mix all ingredients well. Spoon into a greased pan and bake at 350 degrees for 20 to 30 minutes. Do not overbake.

Makes 3 quarts of heavenly corn bread stuffing.

WILD RICE DRESSING

1 cup wild rice
7 slices bread
Butter
1 cup celery, diced
1 medium onion, sliced
1 (4-ounce) can mushrooms, sliced
1 can chicken and rice soup
½ pound bulk sausage

Cook rice in boiling salted water for 30 minutes or until tender. Drain. Toast bread and spread with butter. Cut into cubes. Combine all ingredients. Place in a greased casserole. Bake at 350 degrees for 1 hour.

Super!

Serves 6 to 8

SAGE & ONION STUFFING

2 cups onion, chopped
¼ cup butter or margarine
2 cups mushrooms, coarsely chopped
¼ cup parsley, chopped
2 teaspoons sage
½ teaspoon pepper
1 (16-ounce) package herb stuffing mix
Water, wine, butter or margarine

Saute onions in butter until transparent. Add mushrooms, parsley, sage and pepper. Saute 3 minutes more. Prepare stuffing according to package instructions using water, wine, butter or margarine. Add to onion and mushroom mixture and toss lightly to mix.

Makes 6 cups

TURKEY DRESSING PRIMA VERA

1 package seasoned poultry dressing
¼ cube butter
1 cup chicken broth
2 bunches fresh spinach
5 links sausage
6 stalks celery and tops
1 large onion, chopped
Handful of parsley, chopped
1 small can black olives, chopped
¼ cup Parmesan cheese
2 eggs
Salt and pepper to taste

Warm butter and chicken broth over low heat. Pour over poultry dressing and let stand. Wash and trim spinach. Place in boiling water until limp. Remove and drain thoroughly. Cool. Fry sausage slowly over low heat, pierce with a fork while cooking. Remove from pan and cool. Saute onion, celery and parsley in sausage drippings until soft and set aside. In a large bowl place moistened poultry dressing, chopped spinach, cooked vegetables, sausage, minced olives and Parmesan cheese. Toss. Season to taste. Beat eggs and add to mixture. Stuff turkey and bake. Will stuff a 12 to 16 pound bird.

NEVER FAIL DUMPLINGS

Sift together 2¼ cups flour, 2 teaspoons baking powder and ¼ teaspoon salt. Combine flour mixture, 2 beaten eggs and 1 cup milk and mix well. Drop by teaspoons into boiling chicken, veal or broth stock or onto vegetable stew, even on sauerkraut. Cook for 10 minutes or till done.

Serves 4 to 6

TYROLEAN DUMPLINGS

5 hard crust French rolls cut into ½-inch cubes
½ cup milk
¼ teaspoon salt
2 eggs
8 strips of bacon , crisped and diced
1 tablespoon parsley
1 cup flour

Soak the bread cubes in the milk and add the salt, bacon and parsley. Add eggs and flour and blend well. Divide dough evenly into 5 portions form into balls and put into lightly salted boiling water (uncovered) for 10 minutes.

Makes 5 dumplings

FETTUCINI WITH PARSLEY SAUCE

1 pound fettucini or thin noodles
½ pound unsalted butter or margarine
½ cup heavy cream
½ cup parsley, chopped
1 teaspoon dried basil
½ teaspoon salt
Dash black pepper
2 cups Parmesan cheese, grated

Cook noodles according to package directions. Slice half of the margarine into warm bowl or chafing dish. Add cream, parsley, basil, salt and pepper. Drain noodles quickly and pour into bowl. Slice in remaining margarine. Toss gently turning noodles over and over, until noodles are well-coated. Add cheese and toss lightly until cheese coats noodles. Serve immediately.

Serve 4

SEAFOOD FETTUCINI WITH GARLIC AND MUSHROOMS

1 pound fettucini noodles
½ cup olive oil
½ cup garlic, minced
¼ cup green onions, chopped
½ cup parsley, chopped
½ cup fresh basil, chopped (don't fudge, get fresh)
1 pound fresh mushrooms, sliced
½ cup dry white wine (I love vermouth)
Dash of Tabasco
½ tablespoon chicken stock base
½ tablespoon beef stock base
1 cup Italian tomatoes (use canned, they're better)
1 cup cooked lobster, chopped
1 cup cooked shrimp
1 cup cooked crab, chopped
¼ pound sweet butter
½ cup parsley, finely chopped

In a large skillet add olive oil and saute the garlic, green onions, parsley and basil. Add the mushrooms, saute for a few minutes then add the wine, Tabasco and the tomatoes. Bring to a boil. Add the chicken and beef stocks. Let simmer gently. Add seafood, simmering until just heated through. Boil fettucini until al dente. Drain. Add butter then sauce and top with parsley. Serve immediately.

Mama Mia Is This Good — This is so good it should be against the law. The marriage of fresh basil, garlic and mushrooms make this a memorable occasion, and with the seafood, now you have a fabulous dinner. Serve with a Cabernet, crusty bread and a green salad. For dessert a little sherbert with liqueur over the top and Italian cookies.

Serves 8

HUSH PUPPIES

2 cups corn meal
1 cup flour
1 tablespoon salt
4 teaspoons sugar
2 cups onion, finely chopped
4 teaspoons baking powder
2 eggs, beaten
2 cups (approximately) milk

Mix dry ingredients with onions, add eggs and milk. When paste-like consistency, drop from a teaspoon into deep hot fat. When done, they will float. Drain on absorbent paper and serve.

Fit for a king rather than the hounds. The perfect accompaniment for hot fried catfish.

Serves 4 to 6

KNISHES

Dough

2½ cups sifted flour
1 teaspoon baking powder
½ teaspoon salt
2 eggs
⅔ cup salad oil
2 tablespoons water

Sift the flour, baking powder and salt into a bowl. Make a well in the center and drop the eggs, oil and water into it. Work the flour mixture with your hands and knead until smooth. There are two ways to fill the knishes. In either case, divide the dough in two and roll as thin as possible. Brush with oil. Now you can spread the filling on one side of the dough and roll it up like a jelly roll. Cut into 1½-inch slices. Place on an oiled baking sheet cut side down. Press down lightly to flatten. Or you can cut the rolled dough in 3-inch circles. Place a tablespoon of the filling on each, draw the edges together and pinch firmly. Place on an oiled baking sheet, pinched edges up. Bake in a 375 degree oven for 35 minutes or until browned.

Makes about 24

POTATO

1 cup onions, chopped
6 tablespoons chicken fat or butter
2 cups mashed potatoes
1 egg
1 teaspoon salt
¼ teaspoon pepper

Brown the onions in the fat or butter. Beat in the potatoes, egg, salt and pepper until fluffy.

CHEESE

1½ cups scallions or onions, diced
4 tablespoons butter
2 cups pot cheese
1 egg
1½ teaspoons salt
⅛ teaspoon pepper
2 tablespoons sour cream

Scallions are better than onions for this so try to get them. Brown the scallions in the butter and beat in the cheese, egg, salt, pepper and sour cream until smooth.

POTATO-DOUGH KNISHES

¾ cup onions, minced
6 tablespoons chicken fat or butter
4 cups mashed potatoes
½ cup potato flour
3 eggs
1 teaspoon salt
¼ teaspoon pepper

Brown the onions in 4 tablespoons chicken fat or butter. Cool. Knead together the remaining fat or butter, the potatoes, potato flour, eggs, salt and pepper. Break off pieces (about 2-inches long) and flatten slightly. Place a teaspoon of browned onions on each and cover by pinching the edges together. Place on a greased baking sheet. Bake in a 375 degree oven for 25 minutes.

Makes about 20

LASAGNA

1 pound lasagna
2 tablespoons olive oil
½ pound ground beef
½ pound ground pork
½ pound Italian sausage
1 medium onion, minced
1 clove garlic, minced
1 teaspoon parsley, minced
1½ cans tomato paste
2 cups water
½ teaspoon salt
½ teaspoon pepper
5 quarts water
3 tablespoons salt
1 pound Mozzarella cheese, thinly sliced
¾ pound Ricotta
2 tablespoons grated Romano cheese
1 cup ripe olives, halved

Brown beef, pork and sausage in saucepan with oil, onion, garlic and parsley. Add tomato paste, 2 cups water, salt and pepper and simmer 1½ hours. Bring 5 quarts water to a boil, add salt and lasagna (cut in half) and cook 20 minutes, or until tender, stirring almost constantly to prevent sticking together. Drain. In casserole dish arrange lasagna in layers alternating with meat sauce, mozzarella, olives and Ricotta, until lasagna is all used, and ending in like sequence, ricotta last. Sprinkle with grated cheese. Bake in a 375 degree oven about 20 minutes or until Mozzarella is melted, and serve.
Serves 8

AVOCADO PASTA FOR TWO

1 quart water
4-ounces corkscrew shaped pasta
Homemade pesto sauce or 1 container (4-ounce) frozen pesto sauce, thawed
⅓ cup white wine
1 cup Jack cheese, grated
1 tomato, sliced
1 avocado, cut into wedges

Bring water to a boil. Add pasta and return to a boil. Cook 8 minutes or until done. Return pasta to skillet after draining and add wine and pesto sauce. Toss. Top with cheese. Make a ring of tomatoes around edge and arrange avocado wedges spoke fashion in center. Serve from skillet.
Serves 2

EASY SKILLET PASTA

1 teaspoon oregano
1 envelope onion soup mix
1 pound lean ground beef
1 (28-ounce) can tomatoes, undrained
2 cups water
2 cups uncooked macaroni
⅓ cup Parmesan cheese
Mozzarella cheese

In a large frying pan brown beef, drain off fat. Add soup mix, oregano, tomatoes and water. Bring to a boil, stir in macaroni. Simmer, covered, stirring occasionally for 20 minutes or until macaroni is tender. Stir in Parmesan cheese and top with Mozzarella cheese. Cover and let sit for 10 minutes. This dish is great for back to school . . . easy, good and kind to your pocket book.

Serves 4

MUSHROOM PIZZA

1 cup biscuit mix
⅓ cup milk
1 cup fresh mushrooms, sliced
1 tablespoon margarine
1 tablespoon olive oil
8 ounces Mozzarella or Jack cheese, grated
1 (8-ounce) can tomato sauce
½ teaspoon oregano
Salt and pepper to taste

Blend biscuit mix with milk and roll out on a floured board to form a 14-inch circle. Saute the mushrooms in the margarine 3 minutes. Brush the biscuit dough with the oil and coat with sauce. Put mushrooms on top. Sprinkle with the seasonings and top with the cheeses. Bake 10 minutes at 450 degrees.

Serves 4 to 6

EL CHOLO'S MEXICAN SPAGHETTI

1 package curly spaghetti (capalini)
1 clove garlic, chopped
1 onion, chopped
1 bell pepper, chopped
3 fresh tomatoes, peeled and chopped or 1 can (16-ounce) whole tomatoes
Olive oil
1 (10¾ ounce) can beef bouillon

In a skillet fry garlic, onion and pepper. Add tomatoes and beef broth diluted with a little water. Salt and pepper to taste. Simmer 15 to 20 minutes. Fry spaghetti in olive oil until brown, turning once, they will brown quickly. Add to tomato mixture and simmer for 3 to 4 minutes. Separate spaghetti with a spoon and cook another 2 to 3 minutes.

Serves 4

AVOCADO TOSTADO

4 flour tortillas
Oil
1 (15-ounce) can chili with beans
Fresh salsa
2 avocados, sliced
1 onion, chopped
2 medium tomatoes, chopped
½ pound Monterey Jack cheese, grated
Sour cream
Black olives

Place tortillas on a baking sheet and rub with oil. Bake at 350 degrees for 5 minutes or until crisp. Divide chili amongst the tortillas. Bake at 350 degrees for 20 minutes. Top with remaining ingredients and top with a dollop of sour cream.

Serves 4

RICE OR BULGUR PILAF

2 tablespoons butter
2 tablespoons onion, chopped
1 clove garlic, minced
2 cups rice or 2 cups cracked wheat
2 tablespoons parsley, chopped
½ teaspoon powdered oregano
4 cups chicken stock or light stock
¼ cup pine nuts

In a large casserole melt butter and saute onion and garlic until transparent. Add the rice or cracked wheat and stir well. Add the rest of the ingredients except the stock and pine nuts. Saute 5 minutes, stirring occasionally. Add the stock. Cover the casserole and place in a 350 degree oven for 1 hour. Just before serving sprinkle the pine nuts over all.

Serves 6

INDONESIAN FRIED RICE (NASI GORENG)

½ pound fresh or frozen shelled shrimp
½ pound boneless pork or beef top round steak
2 eggs, beaten
1 tablespoon cooking oil
1 medium onion, finely chopped (¼ cup)
2 cloves garlic, minced
1 teaspoon crushed red pepper or ¼ teaspoon
ground red pepper
4 cups cooked rice, chilled
¼ cup soy sauce
1 teaspoon blachan (shrimp paste)
or anchovy paste (optional)
2 tablespoons cooking oil
1 cup cabbage, coarsely chopped
1 cup fresh bean sprouts or ½ of a 16-ounce can bean sprouts, (drained)
3 green onions, bias sliced into 1-inch pieces
1 medium cucumber, peeled and sliced
2 medium tomatoes, thinly sliced

Thaw shrimp if frozen; halve lengthwise. Partially freeze pork or beef, thinly slice across the grain into bite-size strips. In a 12-inch skillet cook eggs in the 1 tablespoon cooking oil, without stirring, till set. Invert skillet over baking sheet to remove cooked eggs. Cut into short narrow strips. Stir together the onion, garlic, blachan or anchovy paste, if desired and red pepper. In the same skillet cook onion mixture in the 2 tablespoons hot oil until onion is tender but not brown. Add shrimp and pork or beef strips; stir-fry 5 to 6 minutes. Add cabbage, bean sprouts and green onions, stir-fry 2 minutes. Stir in rice, soy sauce and half of the egg strips. Cover and heat through. To serve, spoon the rice mixture onto a heated serving platter. Arrange the remaining egg strips atop the rice mixture, and garnish edge of platter with cucumber slices, if desired. Serve with sliced tomatoes.

Serves 4

MUSHROOM FRIED RICE

1 cup fresh mushrooms, sliced
1 onion, minced
2 tablespoons margarine
1 tablespoon parsley, minced
2 tablespoons pimiento, diced
2 cups cooked rice
2 eggs, beaten

Melt margarine in a large skillet. Saute mushrooms and onion together for 5 minutes. Add parsley and pimiento. Spoon in cooked rice and stir until hot. Just before serving stir in egg and continue cooking until partially set. Garnish with paprika.

Serves 4

salads & dressings

APPLE SNOW SALAD

1 (8¾ ounce) can crushed pineapple, undrained
2 eggs, beaten
½ cup sugar
¼ cup water
3 tablespoons lemon juice
Dash of salt
2 cups unpared apple, diced
½ cup walnuts, chopped
1 cup whipping cream, whipped

In a saucepan combine first 6 ingredients. Cook over low heat, stirring constantly, until thickened. Chill. When cool, stir in apple and walnuts. Fold in whipping cream. Pour into 8x8x2-inch pan. Freeze until firm. Let stand at room temperature 10 to 15 minutes before serving. Cut into squares.

Serves 8

APPLESAUCE GELATIN SALAD

2 cups boiling water
½ cup red cinnamon candies
2 (3-ounce) packages lemon gelatin
2 cups unsweetened applesauce
1 tablespoon lemon rind
½ cup nuts, chopped
Few drops red food coloring
2 (3-ounce) packages cream cheese
¼ cup milk or light cream
2 tablespoons salad dressing

Dissolve candies in boiling water. Add gelatin, applesauce, lemon juice, nuts and food coloring. Place in refrigerator until partially set. Blend together the cream cheese, cream and salad dressing. Swirl into the gelatin mixture to make a marble effect. Chill in a 6-cup ring mold.

Wonderful with pork!

Serves 6 to 8

CHRISTMAS EVE AVOCADO SALAD MOLD

1 small package lime jello
1½ cups boiling water
1 tablespoon onion juice
1 tablespoon lemon juice
½ cup whipping cream
½ cup mayonnaise
1½ cups avocado, diced
½ cup celery, diced
1 tablespoon green pepper, diced

Mix jello and water, cool and let thicken slightly. Add onion and lemon juice. Mix well. Whip jello. Now whip cream and mix with mayonnaise. Add to whipped jello. Mix avocado, celery and green peppers together. Lightly fold into jello mixture. Pour into mold. Garnish with watercress.

Serves 8

AVOCADO AND ORANGE SALAD

1 avocado, sliced
1 cucumber, peeled and sliced
1 head lettuce, torn into pieces
2 tablespoons green onions, chopped
1 (11-ounce) can mandarin oranges, drained

DRESSING

½ cup oil
¼ cup orange juice
2 tablespoons sugar
2 tablespoons red wine vinegar
1 tablespoon lemon juice
½ teaspoon grated orange peel
¼ teaspoon salt

In a salad bowl combine avocado, cucumber, lettuce, onion and the oranges. Mix the dressing ingredients together and pour over the salad just before serving.

Serves 4

AVOCADO APPLE SALAD

1 apple, cored and diced
⅓ cup raisins
¼ cup slivered almonds
¼ cup celery, diced
¼ cup plain yogurt
2 teaspoons honey
1 avocado, diced

Combine all ingredients and serve on a green lettuce leaf.

Serves 2

BANANA SALAD

½ cup lemon juice
½ cup sugar
1 tablespoon sherry
6 bananas
1 small jar Maraschino cherries

Heat the lemon juice with the sugar until the sugar is dissolved. Add the sherry and chill. Chill the bananas. Peel, slice them thinly into a glass bowl and scatter the cherries over them. Pour dressing over the fruit and serve cold.

Serves 4 to 6

HOLIDAY CHEESE SALAD

3 cups cream style cottage cheese
1 (8-ounce) container non-dairy whipped topping
1 (6-ounce) package orange jello
1 (13½ ounce) can pineapple tidbits or crushed pineapple, drained
1 (11½ ounce) can mandarin oranges, drained

Blend cottage cheese and whipped topping. Stir in dry jello. Fold in pineapple tidbits and mandarin oranges. Press into mold. Set for 3 to 4 hours.

Serves 12 to 15

TOMATO-CHEESE ICE

2 tablespoons Roquefort cheese, grated
1 (3-ounce) package cream cheese
¼ teaspoon onion, grated
1 teaspoon Worcestershire
1 teaspoon salt
⅛ teaspoon pepper
2 tablespoons lemon juice
2 cups tomato juice
2 eggs whites, stiffly beaten

Cream together roquefort cheese and cream cheese. Add onion, Worcestershire sauce, salt, pepper and lemon juice. Gradually add tomato juice, blending smoothly. Pour into freezing tray and freeze until all but a portion of the center is frozen. Remove from tray, break up in a bowl and beat smooth with a chilled rotary beater. Quickly fold in beaten egg whites, return to freezing tray and serve in sherbet glasses when frozen. This is a delicious first course.

Serves 6

HOLIDAY CHERRY SALAD

1 (16-ounce) can pitted bing cherries
1 (6-ounce) package orange flavored jello
⅓ cup lemon juice
1 (3-ounce) package cream cheese
¾ cup walnuts, chopped

Heat 1¾ cup liquid (use cherry juice or water). Pour over jello and add lemon juice. When cool add cherries that have been stuffed with a mixture of cream cheese and nuts. I use a circular mold. Give it a light grease so you can unmold it easily.

DRESSING

1 cup shipping cream
2 to 3 tablespoons mayonnaise

Whip whipping cream and fold into mayonnaise. You can add pink coloring if you like. This recipe doubles beautifully.

Serves 6

CREAMY COLESLAW

Slice half a head of cabbage into match stick pieces. Place in a large bowl and toss cabbage pieces with 2 carrots that are finely shredded. Stir in 3 tablespoons dry minced onions, 1 tablespoon seasoned salt and 1 cup milk. Cover and refrigerate 1 hour. In another bowl mix together the dressing ingredients.

2 cups mayonnaise
8-ounces sour cream
3 tablespoons sugar
1 teaspoon Dijon mustard
1 teaspoon celery seed

Pour the dressing mixture over cabbage mixture, coating well. Cover. Refrigerate another hour before serving. Leftover slaw can stay in the fridge up to 2 days.

Serves 6

RANCH SLAW

1 carrot
1 zucchini
½ green pepper
1 celery stalk
¼ head cabbage
¼ head red cabbage

DRESSING

⅓ cup olive oil
2 tablespoons fresh lemon juice
1 egg yolk
1 teaspoon Dijon mustard
Salt and pepper to taste
Minced parsley for garnish

Cut all the vegetables into julienne strips or grate. Wrap green and red cabbage in a towel and refrigerate 1 hour. Combine vegetables into a salad bowl and toss lightly. Whisk all remaining ingredients except parsley in a small bowl until well blended. Pour over vegetables and toss. Sprinkle with minced parsley.

Terrific salad for 2. Great with any type entree.

Serves 2

RED AND GREEN COLESLAW

2 cups green cabbage, shredded
1 cup red cabbage, shredded
1 small onion, cut into rings
½ cup evaporated milk
¼ cup sugar
½ teaspoon salt
¼ teaspoon pepper
¼ cup vinegar
2 firm ripe kiwi fruit, peeled and sliced

Place cabbage and onion in a salad bowl. Toss to mix. Chill. Mix evaporated milk with sugar, salt and pepper. Stir a few minutes until sugar has dissolved. Stir in vinegar. Add dressing to cabbage and toss to coat. Chill at least an hour before serving. At serving time, add kiwi fruit slices, toss gently to mix.

Serve 6 to 8

CURRIED CHICKEN SALAD LUNCHEON

2 cups cooked chicken breasts, diced
1 apple, peeled and diced
1 cup fresh pineapple, cubed
¼ cup white raisins
⅓ cup dates, chopped
2 tablespoons chopped chutney
½ teaspoon salt

Combine all ingredients and refrigerate.

DRESSING

2 teaspoons curry powder
2 tablespoons chicken broth
1 cup mayonnaise

Simmer curry powder in broth for 2 minutes, stirring to a smooth paste. Cool. Add paste to mayonnaise. Stir mayonnaise and curry powder mixture into chicken salad mixture 1 hour before serving.

Serves 4

JACKIE'S 24 HOUR CABBAGE SALAD

This salad should be refrigerated at least 24 hours before using. It will stay crispy for a long time. For the dressing, combine 1 tablespoon unflavored gelatin and ¼ cup cold water, let stand to soften. Heat together 1 cup vinegar and 1½ cups sugar until sugar is dissolved. Add 1 teaspoon celery seed, 1 teaspoon salt, ¼ teaspoon pepper and stir in softened gelatin. Let cool to thickness of cream then beat in 1 cup salad oil. Combine 6 to 8 cups shredded cabbage, 2 cups shredded carrots, 1 grated onion and 2 green peppers, grated. Toss with enough of the dressing to moisten. The remainder of the dressing will keep in the fridge for weeks.

This will be one of your favorites.

Serves 10 to 12

CRANBERRY SALAD

1 (1-pound) can whole cranberry sauce
1 cup boiling water
1 small package cherry gelatin
½ cup mayonnaise
1 apple, diced
¼ cup nuts, chopped

Heat cranberry sauce. Add boiling water to jello, stir until dissolved. Add cranberries and stir until smooth. Cool. Whip in mayonnaise and add apple and nuts. Pour into 1-quart mold and chill until set.

Serves 6

RASPBERRY-CRANBERRY MOLD

1 small package strawberry jello
¾ cup boiling water
1 (1-pound) can whole cranberry sauce
1 (20-ounce) can crushed pineapple, drained
1 pint sour cream
2 small packages raspberry jello
1½ cups boiling water
2 packages frozen raspberries

Dissolve the strawberry jello in the ¾ cup boiling water. Heat the cranberry sauce and add the crushed pineapple. Stir until well combined. Add to the strawberry jello and place in the bottom of a greased 9x13-inch dish. Chill in the refrigerator. Spread the sour cream over the set mixture. Chill 1 hour longer. Dissolve the raspberry gelatin mix in the 1½ cups boiling water. Add the frozen berries. Spoon this mixture over the sour cream and chill until set.

Serves 12 to 14

CUKES IN SOUR CREAM

1 large cucumber
1 cup sour cream
½ teaspoon dill weed
3 tablespoons white vinegar
¼ teaspoon salt
⅛ teaspoon white pepper

Pare skin and score cucumber lengthwise with a fork. Slice thinly. Mix together with the ingredients and chill at least 30 minutes before serving.

Serve 2 to 4

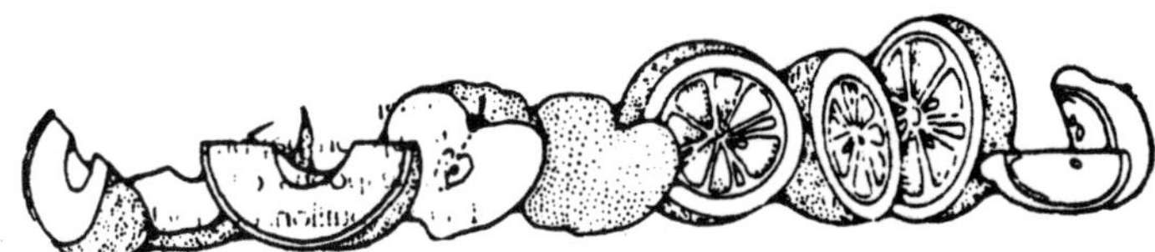

PINEAPPLE CUCUMBER SHRIMP BRUNCH

2 (20-ounce) cans sliced pineapple, chilled
4 cups cucumber slices
2 pounds shrimp, cooked and cleaned
12 hard-boiled eggs, shelled and carefully sliced
2 quarts assorted greens, torn into bite-size pieces
2 packages salad dressing, prepared as directed or
your own favorite creamy dressing

Drain pineapple. Divide and stack pineapple in center of 2 round serving plates. Cover the remaining surface of both serving plates with greens. Arrange shrimp and cucumber around the pineapple on both plates covering most of the lettuce. Use 6 rows (one egg per row) of sliced eggs for each platter, starting from the outer edge of the pineapples to the edge of the platter. Dribble some of the dressing over the stack of pineapple and put the rest in a small serving bowl.

This is so easy and looks so good and can be made way ahead.

Serves 8

HOLIDAY FRUIT SALAD WITH CREAM CHANTILLY

1 large navel orange
1 medium Delicious apple
1 (8-ounce) can chunk pineapple, drained
¼ cup celery, chopped
¼ cup walnuts, chopped
¼ cup Grand Marnier
Dash of cinnamon
Dash of nutmeg
Coconut

Peel orange over mixing bowl to catch the juice. Cut into chunks. Quarter apple and cut into chunks. Mix in remaining ingredients except coconut and stir. Refrigerate until icy cold, stirring now and then. Place in serving bowls and sprinkle with coconut and top with Cream Chantilly.

CREAM CHANTILLY

¼ cup brown sugar
1 cup sour cream
½ cup heavy cream
2 tablespoons lemon juice
2 tablespoons Grand Marnier

Combine all ingredients. (Can add more Grand Marnier, if desired.)

Serves 4

MISSISSIPPI FROZEN FRUIT SALAD

1 can apricots
1 can pears
1 can Queen Ann cherries
1 bottle red cherries
1 can pineapple
4 oranges, sliced
2 bananas
1 cup pecans

DRESSING

2 whole eggs
4 tablespoons vinegar
4 tablespoons sugar
1 jar marshmallow cream
1 cup whipping cream

Drain and chop fruits. Prepare the dressing. Beat eggs, add vinegar, sugar and cook in double boiler until thick, stirring constantly. Remove from heat and add marshmallow cream. Stir until dissolved. When cool, add whipped cream. Fold into the fruit mixture. Freeze for 24 hours. If more dressing is desired to top individual serving, double the recipe.

This is a favorite at every buffet in the South.

Serves a bunch

SPECTACULAR FRUIT SALAD

Mango, peeled and cut into thin strips
Orange, peeled and sliced crosswise
Pineapple, peeled and cut into small chunks
Seedless grapes, cut in half
Bibb lettuce
Watercress

DRESSING

⅓ cup sugar
1 teaspoon toasted sesame seeds
1 teaspoon salt
1 teaspoon dry mustard
4 tablespoons vinegar
1 cup oil
1 teaspoon paprika
1 teaspoon onion, grated

Mix ingredients for dressing in a jar. Cover, shake well and refrigerate. Place fruit, watercress and lettuce in a bowl in refrigerator. Shake dressing and pour over salad. Carefully toss and serve.

Serves the whole family

THANKSGIVING FRUIT SALAD

1 large can crushed pineapple, drained reserving the juice
1 small bottle Maraschino cherries, drained reserving the juice
1 can mandarin orange sections, drained reserving the juice
2 tablespoons butter
½ teaspoon salt
2 eggs, beaten
¾ cup sugar
1 tablespoon flour
½ pint whipping cream, whipped and sweetened
4 large apples, chopped
2 pounds seedless grapes, cut in half
2 navel oranges, cut up
4 bananas, cut

Place reserved juices in a saucepan. Heat to lukewarm. Add butter, salt, eggs, sugar and flour. Cook until smooth and thick. Cool. Add whipped cream and chill. Combine fruits with whipped cream dressing. Any amounts of the fruit can be varied to suit your own personal taste. You may also add chopped walnuts as well.

Serves 20 to 24

PETITE PEA SALAD

2 (10-ounce) packages tiny frozen peas, thawed
1 cup onion, diced
1 cup celery, diced
½ cup water chestnuts, sliced
1¼ cups sour cream
3 tablespoons mayonnaise
Juice of ½ lemon
Salt and pepper to taste
1 cup crisp bacon, crumbled
1 cup salted cashews

Combine all ingredients, except the bacon and the cashews, early in the day. Cover and refrigerate. When ready to serve, add cooked bacon and nuts. You may also add diced chicken breasts, tuna, etc. Just increase sour cream and mayonnaise to moisten. Serve on lettuce lined plate.

This is one of my favorites.

Serves 6

PARSLEY POTATO SALAD

8 medium potatoes, boiled in jackets
1½ cups mayonnaise
1 cup sour cream
1½ teaspoons horseradish
1 teaspoon celery seed
1½ teaspoons salt
1 cup parsley, chopped (do not omit or decrease)
2 medium onions, finely minced

Peel potatoes, cut into ⅛-inch slices. Combine mayonnaise, sour cream, horseradish, celery seed and salt and set aside. In another bowl mix parsley and onion. In a serving bowl arrange a layer of potatoes, salt very lightly, cover with a layer of the mayonnaise mixture and then a layer of the parsley mixture. Do not stir. Cover and refrigerate at least 10 to 12 hours. This salad is better if made the night before.

A different and delicious twist on an old standard.

Serves 8

GRANDMA'S HOT POTATO SALAD

Dice ½ cup bacon and fry until crisp. Remove bacon and let drippings cool to lukewarm. Combine 2 beaten eggs, ¼ cup vinegar, 1 teaspoon sugar, 1 teaspoon salt and beat until light. Stir into lukewarm bacon drippings and cook over low heat continuing to stir, until mixture is thickened. Pour over 1 onion, chopped and 4 cups of sliced, cooked potatoes (potatoes should be warm). Mix to coat potatoes and add crisp bacon, garnish with quartered hard-cooked eggs and parsley.

This is wonderful if served right after mixing.

Serves 6 to 8

THANKSGIVING RING MOLD

2 envelopes unflavored gelatin
½ cup sugar
2 tablespoons lemon juice
2 tablespoons water
3 cups hot cider
1 cup red apple, diced
¼ cup celery, diced
1 cup mincemeat

Mix gelatin with sugar in a saucepan. Add lemon juice and water. Place over low heat and stir until gelatin is dissolved. Add hot apple cider. Remove from heat and chill in refrigerator until the mixture is the consistency of unbeaten egg whites. Add diced apple and celery to the thickened gelatin. Carefully fold in the mincemeat. Pour into a 6-cup ring mold.

Serves 6 to 8

SEAFOOD PLUM SALAD

1 teaspoon Dijon mustard
¾ cup good mayonnaise
1 tablespoon lemon juice
Salt and pepper to taste
1 (7-ounce) can water packed tuna, broken into chunks
1 cup cooked shrimp
3 large plums, sliced
2 stalks celery, thinly sliced
Salad greens

Combine mustard, mayonnaise, lemon juice and seasonings. Add tuna, shrimp, plum slices and celery. Toss to mix. Serve on salad greens.

Delightful summer salad.

Serves 4

WATERMELON BOAT

Envision this picnic still life if you will: A plump watermelon scooped out and brimming with cool, colorful fruit . . . golden peaches, bright strawberries, lush pineapple, bananas, grapes, mmm. What a happy way to tote a melon to a party and have it serve as a container too! If you're ambitious enough, melons can be scooped out and the shells cut into various designs, such as a basket. However, if the melon art is not your forte, cut above a quarter of the watermelon off the top and scoop out the bottom, making a boat. Cut the melon balls and all the lovely fruits of the season. Squeeze a lemon over the fruits to prevent discoloration and toss them well. Cover with top shell and wrap in foil. Refrigerate until ready to depart. Carry along a wonderful light wine dressing in a separate container and mix it with the fruits just before serving.

WINE DRESSING

¾ cup dry white wine
1½ tablespoons sugar
1½ teaspoons salt
1 tablespoon lemon juice
¾ cup salad oil

Combine all ingredients in a jar. Give it a good shake. Chill in refrigerator.

MARIE CALLENDAR'S HOT BACON DRESSING

3 tablespoons cornstarch
1 tablespoon soy sauce
3 tablespoons wine vinegar
⅓ cup water
½ cup brown sugar
1 ¼ cups pineapple juice

Combine ingredients in a saucepan and simmer until thick, stirring frequently.
Add: Bacon bits
Chopped green onions
Chopped red and green pepper
Serve warm.

CHEESE/WINE DRESSING

½ cup Bleu or Roquefort cheese, crumbled
¼ cup white wine vinegar or lemon juice
½ cup oil
¼ cup Chablis or dry white wine
1 teaspoon Worcestershire sauce
¼ teaspoon salt
¼ teaspoon coarsely ground pepper

Stir cheese into vinegar and oil, leaving many large bits. Add remaining ingredients and stir only until mixed. Chill overnight to improve flavor. Serve with green salads, sliced tomatoes or citrus fruits.

Variation: Stir equal parts wine/cheese dressing and sour cream together for a fresh vegetable sauce or dip. Additional salt may be required.

CURRIED CHICKEN SALAD DRESSING

2 teaspoons curry powder
2 tablespoons chicken broth
1 cup mayonnaise

Simmer curry powder in broth for 2 minutes, stirring to a smooth paste. Cool. Add paste to mayonnaise. Stir mayonnaise and curry powder mixture into chicken salad mixture 1 hour before serving. (See Curried Chicken recipe.)

Serves 4

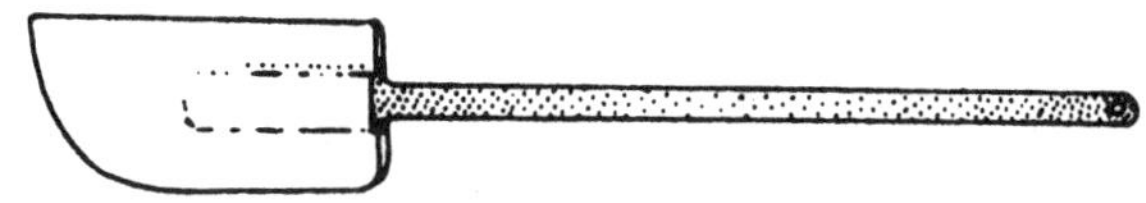

COTTAGE CHEESE DRESSING

1 cup (½ pint) cottage cheese
⅔ cup sour cream
½ medium clove garlic, crushed
2 teaspoons tarragon vinegar
1 teaspoon dry mustard
¼ to ½ teaspoon salt
¼ teaspoon pepper
¼ teaspoon paprika
¼ teaspoon sugar
½ teaspoon Worcestershire sauce

Combine all ingredients in blender jar or electric mixer bowl. Blend or beat until smooth, refrigerate to blend flavors.

Makes about 1⅔ cups low calorie dressing

CHUTNEY DRESSING

1 cup salad oil
⅓ cup wine vinegar
1 clove garlic, crushed
1 teaspoon salt
1 cup chutney, finely chopped

Mix all ingredients in a jar, shake well and store in refrigerator until ready to use. Shake well before serving with mixed green salad, fruit or may be used as a dip.

Makes 2 cups

ANOTHER FRENCH DRESSING

1 teaspoon salt
1 clove garlic
1 to 2 tablespoons red wine vinegar or lemon juice
1 teaspoon Dijon mustard
½ teaspoon Worcestershire sauce
½ teaspoon fresh cracked pepper
6 tablespoons olive oil

Place the salt in the bottom of a small, hard-surfaced mixing bowl, stainless steel or ceramic. Cut garlic clove in half and rub the salt well with it. Discard garlic. Add the rest of the ingredients except the oil and blend well. Stirring constantly, beat in the oil. When using to marinate cooked vegetables such as garbanzo beans, kidney beans etc., finely chopped onion and a little chopped pimiento should be added. Note: Oregano, thyme, or sweet basil and parsley may be added for additional flavor.

Makes ¾ cup

ALL PURPOSE FRENCH DRESSING—MARINADE

1 cup water
1 cup red wine vinegar
1 teaspoon sugar
Juice of ½ lemon
2½ tablespoons salt
1 tablespoon fresh cracked pepper
1 tablespoon Worcestershire sauce
1 teaspoon dry mustard
1 clove garlic, crushed
1 cup olive oil
3 cups salad oil

Blend all ingredients except oils. Add oils and blend well. Variations: Use orange juice or tomato juice in place of water. Mix equal parts of dressing and white wine for chicken or pork or veal. Red wine for beef. Blend equal parts of dressing with soy sauce and sherry or brandy for Polynesian-type dishes.

Makes about 6 cups

FAVORITE OIL & VINEGAR

½ cup vinegar
2 teaspoons salt
1 teaspoon sugar
1 teaspoon pepper
1 teaspoon paprika
1 teaspoon dry mustard
1½ cups salad oil
2 teaspoons prepared mustard
1 teaspoon Worcestershire sauce
8 drops Tabasco
¼ onion

Combine first six ingredients. Shake well then add next four. Shake again. Put ¼ of a cut onion in jar with dressing to season. Do not pour onion out on salad.

Makes about 2 cups

FAR EAST TAMARI DRESSING

1 cup olive oil
½ cup red wine vinegar
2 tablespoons Tamari
2 cloves garlic, crushed
1 teaspoon dried basil
Juice of 1 lemon
2 tablespoons honey
1 teaspoon Worcestershire sauce

Combine all ingredients in jar, shake well and refrigerate.

Makes 1¾ cups

NOTE: Tamari soy sauce is found in Oriental markets or the gourmet section of leading supermarkets.

vegetables

ARTICHOKES WITH DIPPING SAUCE

1 medium onion, minced
1 carrot, minced
1 clove garlic, minced
4 sprigs parsley, minced
6 tablespoons oil
½ teaspoon rosemary
¾ cup white wine
6 artichokes
½ cup mayonnaise

Place the minced vegetables into a large saucepan with the oil, rosemary and the wine. Set the artichokes on top of the mixture, cover the pan, and cook over low heat 45 to 50 minutes, or until the artichokes are done. Remove artichokes and stir the mayonnaise into the sauce remaining in the saucepan. Serve sauce with the artichokes.

Serves 6

AVOCADO FREEZE

4 ripe avocados, mashed
1 (8-ounce) package of cream cheese
2 tablespoons lemon or lime juice
1 tablespoon vinegar
1 tablespoon onion, grated
1 teaspoon salt
Dash of hot pepper sauce

Blend the above ingredients in a blender until smooth. Place in plastic freezer container, filling completely to the top so no air can get into mixture. Freeze. Can be kept in freezer up to six months.

Serves 4 to 6

OLD FASHIONED PORK AND BEANS

1 pound dried pea beans or small white beans
10 cups water
1 tablespoon vegetable oil
1 medium onion, sliced
1 ½ teaspoons salt
1 bay leaf
1 small red pepper, if desired
¼ cup molasses
⅓ cup catsup
1 tablespoon prepared mustard
1 teaspoon Worcestershire sauce
½ teaspoon ground ginger
4-ounces salt pork, thinly sliced
2 tablespoons brown sugar

Sort and rinse beans, do not soak. In a 4-quart pot, combine rinsed beans, water, oil, onion, salt, bay leaf and red pepper, if desired. Bring to a boil, reduce heat. Cover and simmer until beans are almost tender, 1 ½ to 2 hours, checking beans several times. Add hot water as needed to keep beans just covered while cooking. Drain beans, reserving 1 cup cooking liquid. Remove and discard bay leaf and red pepper. Preheat oven to 300 degrees. In a small bowl, combine reserved cooking liquid, molasses, catsup, mustard, Worcestershire sauce and ginger, mix well. Put beans in a 2½ quart bean pot or casserole with a cover. Pour molasses mixture over beans, stir well. Arrange salt pork on top. Sprinkle top with brown sugar. Cover and bake 2 hours.

Serves 6 to 8

SWEET AND SOUR GREEN BEANS

1 pound string beans, julienned and steamed al dente
3-ounces butter
¼ cup onions, finely diced
½ cup chicken broth
1 tablespoon flour
1 tablespoon brown sugar
2 tablespoons malt vinegar
⅛ teaspoon savory
Salt, pepper and a few grains of mace

Heat butter in saucepan, add onions and brown lightly. Blend in flour and heat thoroughly, add hot broth stirring briskly to avoid lumps. Add brown sugar, vinegar and seasoning. Add string beans and simmer very slowly 5 to 10 minutes.

This was my Aunt Grace's favorite way to serve snap beans out of her garden.

Serves 4

SICILIAN STYLE BROCCOLI

1 large bunch broccoli
4 tablespoons olive oil
2 small onions
1 cup black olives
2 anchovy filets
10-ounces Provalone cheese, grated
1 cup dry red wine
Crushed garlic, to taste

Wash and trim a large bunch of broccoli and cut the stalks lengthwise into thin slices. Pour 1 tablespoon olive oil into a skillet and add a layer of thinly sliced onions, scattering of black olives and an anchovy filet cut into pieces. Using ½ amounts, add a layer of broccoli and sprinkle generously with Provalone, olive oil, salt, pepper and garlic to taste. Repeat the process and pour over the dry red wine. Cover the pan and cook over very low heat for 30 minutes or until tender.

This is so good it will make you an honorary Italian.

Serves 4

BROCCOLI SOUFFLE

½ cup mayonnaise
¼ cup flour
1½ cups milk
1 teaspoon
3-ounces Parmesan cheese, grated
1 (10-ounce) package frozen chopped broccoli, thawed and drained
4 eggs, separated

In a saucepan, combine the mayonnaise and the flour. Mix well. Gradually add the milk. Cook, stirring constantly, over low heat until thickened. Add salt and cheese, stirring until melted. Cool. Stir in broccoli and slightly beaten egg yolks. Beat egg whites until stiff peaks form and fold into the cheese mixture. Pour into a 1½ quart casserole. With the tip of the spoon make a slight indentation around the top of the souffle for "top hat". Bake at 300 degrees for 1 hour and 15 minutes. Serve immediately.

Serves 4

BRUSSEL SPROUTS

3 (10-ounce) packages frozen brussel sprouts
¼ pound butter
¼ cup dry white wine
3 tablespoons Dijon mustard
¼ teaspoon sage
1 cup heavy cream
Slivered almonds, toasted and blanched

Cook brussel sprouts in butter and wine until tender, but still slightly crisp. Stir in mustard, sage and cream. Cook until thickened, shaking pan occasionally so that each sprout is coated. Serve sprinkled with warm toasted almonds.

Serves 10

RED CABBAGE

1 head red cabbage, thinly sliced
2 onions, sliced
2 apples, cored and sliced
½ cup red currant jelly
1 bay leaf
Salt
Dash of pepper
¼ pound butter, chicken or bacon fat
4 medium-size ham knuckles
3-ounces vinegar

Mix red cabbage with onions, apples, currant jelly, bay leaf, salt and pepper. Put butter, chicken or bacon fat in heavy casserole with tight-fitting cover. Add red cabbage, ham knuckles and ¼ cup water. Bring to a boil and cook slowly for 2½ hours. Add vinegar at the last minute. Remove the bay leaf.

Serves 6

JACKIE'S RED CABBAGE

2 tablespoons butter
1 apple, peeled and sliced
1 small onion, chopped
4 cups red cabbage, shredded
¼ cup vinegar
2 to 4 tablespoons sugar or can use apple jelly
Pinch of cloves
½ cup burgundy
½ tablespoon cornstarch

Saute apple and onion in butter until tender. Stir in cabbage. Add vinegar, sugar or jelly, cloves and wine. Cover and cook about 12 minutes or until tender. Thicken the sauce with cornstarch that has been pre-mixed with a little water. Simmer until sauce is smooth.

Serves 6 to 8

SPICED RED CABBAGE

3 tablespoons shortening
6 cups (1 medium head) red cabbage, shredded
2 tablespoons molasses
2 cups apple slices
1 cup onion, minced
⅓ cup water
1 teaspoon salt
1 tablespoon red currant jelly

Melt shortening in a heavy skillet. Add cabbage and molasses and cook, turning until cabbage starts to soften. Add remaining ingredients. Cover and simmer 1 to 1½ hours, stirring occasionally.

Shades of my past . . . this is wonderful with pot roast. My kids like this reheated better the second day, they say it has a lot more flavor.

Serve 4 to 6

CARROTS AND ALMOND RING

2½ tablespoons butter
2½ tablespoons flour
¾ cup warm milk
2½ cups carrots, cooked and mashed
⅔ cup almonds, grated
Dash salt
Dash nutmeg
5 eggs, separated
1 buttered 9-inch ring or springform pan
4 cups peas, buttered

Melt butter in saucepan and slowly stir in the flour and whisk until smooth. Slowly add milk, stirring constantly. Reduce heat and simmer 5 minutes, stirring to keep sauce smooth. Remove from heat and add carrots, almonds, salt and nutmeg. Blend a small portion of the carrot mixture into the beaten egg yolks and then combine with the remaining carrot mixture. Cook over low heat 4 minutes. Remove and cool. Beat the egg whites until stiff and fold into the carrot mixture a little at a time. Pour into the mold. Set the mold into a pan of hot water and bake at 350 degrees for 1 hour. Unmold and fill the center with hot buttered peas.

Serves 6 to 8

CARROTS ELEGANTE

1 pound carrots
¼ cup butter
½ teaspoon salt
2 teaspoons sugar
½ teaspoon celery seed
¼ cup orange juice

Peel carrots, slice in thin rounds. Melt butter in a large saucepan, stir in salt, sugar, celery seed and carrots. Cover. Cook over low heat, stirring frequently for 10 minutes. Stir in orange juice, cook for 5 minutes longer or until carrots are al dente.

Serves 4

RAGSDALE CARROT SOUFFLE

1 bunch carrots, peeled
3 tablespoons butter, melted
3 tablespoons brown sugar
3 eggs, separated
1 teaspoon salt
¼ teaspoon ground nutmeg
Dash of Tabasco
Jigger of Grand Marnier

Steam carrots until tender, then puree. Combine with butter, brown sugar, beaten egg yolks, salt, nutmeg, Tabasco and Grand Marnier. Beat egg whites until stiff but not dry. Fold into carrot mixture. Bake in a greased souffle dish at 325 degrees 20 to 25 minutes.

Serves 4 to 6

CAULIFLOWER IN WINE SAUCE

1 large head of cauliflower
¼ cup butter or margarine
¼ cup flour
1 cup half and half
½ cup dry white wine
½ cup water
½ cup blanched almonds, shredded
Salt and pepper to taste
¼ cup Cheddar cheese, grated

Trim and separate cauliflower into flowerettes. Cook in boiling salted water about 8 to 10 minutes, just until al dente. Meanwhile prepare sauce. Melt butter and stir in flour. Add half and half, water and wine. Cook stirring constantly until mixture is thickened and smooth. Add almonds and season to taste. Drain cauliflower and place in greased baking dish. Pour over sauce and sprinkle with cheese. Bake at 350 degrees about 20 minutes or until hot.

One of my family's favorite . . . a real nice way to perk up cauliflower.

Serves 6

ORIGINAL SARATOGA CHIPS

Peel potatoes and slice into uniform paper-thin slices. Use a vegetable slicer or food processor. Soak in cold water or ice water 2 hours. Dry thoroughly and fry in hot oil (375 degrees) until crisp and golden. Drain on paper towels and sprinkle with salt.

DILLED MUSHROOM - CUCUMBER SAUTE

2 large cucumbers
½ pound fresh mushrooms
3 tablespoons butter
1 small onion, thinly sliced
½ teaspoon seasoned salt
1 cup chicken broth
½ cup sour cream
½ teaspoon dill weed

Peel cucumbers and cut into pieces lengthwise about 3-inches long and ½-inch thick. Melt butter and add cucumbers, mushrooms and onions. Saute about 5 minutes, stirring occasionally. Add chicken broth and seasoned salt and cook 3 minutes more. Remove mushrooms, cucumber and onion to hot platter. Let the liquid cook and reduce down by one-third. Remove from heat and add sour cream and dill and pour over vegetables.

Serves 4 to 6

NOPALITOS

1 pound fresh tender cactus, diced

Boil in water with salt, 1 clove garlic and ¼ onion. When tender, drain in colander till natural juice runs out.

SALSA

1 tomato, freshly diced
½ onion, chopped
¼ teaspoon oregano (2 pinches)
Garlic salt
Pepper to taste
Green pepper
1 small hot pepper (optional)
½ cup tomato sauce
½ cup broth or water
2 tablespoons lard or shortening

Stir-fry vegetables and seasonings in hot shortening for 2 minutes. Add broth, tomato sauce and simmer for about 3 minutes. Add the nopalitos to sauce and cover. Simmer for 5 minutes.

Serves 4 to 6

FRENCH FRY SECRETS

To make French fries at home, use only long white Russets. Peel and cut in half lengthwise. It will be easier to manage them if you cut potatoes into strips with a sharp knife. Place cut sides of potatoes on a board and remove a thin slice from the rounded long side of it. Now you have almost a rectangular shape to work with. Slice this into ¼-inch thick strips. Place in deep container. Mix 1 quart water with ½-cup white vinegar, repeating it until you have enough to cover all potatoes. Cover the container and chill the submerged potatoes at least several hours. This draws out the starch that makes a fried potato limp and holds the grease. Drain them well on paper towels. Drop a few at a time into 425 degree oil and let them blanch in the oil rather than fry completely, removing the potatoes after 1 minute. At once drop them into a freezer container or on a cookie sheet and place in the freezer for 10 minutes. Return them to the oil to fry until golden brown, drain on paper towels. Salt them as you wish. Remember if the oil is not hot enough the potatoes will be greasy. A good combination of oils is ½ corn oil and ½ Crisco. Keep your oil about 4 inches deep and at 425 degrees.

This seems like a lot to do; however, I promise you the best French fries ever to grace your table with this little added effort.

STUFFED BAKED POTATOES

Baking potatoes (allow one per serving)
Sour cream
Chopped chives
Chopped parsley
Celery salt or seasoned salt
½-inch wide strips of Cheddar cheese
Paprika

Bake the potatoes until done. Cut top fourth of potato off lengthwise. Scoop out the meat of the potato including the top. Mash the potato meal into small chunks. Add rest of ingredients except the cheese and blend well. Return mixture to potato jackets and garnish with a couple of strips of the cheese. Dust with paprika. This may be done far in advance and kept in the refrigerator. To serve, place in a very hot oven until potato is thoroughly heated and cheese is melted.

SWEET POTATO MAGIC

3 cups sweet potatoes, cooked and mashed
1 cup granulated sugar
2 eggs, well-beaten
1 teaspoon vanilla
¼ cup milk
½ cup butter

TOPPING

1 cup brown sugar, packed
⅓ cup flour
1 cup pecans, chopped
⅓ cup butter

Mix all ingredients together except topping and pour into buttered casserole. Mix topping ingredients together and sprinkle over casserole. Bake at 350 degrees for 30 minutes.

Serves 8 to 10

SWEET POTATO PONE

2½ pounds sweet potatoes or yams
¼ cup butter or margarine, melted
2 eggs
¼ cup light brown sugar, firmly packed
½ cup milk
¼ cup light molasses
½ teaspoon salt
½ teaspoon cinnamon
¼ teaspoon nutmeg
⅛ teaspoon ground cloves

Wash potatoes. Place in kettle and cover with water. Bring to a boil. Simmer covered 30 minutes or until tender. Drain. Let cool until they are easy to handle. Peel and mash potatoes, stir in butter. Preheat oven to 375 degrees. Place eggs and sugar in a bowl and beat thoroughly. Add milk, molasses, salt, cinnamon, nutmeg and cloves and beat until well blended. Stir into mashed potatoes until well blended. Turn into a buttered, 1½ quart casserole. Bake uncovered 50 to 60 minutes, or until heated through.

Serves 6 to 8

SWEET POTATO SOUFFLE

1 cup milk
½ cup sugar
½ teaspoon salt
3 tablespoons butter
1 teaspoon nutmeg
2 cups mashed sweet potatoes, drained
2 eggs, separated
½ cup crushed pineapple, drained
½ cup pecans
Marshmallows

Scald milk and add sugar, salt, butter and nutmeg. Beat until stiff with 2 cups sweet potatoes and egg yolks. Beat egg whites separately and fold into mixture along with pineapple and pecans. Place in a greased baking dish and bake at 350 degrees for 50 to 60 minutes. Top with marshmallows.

Serves 6 to 8

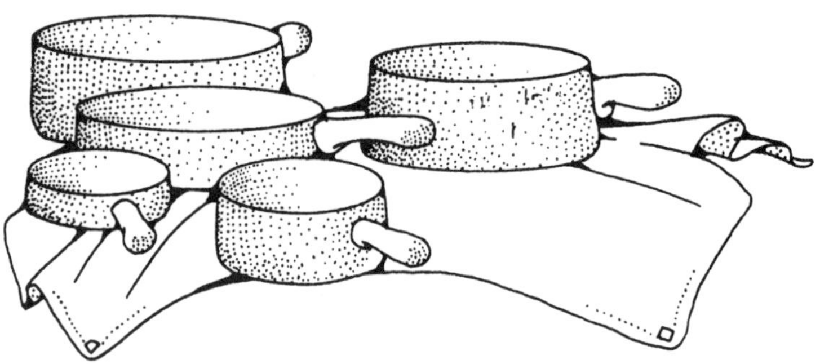

STUFFED EGGPLANT

1 large eggplant (cook 1 hour in 350 degree oven)

Let cool. Cut in half and scoop out pulp leaving ¼-inch ridge. Save the pulp.

2 tablespoons olive oil
1 onion, finely chopped
1 clove garlic, chopped

Saute this until transparent. Add eggplant pulp and cook until done.

¾ teaspoon pepper, or to taste
½ teaspoon seasoned salt
1 teaspoon bouquet garni (equal parts of cinnamon, nutmeg and oregano)
1 tablespoon parsley, freshly chopped
¼ cup green chiles, chopped
2 tablespoons capers
2½ tablespoons garlic flavored red wine vinegar

Add these ingredients to the eggplant pulp and simmer. Then add ½ cup Parmesan, 1 cup soft bread crumbs and 1 cup grated Cheddar cheese. Place mixture back into the eggplant rind and put in 350 degree oven for 45 minutes.

Serves 6 to 8

SPINACH CASSEROLE

2 bunches spinach, washed and steamed
2 tablespoons onions, chopped
1 (6-ounce) jar marinated artichoke hearts
Salt and pepper to taste
1 (3-ounce) package cream cheese, softened
⅓ cup Parmesan cheese, grated
½ cup sour cream

Cook spinach and drain. Turn into a 1-quart casserole. Add onion, undrained artichoke hearts, salt and pepper. Combine cream cheese and sour cream and spread over the top of casserole using the back of a spoon to cover, sprinkle Parmesan on top. Bake at 350 degrees for 20 to 25 minutes.

Serves 4 to 6

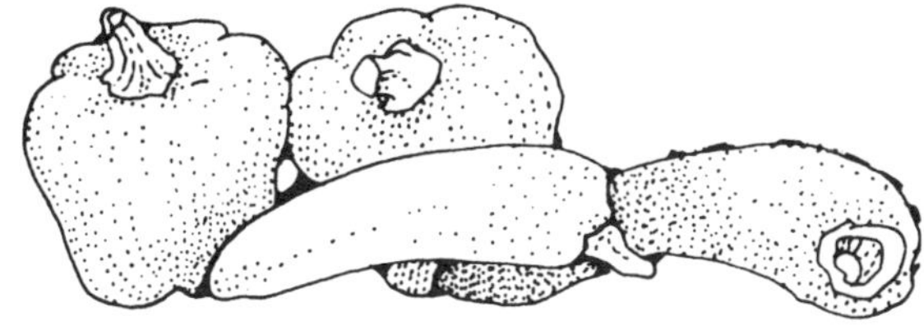

CREAMED SPINACH

1½ pounds fresh spinach
4 strips bacon
1 clove garlic, minced
1 small onion, minced
1½ teaspoons seasoned salt (or to taste)
¼ teaspoon white pepper
4 tablespoons flour
2 cups half and half

Cook spinach and drain. When cool, chop. Set aside. Grind bacon finely and saute with garlic. Add onion, seasoned salt and pepper. Saute until all the moisture is gone. Melt butter in skillet, add flour and blend thoroughly. When smooth, add half and half and cook a few minutes. Add spinach and onion mixture and slowly bring to a soft boil. Serve immediately with a sprinkle of nutmeg. Scrumptious.

Serves 6

EASY CREAMED SPINACH

1 (10-ounce) package frozen chopped spinach
2 slices bacon, finely chopped
½ cup onion, finely chopped
2 tablespoons flour
1 teaspoon seasoned salt
¼ teaspoon seasoned pepper
1 garlic clove, minced
1 cup milk

Cook spinach according to package directions. Drain well. Fry bacon and onions together until onions are tender, about 10 minutes. Remove from heat. Add flour, seasoned salt, seasoned pepper and garlic. Blend thoroughly. Slowly add milk, return to heat and stir until thickened. Add spinach and mix thoroughly.

Serves 4

SPINACH IN CREAM SAUCE

3 pounds young tender spinach
1 heaping tablespoon butter
1 tablespoon flour
1 tablespoon onion, finely grated
¼ cup whipping cream
Salt and pepper to taste

Prepare spinach by washing carefully and discarding all tough stems. Throw spinach into a kettle of boiling water for 3 minutes— no longer. Remove from heat and drain. In a heavy pan, place butter and shake on the flour. Blend well. Add spinach, onion, cream, salt and pepper. Heat thoroughly and serve immediately. This is equally good if sour cream is used in place of whipping cream.

Serves 8

CHEESY TOMATO PIE

4 cups day-old bread, crust removed and cut into 1-inch cubes
3 medium-ripe tomatoes
1½ cups Swiss cheese, grated
2 eggs
1 teaspoon seasoned salt
Few drops Tabasco
½ teaspoon dry mustard
1½ cups milk
½ teaspoon basil

Press bread crumbs into a well-oiled 9-inch pie pan. Sprinkle with basil. Skin, core and slice tomatoes ¼-inch thick and starting at the outer edge of the pan, overlap the slices until top is covered. Top with grated cheese. Combine remaining ingredients and pour gently at the edge of the pan so that the liquid will be absorbed by the bread. Bake about 35 minutes in a 375 degree oven or until the cheese is puffy and brown.

Serves 4

TOMATO LENTEN PIE

1 9-inch pie crust
2 to 3 medium tomatoes, peeled, cored and thickly sliced
½ teaspoon salt
¼ teaspoon pepper
½ teaspoon basil
¼ cup chives, chopped
¼ to ½ cup mayonnaise
1½ cups sharp Cheddar cheese, grated

Preheat oven to 425 degrees. Bake crust for 5 minutes. Remove from oven and reduce heat to 400 degrees. Line bottom of crust with the tomatoes. Now sprinkle with the salt, pepper, basil and chives. In a small mixing bowl combine the mayonnaise and the cheese. Carefully spread the cheese mixture over the tomatoes, making sure to seal the edges of the pie crust completely. Bake for 35 minutes. Serve at once while hot and bubbly.

Serves 6

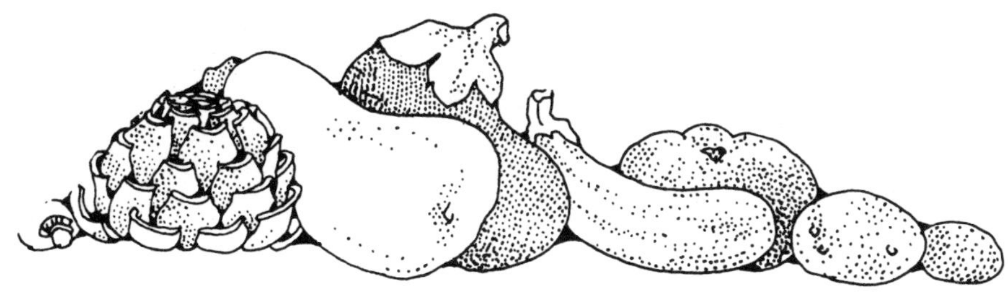

VEGETABLE BOUQUET

1 cup cauliflower, cut into flowerettes
1 cup zucchini squash, sliced ¼-inch thick
1 cup fresh carrots, sliced
1 cup turnips, diced
1 cup celery, sliced
1 cup purple onion, diced
1 cup broccoli, cut into pieces
½ cup olive oil
Salt and white pepper to taste
2 cloves garlic, crushed

Cut all vegetables and cook each in separate batches of salted water until barely tender (do not overcook), drain and toss together. Saute vegetables in olive oil seasoned with salt, pepper and garlic.

Serves 4 to 6

FAVORITE VEGETABLE CASSEROLE

1 cup almonds, slivered
¼ pound bacon, cut into 1-inch pieces
1 pound zucchini, sliced
1 pound eggplant, diced
1 large onion, cut into wedges
1 tablespoon flour
1 (1-pound) can tomatoes, undrained
2 cloves garlic, minced
Salt and pepper to taste
1 teaspoon basil
1 cup Swiss cheese, grated

Saute the almonds with the bacon pieces until the bacon is crisp and the almonds are lightly toasted. Remove and drain on paper towels. Add zucchini, eggplant and onion to pan. Cover and cook over low heat for 15 minutes, shaking pan often to prevent sticking. Add flour and mix. Add tomatoes breaking up chunks with a spoon. Stir in garlic and seasonings. In a 2-quart baking dish, layer vegetables, almonds, bacon and cheese, saving some bacon and almonds for the top. To serve right away you can bake at 400 degrees for 15 to 20 minutes, uncovered. Or to serve later, cover and refrigerate. To heat simply uncover casserole and bake in a 400 degree oven 30 to 35 minutes or until hot and bubbly.

All that's needed for this vegtable delight is a green salad, some French bread and a little wine. Super!

Serves 6

VEGETABLES WITH CREAMY DILL SAUCE APPETIZERS

1 cup sour cream
¼ cup mayonnaise
1¼ teaspoons celery salt
1 tablespoon dill weed
1½ teaspoons parsley flakes
¼ teaspoon onion powder
1 clove garlic, minced
½ teaspoon prepared horseradish

Combine all ingredients and chill for at least 2 hours. Serve with raw carrot or celery sticks, cauliflower pieces, zucchini strips, etc . . .

Easy, and soooo good.

Makes about 1½ cups

HARVEST VEGETABLES IN THE WOK

1 bunch broccoli
1 small cauliflower
2 cups fresh mushrooms, sliced
2 tablespoons lemon juice
2 tablespoons peanut oil
1 small slice ginger root
½ cup green pepper, sliced
2 cups celery, diagonally sliced
1 clove garlic
1 teaspoon salt
1 teaspoon pepper
2 tablespoons soy sauce
⅓ cup Cheddar cheese, grated

Trim stems and leaves from broccoli and cauliflower. Divide into small flowerettes. Pour lemon juice over mushrooms and set aside. Measure oil into wok, rub ginger root around sides of wok and discard. Toss broccoli and cauliflower with green pepper and celery and arrange on bottom and sides of wok. Add garlic and all seasonings except soy sauce. Cover and cook for about 10 minutes or until vegetables are cooked, but still crisp. Add soy sauce and cheese. Cook until cheese is melted.

Wonderful way to serve a fall harvest of vegetables.

Serves 6

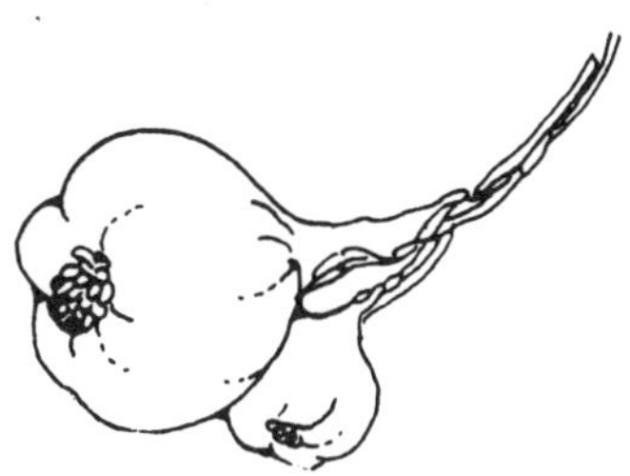

ZUCCHINI-EGGPLANT PIE

1 medium onion, sliced
1 clove garlic, minced
¼ cup olive oil
5 medium tomatoes, cut into wedges
3 large zucchini, sliced
1 small eggplant, diced
1 green pepper, sliced
15 fresh okra, sliced or 1 (10½ ounce) package
frozen okra
1 tablespoon salt
½ teaspoon oregano
½ teaspoon pepper
Bread shells

Cook onion and garlic in oil until transparent. Stir in remaining ingredients. Simmer, covered, over low heat about 30 minutes, stirring occasionally. Uncover and simmer 20 minutes longer. Prepare bread shells and fill with vegetable mixture.

BREAD SHELLS

48 slices of bread, trimmed
¼ cup water
⅓ cup butter, melted

Flatten slices of bread with rolling pin. Place 4 pieces together over the bottom and up sides of twelve 5-inch pans to form shell. Brush edges with water, overlap and seal well. Trim. Brush with melted butter. Bake in preheated 350 degree oven 25 to 35 minutes or until crisp and golden brown.

Serves 8

EGGPLANT AND ZUCCHINI

3 medium zucchini, sliced
1 medium eggplant, peeled and diced
1 (16-ounce) can tomatoes
1 cup onion, diced
3 tablespoons all-purpose flour
3 envelopes chicken bouillon
2 teaspoons oregano leaves
½ teaspoon sugar
½ teaspoon salt
½ teaspoon garlic powder

Drain tomatoes, reserving juice and set both aside. Toss remaining ingredients together until vegetables are coated. Heat ½ cup water and reserved tomato juice to boiling. Add coated vegetables and top with tomatoes. Reduce heat. Cover and simmer about 30 minutes, stirring occasionally. Uncover and continue cooking until vegetables are tender and liquid is reduced.

Serves 6 to 8

ZUCCHINI AND MUSHROOM BAKE

2 medium-sized zucchini, washed and trimmed
⅛ teaspoon dried dill, chopped
1 clove garlic
Boiling salted water
½ pound mushrooms, sliced
3 tablespoons butter
2 tablespoons flour
1 cup sour cream
Buttered bread crumbs

Cut the zucchini into 1-inch slices. Add the dill and garlic and boiling salted water to cover. Return to a boil. Reduce the heat, cover and simmer gently until the zucchini is tender—do not overcook. Drain, reserving 2 tablespoons of the cooking liquid. Remove and discard the garlic. Saute the mushrooms in butter 5 minutes, stirring occasionally. Stir in the flour and cook two minutes longer. Add the sour cream, zucchini and reserved cooking liquid, stirring constantly. Correct the seasonings and heat thoroughly but do not boil. Place the mixture in a casserole and top with buttered bread crumbs. Brown quickly under high broiler heat.

Serves 4

ZUCCHINI NICOISE

1 onion, diced
3 tomatoes, peeled and diced
1 eggplant, diced
3 zucchini, diced
1 tablespoon tomato puree
2 tablespoons Parmesan cheese, grated
¼ cup olive oil
Salt and pepper to taste
2 garlic cloves, crushed

Saute onion in olive oil. Add eggplant, tomatoes and zucchini. Saute together and season with salt, pepper and garlic. Add tomato puree. Place in a casserole and bake at 350 degrees for 20 minutes. Sprinkle with Parmesan and brown under broiler.

Serves 4

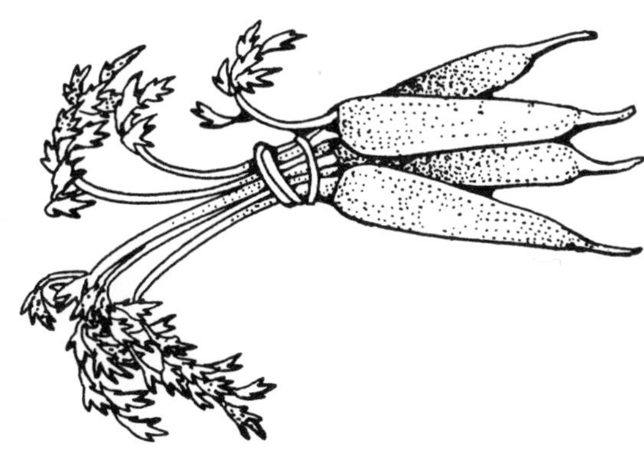

ZUCCHINI IN SOUR CREAM

6 small zucchini, cut in ½-inch slices
⅔ cup sour cream
2 tablespoons butter or margarine
⅓ cup sharp Cheddar cheese, shredded
½ teaspoon salt
3 tablespoons bread crumbs

Simmer zucchini 10 minutes in water to cover. Drain. Place in 8-inch pie plate. Combine sour cream, butter, half of the cheese and salt. Heat, stirring until blended. Pour over zucchini. Top with bread crumbs and remainder of the cheese. Bake at 375 degrees about 10 minutes or until crumbs are golden brown. Let stand 5 minutes before serving.

Serves 4

ZUCCHINI STUFFED WITH RICE

4 medium zucchini
1 small tomato, chopped
½ cup Cheddar cheese, shredded
1 (8-ounce) package flavored rice mix

Prepare rice mix as directed on package. In a large saucepan, heat 6 cups water and 1½ teaspoons salt to boiling. Cut zucchini in half lengthwise and add to water. Cook over medium heat 5 to 7 minutes until tender-crisp. Drain and cool zucchini under running cold water for a few seconds. Preheat oven to 375 degrees. Scoop out and discard seeds from zucchini leaving shells about ¼ to ½-inch thick. In an oiled baking dish (13x9-inch) arrange zucchini halves crosswise in a row. Sprinkle lightly with salt. Pile rice into zucchini shells and top each with some tomato and cheese. Bake 10 minutes or until cheese melts and rice is heated.

Serves 8

seafood

WEST COAST BOUILLABASSE

(If possible add a 2-foot length of seaweed or kelp to the mixture during the cooking time and remove before serving. Taste before salting as the seaweed adds some salt to the stew. Also any combination of shellfish or fish in the amounts given will do.)

½ cup carrots, sliced
¾ cup onion, chopped
½ cup olive oil
1 (# 2½) can tomato puree
3 cloves garlic, diced
2 tablespoons parsley, chopped
⅛ teaspoon saffron
¼ teaspoon oregano
¼ teaspoon thyme
¼ teaspoon marjoram
¼ teaspoon fennel (optional)
1 tablespoon salt
Freshly ground pepper
8 lobster tails
7 cups water
1 cup dry white wine
8 slices sea bass, cut into 1-inch cubes
8 slices red snapper
1 pound shrimp, shelled and deveined
1 (8-ounce) can whole clams

Saute carrots and onions in oil about 10 minutes. Add tomato puree, garlic and other seasonings. Add lobster, water and wine and bring to boiling. Reduce heat and simmer 15 minutes. Add bass and snapper and cook 10 minutes. Add shrimp and clams and heat thoroughly.

Makes about 20 to 24 servings

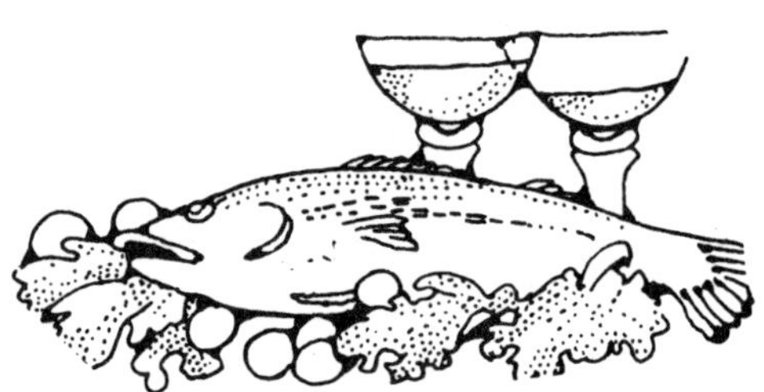

CRAB DELMONICO

Arrange crab legs and pieces of crab attractively on a platter of crushed ice. Garnish with lemon, parsley, and other suitable vegetables.

SAUCES:

RED COCKTAIL SAUCE

½ cup catsup
½ cup chili sauce
1 tablespoon (or to taste) horseradish
1½ teaspoons lemon juice
1½ teaspoons Worcestershire sauce
Few drops Tabasco (or to taste)

Mix all ingredients well and allow to stand in refrigerator before serving, approximately 4 hours.

MAYONNAISE-MUSTARD SAUCE

½ cup mayonnaise
1½ teaspoons Worcestershire sauce
½ teaspoon dry mustard (or to taste)
2 tablespoons stale beer

Blend all ingredients well and chill.

THOUSAND ISLAND DRESSING

½ cup mayonnaise
½ cup red hamburger relish
1 tablespoon onion, grated
½ clove garlic, crushed
1 teaspoon celery juice (made by rubbing a stalk of celery against fine side of grater)
1½ teaspoons capers, chopped
Few drops Angostura bitters

Blend all ingredients well and chill.

TARTAR SAUCE

¾ cup mustard
1 tablespoon grated onion juice
1 tablespoon lemon juice
1½ teaspoons Worcestershire sauce
1½ tablespoons capers, chopped
1½ tablespoons sour or dill pickles, finely minced
1½ teaspoons horseradish

Blend all ingredients well and chill.

ALASKA KING CRAB MEAT CAKES

1 cup butter, melted
1 cup onions, finely chopped
2 cups mushrooms, finely chopped
½ cup green peppers, finely chopped
2 cups bread flour
2 tablespoons dry mustard
1 tablespoon paprika
½ teaspoon cayenne pepper
1 quart half and half, hot
8 pounds fresh Alaska king crab meat chunks, finely chopped
2 quarts fresh bread crumbs
1 cup white wine
½ cup parsley, finely chopped
2 tablespoons Worcestershire sauce
Salt to taste
6 eggs, separated
2 pounds bread flour
1 quart cooking oil

Pour melted butter into saucepan and heat. Add onions, mushrooms and green peppers and cook until soft. Add flour, dry mustard, paprika and cayenne pepper. Stir until smooth. Cook 15 minutes. Blend in hot cream and stir until smooth. Remove from heat, add crab meat, bread crumbs, white wine, parsley, Worcestershire sauce and salt. Mix well. Beat egg yolks until light and lemon colored. Fold into crab mixture. Beat egg whites until stiff. Fold into crab mixture. Allow mixture to cool. Portion 100 cakes using # 24 ice cream scoop. Shape into patties and dredge in the 2 pounds of flour. Fry in oil until golden brown. (May also be fried in deep fat at 350 degrees until golden brown.) Remove and place on paper towels to absorb grease. Serve hot.

Makes 50 portions — 2 cakes per portion

CRAB MUFFINS

4 English muffins
1 cup crab meat
3 cups Cheddar cheese, grated
3 green onions, sliced
1 cup mayonnaise
1½ teaspoons Worcestershire sauce

Toast muffins on torn or split side. Combine remaining ingredients and spread on muffins. Bake in 350 degree oven about 30 minutes until hot and bubbly.

Serves 2 to 4

COUNTRY HALIBUT

2 pounds halibut steaks, 1-inch thick
½ teaspoon salt
¼ teaspoon white pepper
¼ cup catsup
1 (6-ounce) can sliced mushrooms
½ cup green onions, sliced

Place steaks in greased baking dish and season with salt and pepper. Brush top of each steak with catsup. Top with mushrooms and sprinkle with green onions. Bake in preheated 450 degree oven allowing 10 minutes cooking time per-inch thickness for fresh fish and about 30 minutes per-inch thickness if fish is frozen.

Serves 6

JAMBALAYA

¾ pound hot Italian sausage
2 onions, chopped
1 green pepper, chopped
2 garlic cloves, minced
2 (16-ounce) cans tomatoes
1½ cups chicken broth
1 cup uncooked rice
½ cup dry white wine
1 tablespoon Worcesterchire sauce
½ teaspoon thyme
½ pound raw shrimp, cleaned
1 cup cooked chicken, diced into bite-sized pieces
Tabasco to taste

In a large skillet saute the sausage after removing the casings. Add onions. Drain off excess fat. Add pepper and garlic and saute a minute more. Add remaining ingredients except shrimp, chicken and Tabasco. Cover and simmer 15 minutes. Add shrimp, chicken and Tabasco to taste and continue cooking until rice is tender and shrimp are pink.

Serves 6

LOBSTER BISQUE

1 medium onion, sliced
1 quart milk
4 tablespoons butter, melted
4 tablespoons flour
1 teaspoon salt
⅛ teaspoon pepper
¼ teaspoon nutmeg
¼ teaspoon celery salt
1½ cans lobster meat
½ cup cream
Chopped pimientos

Mix onion and milk in top of double boiler and heat. Combine melted butter, flour, salt, pepper, nutmeg and celery salt in a 2 quart sauce pan. Strain onions from milk. Stir milk into flour mixture gradually. When thickened slightly, add lobster meat and the pimientos. Simmer 10 minutes. Add the cream and additional salt to taste.

Serves 6

LOBSTER COCKTAIL

1 can lobster meat
½ cup chili sauce
¼ cup catsup
1 tablespoon horseradish
1 tablespoon lemon juice
2 drops Tabasco
1 tablespoon onion, minced
2 tablespoons celery, minced
or ½ teaspoon celery salt
Salt to taste
Green pepper
Crisp lettuce

Drain lobster meat. Cut into large dices and chill. Mix remaining ingredients and chill. Combine lobster meat with sauce. To serve, line cocktail glasses with crisp lettuce, fill with mixture and garnish with sliced green pepper.

Serves 4

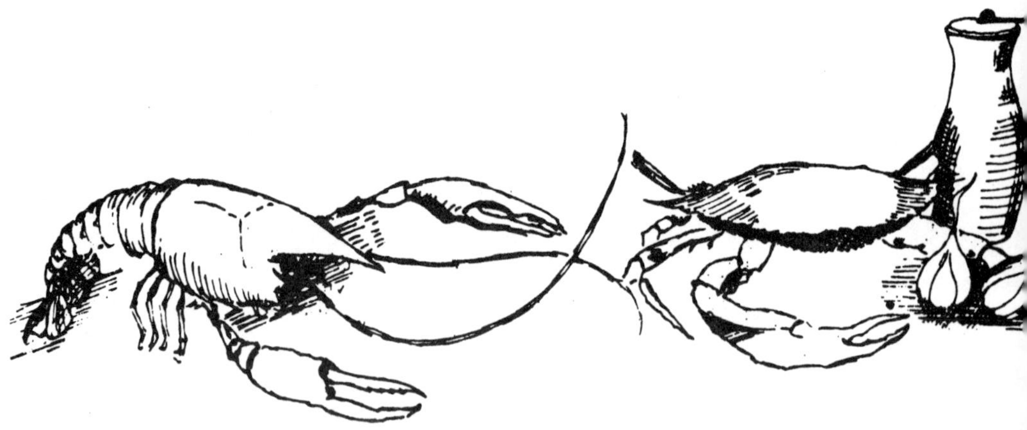

LOBSTER A LA KING

1 can lobster meat
4 tablespoons butter or margarine
1 cup fresh or ½ can sliced mushrooms
2 tablespoons green peppers, sliced
3 tablespoons flour
1 teaspoon salt
⅛ teaspoon pepper
1 cup lobster liquor and milk (approximately ½ cup each)
½ cup cream
1 tablespoon lemon juice
Halved and toasted English muffins or toasted rounds

Drain lobster. Reserve liquor and flake meat. Melt butter or margarine, add mushrooms and green pepper. Stir over low heat for 2 minutes. Stir in flour and seasonings. Add lobster liquor and milk and cream gradually while stirring constantly. Beat in lemon juice and add flaked lobster. Heat thoroughly and add more salt if necessary. Serve over toasted English muffins or toasted rounds.

Makes 6 medium servings or 4 generous servings

LOBSTER NEWBURG

4 tablespoons butter, melted
¼ cup sherry or marsala
2 cans lobster meat, diced
¼ teaspoon salt
½ teaspoon paprika
4 egg yolks, slightly beaten
1 cup thin cream
2 drops Tabasco

Melt butter and add sherry, salt and paprika. Mix lightly and cover. Cook over hot water for 3 minutes. Mix egg yolks and cream thoroughly. Stir gradually into hot mixture. Add Tabasco. Continue cooking, stirring gently about 3 minutes or until sauce thickens slightly. Garnish with sprigs of parsley. Serve at once with toast points.

Serves 4 to 5

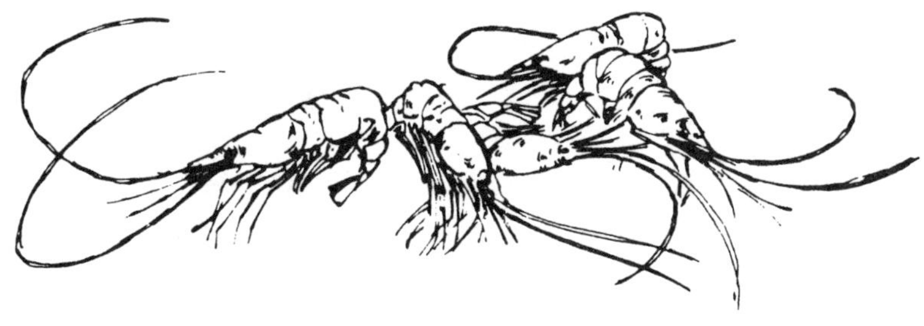

BOXED OYSTERS

1 loaf white bread, unsliced
4 tablespoons butter, melted
with 1 clove garlic
4 tablespoons additional butter
1 pint oysters
10 dashes Maggi's seasoning
¼ cup sherry
2 tablespoons onion juice
6 tablespoons green pepper, chopped
3⅓ tablespoons flour
½ cup cream

Cut crust off bread. Cut thick slice off top and pull out center of loaf. Melt butter with garlic. Brush top and sides of bread shell with butter. Place on lightly buttered cookie sheet. Pour creamed oysters into box and fasten top on box with toothpicks. Bake in 450 degree oven for 20 minutes. Slice with very sharp knife. TO CREAM OYSTERS: Melt butter. Add oysters and cook until edges are curled. Remove oysters and add seasoning, sherry, onion juice and green pepper. Cook until pepper is tender. Add flour and stir until blended. Add cream and cook until thickened. Combine with oysters.

Serves 6

SALMON LOAF

1 can condensed cream of celery soup
⅓ cup mayonnaise or salad dressing
1 egg, beaten
½ cup onion, chopped
¼ cup green pepper, chopped
1 (16-ounce) can salmon, drained, boned and flaked
1 cup cracker crumbs

Mix all ingredients. Place in greased loaf pan and bake uncovered at 350 degrees for 1 hour. Unmold and slice.

Serves 4 to 6

SCALLOPS FETTUCINI

1 (8-ounce) package fettucini or spiral noodles
2 tablespoons butter or margarine
1 medium onion, chopped
1 green pepper, chopped
3 cups fresh mushrooms, sliced
2 cups fresh tomatoes, coarsely chopped
1 pound scallops, cut into half
1 cup sour cream
¼ cup dry white wine
½ cup grated Parmesan cheese

Cook pasta according to package instructions, drain well. Keep pasta hot. Meanwhile melt butter in a large skillet. Add onion and pepper. Saute until onion is transparent. Add mushrooms, tomatoes and scallops. Cook 3 to 5 minutes or until scallops are cooked through. Blend in sour cream and wine. Heat until warm. Toss scallop mixture with fettucini and top with Parmesan.

Serve with green salad . . . Just great.

Serves 4

SEAFOOD CHEESE LOAF

2 cups canned salmon or tuna
1 ¼ cups Cheddar cheese, grated
1 egg, beaten
½ cup evaporated milk or light cream
½ teaspoon salt
1 cup bread crumbs
2 tablespoons butter or margarine, melted
1 tablespoon lemon juice
⅛ teaspoon pepper
½ teaspoon dill weed

Combine all ingredients and place in a buttered glass loaf pan. Cover with wax paper. Cook on MEDIUM 18 to 20 minutes.

This is lovely cold the next day on a lettuce leaf with a little dill sauce or served hot with a Bechamel sauce. Just great and so easy.

Serves 6

CURRIED SEAFOOD

Saute:

¼ cup onion, chopped
¼ cup apple, chopped
¼ cup butter

Add:

1½ tablespoons flour (do not let flour brown)
2 teaspoons curry powder
1 cup chicken broth
1 cup cream
½ teaspoon grated lemon rind

Simmer 20 minutes. Add lobster, shrimp or crab meat and serve over steamed rice.

Makes 2 cups of sauce.

SHRIMP KEBOBS

1½ pounds fresh shrimp or frozen shrimp, thawed
4 slices bacon, cut in squares
1 (4-ounce) can button mushrooms, drained
½ teaspoon salt
⅛ teaspoon pepper
3 tablespoons butter or margarine
1 tablespoon lemon juice

Combine butter, lemon juice and salt and pepper. Peel, devein and wash shrimp and pat dry with paper towels. Alternate shrimp, bacon squares and mushrooms on skewers and brush with seasoned butter. Place on preheated grill. Cook on medium about 5 minutes. Turn and brush with more butter and broil 3 to 5 minutes longer. Serve with lemon wedges.

Serves 4

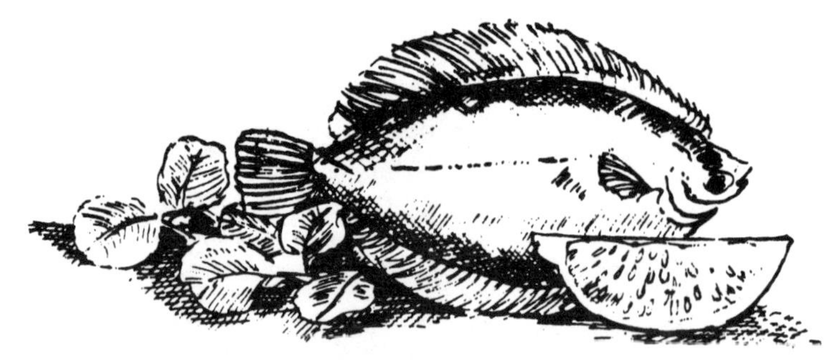

SHRIMP FLORIDIAN CASSEROLE

2 pounds shrimp
½ pound Bleu cheese, Roquefort or Gorgonzola
1 (8-ounce) package cream cheese
1 tablespoon chives, chopped
1 tablespoon parsley, chopped
1 clove garlic, minced
¾ cup dry white wine

Mash cheese and cream cheese and add parsley, chives, garlic and wine to make sauce. Pour over raw, cleaned and shelled shrimp. Bake in a covered baking dish at 400 degrees for 30 minutes.

This is so easy and so wonderful . . . we are so lucky here in California to be able to get good shrimp that is fresh. This will be one of your favorites.

Serves 4 to 6

DRIED SHRIMP PATTIES

4 eggs, separated
3 tablespoons dry shrimp (grated)
3 tablespoons butter or lard
Salt and pepper

Beat the egg whites until stiff. Fold in yolks and shrimp. Heat butter or lard in a skillet and drop shrimp batter, 1 teaspoon at a time, to form cakes. Brown on both sides.

Serve hot with parsley garnish or with Nopalitos (cooked cactus).

Serves 2

SHRIMP TEMPURA

1½ pounds large shrimp, fresh or frozen
½ cup cornstarch
½ cup flour
1 teaspoon salt
1 egg
½ cup water
1½ cups salad oil

Shell and clean shrimp leaving tails on. Split shrimp through back, cutting almost through. Open to butterfly shape. Sift flour, cornstarch and salt together. Beat egg with water. Blend together for batter. Heat oil to 375 degrees, dip through batter holding tail and drop gently into oil. When shrimps rise to surface turn and continue cooking until golden brown. Drain on paper towel and serve immediately with Hot Shoya Sauce or Chinese mustard.

Serves 4 to 6

FISH STEAKS IN BEER

1½ pounds boneless fish steaks
2 cans beer
1 onion, chopped
1 lemon
2 bay leaves
2 tablespoons butter
2 tablespoons flour
½ tablespoon paprika
½ teaspoon seasoned salt
⅛ teaspoon seasoned pepper

Lay fish steaks in heavy saucepan with a cover. Pour over beer, add onion, lemon cut in half, bay leaves, paprika, and seasoned salt. Bring to a boil. Cover and turn heat to low and simmer 5 minutes. Lift fish steaks from broth and discard seasonings. Blend butter and flour together and stir into broth, stirring constantly until sauce boils and thickens. Add pepper and return steaks to sauce just long enough to reheat. Serve immediately with rice or noodles.

Serves 4

FISH STEAKS WITH KIWI FRUIT SAUCE

4 fish steaks (about 2½ pounds)
2 tablespoon cooking oil
Salt and pepper to taste
2 kiwi fruit for garnish
Kiwi fruit sauce

Preheat broiler to high. Brush fish with oil and sprinkle with salt and pepper. Broil 5-inches away from heat for 5 minutes. Turn and brush with oil and finish cooking on other side, about 5 to 8 minutes or until fish flakes. Top each steak with sauce.

KIWI FRUIT SAUCE

4 tablespoons green onions, chopped
¼ cup white vinegar
¼ cup white wine
¼ cup heavy cream
6 tablespoons butter, cut into small pieces
1 Kiwi fruit, peeled and chopped

Combine onions, vinegar and wine in a saucepan and cook until most of the liquid is gone. Add cream and cook a minute or two, stirring constantly. Gradually add butter, one piece at a time, continue stirring. Cook only until butter is melted. Add chopped Kiwi fruit. Pour over fish steaks and add sliced Kiwi fruit for garnish.

Serves 4

FILET OF FISH TERIYAKI

¼ pound onions
2 green peppers
¼ pound mushrooms
¼ pound tomatoes
2 pounds fish filets, cut in 1¼-inch cubes

SAUCE

½ cup soy sauce
½ cup sherry
1 teaspoon sugar

Cube onion, green pepper, mushrooms, tomatoes and any other green vegetable desired. Combine sauce ingredients. Thread fish on skewers, brush with sauce and let stand for 30 minutes. Broil in oven or barbeque, turning often and brushing with sauce for about 15 minutes.

Delightful with rice or baked potato and a fruit salad.

Serves 6 to 8

SWORDFISH STEAK WITH LEMON AND CAPERS

3 to 4 lemons
6 slices swordfish (about 8-ounces each)
Salt and freshly ground white pepper
Milk
All-purpose flour
12 tablespoons peanut oil
1 teaspoon butter
5 tablespoons unsalted butter
¼ cup drained capers
2 tablespoons fresh parsley, chopped (garnish)

Carefully peel lemons, discarding all of white pith. Cut white membrane from lemon sections. Remove segments, then dice and set aside. Generously season swordfish with salt and white pepper to taste. Dip each slice in milk. Coat with flour, shaking off excess. Heat 6 tablespoons oil in large skillet over medium-high heat. Stir in ½ teaspoon butter. Add 3 slices of fish and saute until lightly browned on both sides. Reduce heat and continue cooking until fish is opaque and feels firm to touch. Transfer to heated serving platter and keep warm. Repeat with remaining oil, ½ teaspoon butter and fish. Wipe out skillet. Add remaining butter and cook over medium heat until lightly browned. Stir in reserved lemon and capers. Pour over fish, garnish with parsley and serve immediately.

Serves 6

TORTILLAS WITH TUNA FLORENTINE

2 tablespoons butter or margarine
1 medium onion, chopped
1 cup celery, chopped
3 (6-ounce) cans water packed tuna
1½ cups fresh mushrooms, sliced
1 (10-ounce) package frozen chopped spinach, thawed and drained
1 (8-ounce) can water chestnuts, sliced
¼ cup cornstarch
3 cups chicken broth
2 tablespoons soy sauce
1 tablespoon Dijon mustard
12 (8-inch) flour tortillas, warmed

Melt butter in a skillet. Add onion and celery and saute until tender. Add tuna, mushrooms, spinach, and water chestnuts. Cook 2 minutes. Blend cornstarch into chicken broth. Stir into tuna mixture. Add soy sauce and mustard. Cook stirring constantly over medium heat until thickened. Spread filling evenly over center of warmed tortilla. Roll tortilla. Repeat with remaining tortillas.

Serves 6

TERRIFIC TUNA MUFFINS

2 tablespoons butter or margarine
2 tablespoons flour
1 cup milk
¼ teaspoon salt
1 teaspoon Dijon mustard
½ cup Cheddar cheese, grated
3 English muffins, sliced in half
1 (6½ ounce) can water-packed tuna, drained
¼ cup mayonnaise
1 (8-ounce) can crushed pineapple, drained
½ cup fresh bean sprouts

Melt the butter in a small saucepan. Stir in flour and cook over medium heat for 1 minute. Slowly add milk, stirring until smooth. Cook until slightly thickened. Stir in salt, mustard and cheese. Cook until sauce starts to simmer. Toast muffins. In a medium saucepan combine tuna, mayonnaise, pineapple and bean sprouts. Cover and cook over medium heat until heated through. Spoon hot tuna mixture over toasted muffins. Ladle Cheddar cheese sauce over top.

Serves 4 to 6

TUNA AND MUSHROOM PIE

⅓ cup margarine
4 cups fresh mushrooms, sliced
½ cup onion, chopped
⅔ cup celery, sliced
2 tablespoons lemon juice
⅓ cup flour
3½ cups milk
2 (7-ounce) cans tuna
1 tablespoon Worcestershire sauce
1 package pie crust mix

Melt margarine and saute mushrooms, onion, celery and lemon juice 5 minutes. Blend in flour and gradually stir in milk, cooking until thickened. Add tuna and Worcestershire sauce. Turn into a buttered 2-quart casserole and top with prepared pie crust. Bake at 425 degrees for 30 minutes or until crust is browned.

Serve 6 to 8

poultry

CHICKEN WITH ALMONDS AND GRAPES

6 chicken breasts
½ cup flour
¾ teaspoon salt or 1 teaspoon seasoned salt
½ teaspoon pepper
1 teaspoon paprika
2 tablespoons butter
2 tablespoons oil
2 tablespoons finely chopped shallots or 3 tablespoons chopped onion and 1 clove finely chopped garlic.
½ cup sliced mushrooms (optional)
¼ cup brandy
¼ cup dry vermouth
½ cup chicken stock
½ cup seedless grapes (can use canned grapes)
½ cup almonds or cashews or walnuts

Mix together the flour, salt and pepper and paprika and lightly flour the chicken breasts. Combine oil and butter in heavy pan and when bubbly and hot add the chicken pieces. Add the shallots (or onion and garlic) and the mushrooms. Turn chicken so it browns evenly on both sides. When nice and brown add the brandy. Allow to heat and flame it. When the flame dies down add the wine, stock and grapes. Cover and simmer 15 minutes. Add the nuts and serve immediately.

Serves 6

This can be prepared ahead of time waiting for the nuts until the last minute, when you reheat.

SHERRIED ARTICHOKE CHICKEN

1 (3-pound frying chicken, cut up)
Salt, freshly ground pepper and paprika
2 tablespoons flour
4 tablespoons butter
¼ pound fresh mushrooms, sliced
1 cup chicken stock
3 tablespoons sherry
¼ teaspoon rosemary
1 (16-ounce) can artichoke hearts, drained

Preheat oven to 375 degrees. Sprinkle the chicken pieces with salt, pepper, flour and paprika. Melt butter in a heavy skillet and brown chicken pieces on both sides. Remove to casserole with cover. Add the mushrooms and gradually stir in chicken stock and sherry. Season with rosemary and deglaze the pan. Arrange the artichoke hearts among the chicken pieces, pour sauce over chicken, cover and bake for 40 minutes or until the chicken is tender.

Serves 6

BAKED CHICKEN WITH BUTTER AND CREAM

½ cup flour
1½ teaspoons salt
½ teaspoon paprika
¼ teaspoon pepper
1 fryer, cut into serving pieces
¼ cup butter
1½ cups hot water
½ cup nonfat dry milk powder

Dip chicken into water. Coat with mixture of flour and seasonings. Put skin side down in a 9x13-inch baking pan. Dot with butter. Bake at 350 degrees for 30 minutes. Mix hot water and milk powder. Pour around chicken. Bake 1¼ hours longer or until chicken is tender.

Serves 4

CHICKEN WITH BRANDY

1 chicken, cut for frying
¼ pound butter
4 medium-sized onions, diced
2 heaping teaspoons curry
2 cups fresh cream
3-ounces brandy or rum
Salt and pepper to taste

Brown onions in butter, add chicken, sprinkle with salt and pepper and cook slowly for 35 minutes. Just before serving remove chicken from pan. Mix and add cream, spirits and curry. Bring to a boil in same pan and pour over chicken. Serve with rice.

Serves 4

CHICKEN BREASTS IN A HEAVENLY SAUCE

4 small whole chicken breasts, split, boned and skinned
¼ cup flour
1 teaspoon each salt and pepper
1 cube butter (¼ pound)
2 tablespoons oil
½ pound mushrooms
½ pint whipping cream
¼ cup champagne

Place chicken breasts in a plastic bag with the flour, salt and pepper. Shake until breasts are lightly coated. Melt the butter and oil over medium-high heat in a skillet. Lightly brown the chicken breasts on both sides. Quarter the mushrooms and add to the pan with the breasts. Cover pan, lower heat and cook slowly for ten minutes. Remove the breasts and add the cream and champagne to the skillet. When the mixture is as thick as you like, pour the sauce over the chicken breasts and serve.

Serves 4 to 6

FAVORITE BROILED CHICKEN

½ cup butter
½ cup sherry
½ cup soy sauce
2 broilers, cut in half

Melt the butter in a saucepan and add sherry and soy sauce. Wash and pat dry chicken. Brush with butter marinade. Broil for 30 to 40 minutes, turning chicken often and basting with the marinade. Serve with fresh fruit kabobs, cooked rice and a tossed green salad.

Variation: Can be barbecued over medium coals 30 to 40 minutes turning chicken occasionally and basting frequently with marinade.

Serves 4

GOLDEN BROWN CHICKEN CASSEROLE

1 stick butter
Salt and pepper
1 chicken, cut into serving pieces
1 (4-ounce) can mushrooms
1 tablespoon flour
2 tablespoons Worcestershire sauce
1 bay leaf
Lemon juice to taste
1 (10½ ounce) can condensed beef bouillon

Melt butter in skillet. Salt and pepper chicken and brown well in butter. Transfer chicken to a large casserole dish. Brown mushrooms in same butter. Take out and place with chicken. Add flour to the butter and mix well. Add Worcestershire sauce, bay leaf, lemon juice and beef bouillon. Pour over chicken and mushrooms and cook 1 hour in the oven at 350 degrees. The chicken and mushrooms get brown and the gravy thickens. The gravy is wonderful for rice or mashed potatoes. It's great because you can prepare this the day before. Next day just cook in oven until hot and bubbly.

One of my favorites.

Serves 4

CHICKEN WITH CHERRY WINE SAUCE

2½ to 3-pounds chicken parts
¼ cup flour
Salt and pepper to taste
3 tablespoons butter or margarine
1 cup dry red wine
1 tablespoon sugar
1 teaspoon cinnamon
½ teaspoon allspice
2 cups pitted sweet red cherries

Coat chicken with mixture of flour and salt and pepper. Brown in butter in a large skillet. Stir in red wine, sugar, cinnamon, allspice and cherries. Cover and simmer, stirring occasionally, 35 to 40 minutes or until chicken is tender.

Serves 4

BETTY DEBORAH ULIUS'S SIAMESE COCONUT CHICKEN

2 cups milk
2 cups dried coconut (preferably unsweetened)
4 large chicken breast halves, skinned
½ onion, grated
1 teaspoon red pepper flakes
2 cloves garlic, crushed
1 teaspoon cumin
4 tablespoons crunchy peanut butter
2 tablespoons lemon juice
2 tablespoons lime juice
2 tablespoon soy sauce
2 tablespoons lemon rind
2 teaspoons sugar (if coconut is unsweetened)
2 teaspoons curry powder

Combine milk and coconut in saucepan, bring to a simmer, remove from heat and soak 30 minutes. Press all the liquids from the coconut (this is what Thais' call coconut cream), reserve the liquid and also the shredded coconut. Combine the liquid with the skinned chicken breasts in a saucepan. Put in about 4 tablespoons of the coconut and the crushed garlic. Cover and cook over medium-low heat, simmering for 30 minutes. Add remaining ingredients, stirring until well-mixed. If you want more sauce, add ½ to 1 cup more milk. Salt if needed. Cook for another 15 minutes, until thickened. Coat the chicken as it cooks. Marvelous served with rice pilaf in which you've put some white raisins the last few minutes of cooking.

Serves 4

CHUTNEY CHICKEN (Microwave)

1 (3-pound) fryer cut into serving pieces
1 teaspoon salt
1 (8¼ ounce) can crushed pineapple
½ cup chutney, chopped
½ cup pecans, coarsley chopped
¼ cup prepared mustard

Salt chicken pieces and place skin side up in a 12x8-inch baking dish. Mix together remaining ingredients and spoon over chicken. Cook on HIGH 10 minutes. Rotate dish. Reduce setting to MEDIUM and cook 18 to 20 minutes. Let stand a few minutes before serving.

Serves 4

CHICKEN DIABLO

Quarter 2 chickens, weighing about 2½ pounds each. Rub them with lemon and brown in melted butter and oil. When the chicken is brown, add 2 tablespoons chopped onion, ½ teaspoon chopped garlic, 4 large mushrooms sliced and ½ teaspoon thyme. Simmer until vegetables are soft and transparent. Sprinkle with 1½ teaspoons paprika, add ¼ cup sherry, cover and let steam for 25 minutes or until chicken is done and tender. Remove chicken pieces to a hot platter.

SAUCE

Add 1 cup brown sauce to skillet with 1 teaspoon Worcestershire sauce, ½ teaspoon dry mustard, 1 teaspoon lemon juice and 2 tablespoons heavy cream. Let simmer slowly for 5 minutes. Serve over chicken pieces.

Serves 4 to 6

BROILED DIJON CHICKEN BREASTS

⅓ cup Dijon mustard
1 clove garlic, crushed
Salt and pepper to taste
1 tablespoon green onion, chopped
3 pounds chicken breasts, halved

Preheat broiler and grease broiler pan. In a small bowl combine mustard, garlic and onion. Season chicken to taste. Place chicken pieces skin side down on a broiler pan. Broil 6 inches from heat for 6 to 8 minutes. Turn chicken, brush with mustard mixture and broil 6 to 8 minutes or until done.

Sooo easy and sooo good.

Serves 4

KNOTT'S BERRY FARM FRIED CHICKEN

2 (3-pound) frying chickens, cut in eighths
2 cups unbleached flour
1 quart oil (or enough to cover chicken)

Cover chicken with salted water and soak for 45 minutes. Drain chicken and pat dry. Coat each piece of chicken with flour and shake off any excess flour. Bring oil to a boil in an 8½ quart saucepan and drop in chicken pieces. (Do not overcrowd chicken in the pot). Cover and fry for 45 minutes. Remove chicken with slotted spoon and drain out on paper towels. Fifteen minutes before serving, heat ¼ cup oil in a large skilled and refry for 15 minutes.

Serves 6

HOLIDAY CHICKEN

24 pieces of chicken (breasts, legs, and thighs)
Butter or margarine
1 can cream of mushroom soup
2 cans cream of chicken soup
¼ cup dry white wine
1 pound fresh mushrooms, sliced or 2 cans mushrooms

Brown chicken in butter or margarine. Place in a large pan so as to have just 1 layer. Mix soups and wine and pour over chicken. Saute mushrooms in a little additional butter for a few minutes and sprinkle on top of chicken. Can be refrigerated overnight with no problem. When ready to bake bring up to room temperature. Cover with foil and bake at 350 degrees for 1½ hours.

Serves 12

INDIAN CHICKEN

1 can chicken broth
½ cup chunk peanut butter
⅛ teaspoon cayenne pepper
1 cooked, skinned and boned chicken
Salt
3½ cups cooked rice (brown or white)
½ cup each of 5 or more diced accompaniments:
Green onion, raw onion, tomato, oranges, avocado, banana, dates, crisp bacon, coconut, peanuts, peppers, currants, sesame seeds, sunflower seeds

In a saucepan combine broth, peanut butter and pepper. Bring to a boil, reduce heat. Simmer 20 minutes, stirring occasionally. Pour over chicken, heat. Season to taste with salt. Serve over rice with accompaniments.

Serves 4 to 6

MISSISSIPPI CHICKEN JAMBALAYA

1 cup onions, chopped
1 cup green pepper, chopped
2 cloves garlic, minced
2 tablespoon oil
1 cup cooked ham, diced
12 small pork sausage links, cut into rounds
1 cup cooked chicken, diced
2 (16-ounce) cans tomatoes
1 cup uncooked rice
1½ cups chicken broth
½ teaspoon thyme
1 teaspoon salt
1 tablespoon parsley, chopped

Saute onions, green pepper and garlic in oil, stirring frequently until tender crisp. Stir in meats and cook for 5 minutes. Add remaining ingredients and place in a 2-quart greased casserole dish. Cover and bake at 350 degrees for 1 hour.

Serves 8

CHICKEN LEGS WITH KIWI FRUIT AND WALNUTS

6 whole chicken legs (thigh with drumstick)
3 tablespoons butter
3 tablespoons oil
1 small onion, chopped
1 cup walnuts, chopped
1 cup chicken stock (may use part white wine)
Salt and pepper to taste
4 kiwi fruit
¼ cup toasted walnut halves

In a large skillet saute chicken in butter or oil until browned. Add onions, walnuts and stock. Salt and pepper to taste. Cover and cook chicken 25 minutes, turning once. Remove cover and cook 10 minutes or until chicken is tender. Place chicken on a warmed serving platter. Reduce liquid in pan to ½ cup or add stock to make ½ cup. Peel kiwi fruit. Chop two and add to pan liquid and warm, do not boil. Pour immediately over chicken. Slice remaining two kiwi fruit and garnish with kiwi fruit slices and toasted walnuts.

Serves 4

LEMON CHICKEN

6 tablespoons butter or margarine
2 tablespoons fresh lemon juice
Rind of 1 lemon, grated
4 boneless chicken breast halves, skinned
1½ cups fresh mushrooms, sliced
1 tablespoon cornstarch
¾ cup chicken broth
1 cup whipping cream

In a large skillet, melt 3 tablespoons butter. Stir in 1 tablespoon lemon juice. Add chicken and brown over medium heat. Remove to a warmed platter. Cover to keep warm. In same skillet add 3 tablespoons butter. Stir in remaining lemon juice and mushrooms. Saute quickly until slightly cooked. In a small bowl dissolve cornstarch in the chicken broth. Stir into the mushrooms. Add cream. Cook 2 to 3 minutes until slightly thickened. Do not boil. Pour sauce over cooked chicken.

Serves 4

MRS. HIVELY'S CHICKEN MAXIN

1 whole chicken plus 2 chicken breasts cooked and cubed
1 cup butter or margarine
1 bag seasoned dressing mix
1 pint sour cream
1 can cream of mushroom soup
1 large can mushrooms, undrained

Melt butter and brown ½ of the dressing and place in the bottom of a 9x13-inch baking dish. Combine chicken, sour cream, soup and mushrooms. Spread mixture over dressing and top with remaining dressing mix. Bake at 350 degrees for 45 minutes.

Serves 6 to 8

CHICKEN ORIN IN THE MICROWAVE

1 (6-ounce) package wild rice mix
1 (10¾ ounce) can cream of mushroom soup
¾ cup hot water
1 (16-ounce) can Chinese vegetables, drained
4 chicken breasts, halved and skinned or a 2½ pound chicken, cut up and skinned
Soy sauce

In a 10-inch baking dish, mix together rice mix, soup and water. Gently fold in drained vegetables. Cook on HIGH 5 minutes. Stir. Place chicken on top of rice mixture. Put a small amount of soy sauce on each piece of chicken. Cover with wax paper. Cook on HIGH 10 minutes. Turn chicken over. Cover. Cook on HIGH 10 minutes. Let stand a few minutes before serving.

Serves 4 to 6

PARSLEY 'N' CHEESE BAKED CHICKEN

¼ cup bottled Italian salad dressing
3 (3½ pound) fryers, cut into serving pieces
1 egg, lightly beaten
2 tablespoons water
½ cup Parmesan cheese
⅓ cup fine dry bread crumbs
2 tablespoons parsley, chopped
½ teaspoon salt
½ teaspoon paprika
⅛ teaspoon pepper

Pour salad dressing into a 9x13-inch baking pan. Add chicken and turn to coat on all sides. (May need to add more.) Cover and refrigerate for 4 hours, occasionally spooning dressing over all. Drain and reserve dressing. Combine egg and water. In a plastic bag, combine cheese, bread crumbs, parsley and seasonings. Dip chicken into egg mixture then shake chicken a few pieces at a time in crumb mixture to coat. Return coated chicken to baking dish. Spoon reserved dressing on top. Bake in a 350 degree oven for 45 to 50 minutes.

Serves 10

POULET SAUTE AU RIESLING

1 (2½ to 3-pounds) fryer
1 tablespoon peanut oil
4 tablespoons butter
¼ pound mushrooms, sliced
3 ripe tomatoes, peeled, sliced and chopped
½ bottle dry white wine
2 tablespoons brandy
2 tablespoons consomme
Salt
Cayenne pepper
3 tablespoons parsley, chopped
2 cloves garlic, chopped

Cut the chicken into serving pieces. Heat oil and butter in casserole. Brown the chicken until golden on all sides, add the mushrooms and the tomatoes. Reduce the heat slightly and cook for 5 minutes. Add the wine, brandy and consomme. Season with the salt and pepper and a little cayenne. Bring to a boil. Cover the casserole and simmer for 25 minutes. Transfer the chicken to a hot serving dish and keep warm. Skim the fat off the pan juices. Add the parsley and the garlic. Bring it to a boil and cook over high heat until the sauce has reduced. Pour over chicken and serve very hot.

Serves 4

SWEET AND SOUR CHICKEN

3 tablespoons oil
3 chicken breasts, boned, skinned and cut into ½-inch strips
1 cup chicken broth
1 can (13½ ounce) pineapple chunks, syrup reserved
1 cup vinegar
2 tablespoons soy sauce
¼ cup brown sugar
3 tablespoons cornstarch
1 large green pepper, cut into chunks
4 small tomatoes, cut in eighths

Heat oil in pan over high heat. Add chicken and cook until chicken turns white and is cooked through stirring frequently. Add syrup, ½ cup broth, vinegar, soy sauce and brown sugar. Continue heating until it boils. Combine cornstarch and remaining broth, add to sauce while stirring and cook until thickened. Add pineapple, green pepper and tomatoes and cook over low heat only until heated through. Serve with rice or chow mein noodles.

Serves 4 to 6

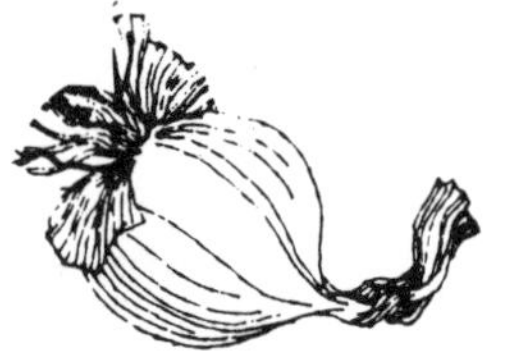

TOUCHDOWN CHICKEN ROLLS

1 (3-ounce) package cream cheese, softened
2 tablespoons margarine, melted
2 cups chicken, cooked and cubed
¼ teaspoon salt
1 tablespoon green onion, chopped
2 tablespoons milk
1 package refrigerated crescent rolls
1 cup seasoned croutons, crushed or wheat germ

Blend cream cheese and margarine. Add chicken, salt, onion, and milk. Separate the rolls into 8 wedges. Spoon ½ cup chicken mixture on each. Roll up tucking points in to close ends. Dip in extra melted butter and roll in croutons. Bake on a cookie sheet in a 350 degree oven until golden brown, about 20 to 25 minutes.

CREAMED CHICKEN TACOS

1 cup green chiles
1 onion
3 tablespoons butter
2 tablespoons flour
2 cups tomato juice
2 cups Cheddar cheese, grated
2 cups cream
1 boiled chicken
12 tortillas

Chop chiles and onions and saute in butter. Add flour and tomato juice. Fry the tortillas in oil until limp, then cut into strips. Cut up chicken. Make alternate layers: Tortillas, tomato sauce, chicken, cream and cheese. Bake in a 350 degree oven until heated through, about 30 minutes.

Simply wonderful.

Serves 6 to 8

SLOW TURKEY COOKING METHOD

Rub turkey inside and out with butter. Sprinkle inside and out with salt and pepper. Place on roasting rack breast side down. Roast at 275 degrees 23 minutes per pound . . . or until meat thermometer reaches 175 degrees. Do not baste, tent or turn. Allow 30 minutes for turkey to set before carving.

NOTE: Time may change for very large or smaller turkeys . . . rely on thermometer for doneness. (I do not reccomend this cooking version for birds under 12 pounds.)

STRAWBERRY GAME HENS

4 Cornich game hens
Salt and pepper to taste
4 cups strawberries, hulled
3 tablespoons corn starch
½ cup water
⅔ cup orange juice
2 tablespoons lemon juice

Preheat oven to 350 degrees. Wash game hens and season with salt and pepper. Place hens in a roasting pan. Mash strawberries and combine corn starch and water and mix until smooth. Add strawberry pulp and orange and lemon juice. Pour over hens and roast, basting frequently with sauce for 1½ hours or until done.

This is a delightful entree any time of the year. A new twist on an old standby.

Serves 4

MOCK ABALONE STEAKS

Pound sliced turkey breast meat until thin. Soak overnight in clam juice, refrigerated. Next day, pat dry, dredge in seasoned flour and pan fry in butter until lightly browned on both sides.

TURKEY CUTLETS

I've found ground turkey available at almost all my favorite supermarkets and I like to use it because it is high in protein and low in calories. Another big plus, it's inexpensive. You can add calories to this dish according to how much sour cream and butter you use.

3 large slices stale white bread, crusts removed
Milk
1 ½ pounds raw ground turkey meat
1 tablespoon onion, finely chopped
1 egg, lightly beaten
Salt and pepper to taste
Butter or margarine for frying
1 cup fresh or canned mushrooms, sliced
2 tablespoons flour (for thickening)
1 (10½ ounce) can beef or chicken consomme
½ cup sour cream
Minced dill or parsley

Soak the bread in a small amount of milk (about ½ cup). When soft, squeeze out excess milk. Add to turkey with chopped onion and egg. Season with salt and pepper. Mix thoroughly with your hands. It will be quite mushy. Have frying pan ready with several tablespoons of butter (don't let it burn). Shape the mixture into plump oval cutlets. Fry evenly until brown on both sides. Arrange in warmed casserole dish. Saute mushrooms in butter for a few minutes. Season with pepper. Dissolve flour in ½ cup undiluted consomme. Add remaining consomme to pan you fried the cutlets in. Simmer, add dissolved flour mixture and the mushrooms. Remove from heat and cool slightly. Add sour cream. Mix and pour over cutlets. Sprinkle with dill. Cover and bake 325 degrees for 20 to 25 minutes.

Serves 4 to 6

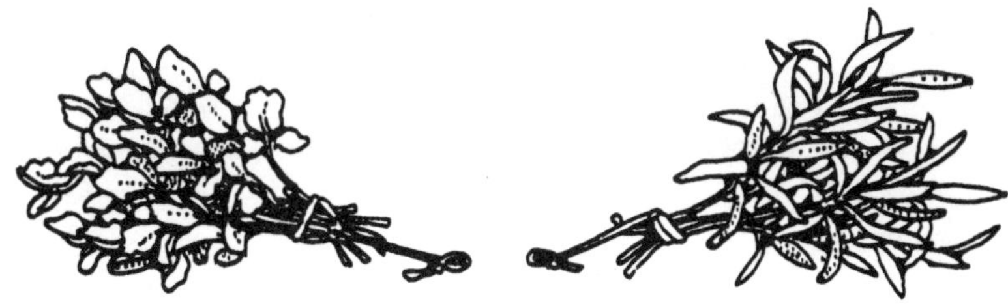

OVEN BROILED TURKEY CUTLETS

1 pound turkey cutlets
½ cup flour
1 egg
Seasoned bread crumbs
5 tablespoons butter or margarine
1 clove garlic, crushed
1 tablespoon parsley, chopped
Parmesan cheese
Salt and pepper to taste
1 lemon

Heat broiler. Coat cutlets by dipping them in flour, then in the egg and then in seasoned bread crumbs. Fry until almost cooked. Place in a single layer on a cookie sheet. Melt butter, saute garlic and add parsley. Pour over cutlets. Sprinkle with Parmesan, salt and pepper. Squeeze lemon juice over all. Broil until crisp on each side.

This is wonderful with rice pilaf, a green vegetable and a peach half for each plate.

Serves 2

JELLIED TURKEY AND HAM LOAF

1 pound cooked turkey
½ pound cooked ham
1 quart chicken broth
2 tablespoons pickling spices
1 cup stuffed green olives, drained
2 tablespoons sliced pimientos
4 envelopes unflavored gelatin
1 teaspoon salt
¼ cup vinegar

Cut turkey into ¾-inch cubes. Slice ham into pencil-thick strips, 1 inch-long. Coarsely chop olives and pimientos. Heat chicken broth with pickling spices. Soften gelatin in a little cold water and stir into hot broth. When gelatin has dissolved, stir in vinegar and salt. Add meat and olives and pimientos and bring mixture to a boil. Simmer 5 minutes. Pour into loaf pans and cool to room temperature. Refrigerate overnight. Serve in ½-inch slices.

Serves 10 to 12

TURKEY MIX UP

2 cups cooked turkey, chopped (may use tuna)
2 cups mashed potatoes
2 tablespoons parsley, chopped
2 eggs
½ cup onions, chopped
Garlic
Basil
Tarragon
Salt and pepper to taste

Mash all ingredients together. Form 6 patties. Saute in oil approximately 5 minutes per side. Wonderful served with cheese or hollandaise sauce.

Great way to get rid of leftovers, you don't have to make a trip to the store . . . as the old song says, "ANYTHING GOES".

Serves 6

TURKEY BREAKFAST SAUSAGE

2 pounds ground turkey
2 teaspoons salt
½ teaspoon coarsely ground pepper
¼ teaspoon ginger
½ teaspoon sage
½ teaspoon marjoram
1 egg, beaten

Mix all ingredients thoroughly. Refrigerate overnight to blend flavors. Form into patties and fry in butter or oil until browned on both sides.

Makes 10 to 12 patties

Variation: For spicy sausage, substitute cayenne pepper for ginger

TURKEY TETRAZZINI

1 (8-ounce) package spinach noodles
¼ cup butter or margarine
½ medium onion, cut into strips
½ cup carrots, thinly sliced
1 cup fresh broccoli flowerets
8-ounces fresh mushrooms, sliced
¼ cup flour
Salt and pepper to taste
¼ teaspoon nutmeg
2 cups milk or half and half
3 cups cooked turkey, diced

Cook noodles according to package instructions. Keep noodles warm. Meanwhile in a large skillet or wok, melt butter. Add onion, carrots and broccoli and stir until al dente. Add mushrooms and cook 1 minute. Stir in flour and seasonings. Add milk, stir until thickened. Add turkey and cook until turkey is warmed. Serve over hot spinach noodles.

Serves 6

meats

PICKLED BOLOGNA

1 pound chub bologna
1 cup vinegar
1 tablespoon pickling spice
1 teaspoon salt
6 whole peppercorns
1 bay leaf
Water

Cut bologna into bite-sized cubes. Combine vinegar and seasonings in a saucepan and bring to a boil. Pack bologna into a quart jar and pour hot brine over it. Add water if necessary to cover bologna with liquid. Cover and shake well. Refrigerate several days to properly pickle cubes. Serve as appetizers or snacks.

Serves 8

BRISKET IN FOIL

4 pounds brisket of beef
Salt and pepper to taste
Steak sauce
6 small red potatoes, washed
6 carrots, washed and pared
3 celery stalks, chopped
½ cup dry red wine
1 large onion, chopped

Season brisket with salt and pepper to taste. Baste entire surface of brisket with your favorite steak sauce. Place a large sheet of heavy-duty foil on baking sheet. Place meat in the center, arrange vegetables around the meat and sprinkle onions over all. Pour wine around the sides of meat. Fold foil up around the meat and vegetables loosely, but seal, closing edges tightly. Bake in a 325 degree oven 3½ to 4 hours. When tender, open foil. Remove meat to a platter, slice across the grain and serve with the vegetables and pan juices.

Serves 4 to 6

BUFFET BEEF BRISKET

1 (4-pound) beef brisket
1 tablespoon instant meat tenderizer
2 cups water
2 cups onions, coarsely chopped
1 cup celery leaves, chopped
1 bay leaf
1 tablespoon salt
1 teaspoon pepper
2 cups soft bread crumbs
¼ cup Dijon mustard
¼ cup maple syrup

Moisten brisket on both sides with water and sprinkle both sides with meat tenderizer. Pierce meat all over with sharp tined fork. Place meat in a heavy skillet or Dutch oven and add the next 6 ingredients. Bring to a boil, reduce heat, cover and simmer 2 hours until meat is tender. Combine remaining ingredients. Remove meat from liquid and drain. Spread crumb mixture over top of meat and broil 5 minutes.

Serves 6 to 8

JACKIE'S CORNED BEEF ON A SPIT

1 (3 to 4-pound) corned beef
Water
4 bay leaves
4 small hot whole red chiles
3 pieces stick cinnamon, broken up
12 peppercorns
3 cloves garlic, cut in half
1 large onion, sliced
½ cup brown sugar
½ teaspoon ground cloves
½ teaspoon ground ginger
½ teaspoon dry mustard
¼ teaspoon celery salt
¼ teaspoon cracked caraway seed

Place corned beef in a large pot and cover with cold water. Add bay leaves, chiles, cinnamon, peppercorns, garlic and onion. Bring to a boil, cover and lower heat and simmer slowly 4 to 4½ hours or until meat is tender. Drain, then blot dry. Blend together remaining ingredients and rub into meat. Place in a rotary basket or on a spit and let rotate over a slow charcoal fire for 1 hour. Slice this thin and serve with sourdough buns. Potato salad and baked beans, a green salad and a lot of cold beer makes a great outdoor feed.

Serves 4 to 6

BEEF ROLLUPS FOR THE ACADEMY AWARDS

½ cup Cheddar cheese, grated
1 (2½ ounce) jar dried chipped beef, finely chopped
(1 teaspoon horseradish)
1 teaspoon Worcestershire sauce
1 (8-ounce) package refrigerated crescent rolls
2 tablespoons butter or margarine, melted

Combine the first 4 ingredients and mix well. Separate the crescent rolls into 4 rectangles. Pinch perforations together. Brush each with the melted butter. Spread mixture evenly over 4 rectangles. Roll up each piece and cut into 4 pieces using a serrated knife. Place seam side down on a greased baking sheet. Bake at 375 degrees for 12 to 14 minutes.

Makes 16

SPICED APPLES AND BEEF

2 pounds beef chuck, cut into 1-inch cubes
2 tablespoons oil
1½ cups water
¼ cup lemon juice
2 cups onions, sliced
1½ teaspoons curry powder
¼ teaspoon cloves
¼ teaspoon cinnamon
1 teaspoon salt
3 cups cooking apples, peeled and cut into 1-inch wedges
Buttered hot cooked rice

Brown beef cubes in the oil. Add 1 cup water, lemon juice, onion and seasonings. Cover and simmer 40 minutes. Add apple wedges and remaining water, mix and cook covered 40 minutes more, or until meat is tender. Serve on the hot buttered rice.

Serves 6

PRECOOKED HAMBURGER MIX

This recipe is the basis for a number of fabulous casseroles.

4 onions, chopped
1 teaspoon garlic salt
2 cups celery, chopped
¼ cup bacon fat
4 pounds lean ground beef
2 teaspoons salt
½ teaspoon pepper
3 tablespoons Worcestershire sauce
2 (12-ounce) bottles catsup

Fry onions, garlic salt and celery in bacon fat until soft. Add hamburger and cook until lightly browned. Add remaining ingredients and simmer 20 minutes. To freeze, cool, skim off fat and ladle into 5 (1-pint) containers. Seal, label and freeze.

ST. PATTY'S DAY HAMBURGER

2 cups ground ham
½ cup mayonnaise
1 tablespoon parsley, chopped
1 tablespoon Dijon mustard
1 tablespoon celery, chopped
6 pineapple slices
Garnish: Ripe olive slices and watercress

Combine ham with all the seasonings and form into 6 patties. Place pineapple slices on a baking sheet, top each with a ham patty. Bake at 375 degrees 8 to 10 minutes. Serve with the garnish on your favorite bun.

Serve 6

OLD FASHIONED BEEF HASH

This recipe is from the days when hash was a lot better on Monday night than the roast beef on Sunday.

3 tablespoons bacon drippings or shortening
2 cups beef, cooked and diced
3 medium potatoes, boiled and diced
2 onions, diced
1 teaspoon salt
¼ teaspoon pepper
Hot water or beef bouillon

Heat drippings in skillet. Add the beef, potatoes, onions, salt and pepper. Cook stirring occasionally, until mixture begins to brown. Moisten lightly as it cooks with water or bouillon.

Serves 4 to 6

INDIVIDUAL MEAT LOAVES WITH SAUCE

1 cup dry bread crumbs
1 medium onion, chopped
2 teaspoons salt
¼ teaspoon pepper
1 teaspoon dry mustard
1 teaspoon Worcestershire sauce
¼ cup catsup
2 eggs
2 pounds ground beef

Combine all ingredients. Shape into 6 loaves. Place on lightly greased baking pan. Bake, basting with sauce in a 350 degree oven for 45 minutes.

Serves 6

SAUCE

1 cup catsup
1 small onion, chopped
¼ cup vinegar
1 tablespoon sugar
½ teaspoon dry mustard

Combine all the ingredients, use to baste loaves.

PIZZA MEAT LOAF

6-ounces Mozzarella cheese
6 slices stale bread, crusts removed
½ cup milk
1½ pounds ground meat
1 small onion, sauteed
1 small can mushrooms, drained
1 tablespoons parsley
Dash oregano or thyme
Salt and pepper
1 clove garlic, mashed
1 small can tomato sauce
Additional oregano, salt and pepper

Cut ½ the cheese into slices, chop the rest in chunks. Soak the bread in milk. Put the bread, meat, onion, mushrooms, chopped cheese, parsley, spices, ½ clove garlic and ⅓ can tomato sauce in large bowl. Mix by hand. Shape into a loaf and bake 45 minutes. Top with pizza topping made of remaining tomato sauce, seasoning and garlic. Pour over meat. Put sliced cheese on top and bake an additional 15 minutes at 350 degrees.

Serves 6 to 8

APPLE EASY POT ROAST

1 envelope onion gravy mix
1 cup apple juice
½ cup water
2 tablespoons Worcestershire sauce
4 pounds boneless rump or chuck roast
3 large baking apples, halved and cored

Combine gravy mix, apple juice, water and Worcestershire sauce. Pour over roast in a large dutch oven or roasting pan. Cover and bake at 325 degrees for 2 to 2½ hours, just until tender. Arrange apples around roast and baste with the gravy. Continue to bake, uncovered, basting frequently, 20 to 30 minutes longer, or until roast and apples are tender. Remove roast and apples to a serving platter. Cook gravy over medium heat to thicken slightly. Serve with the roast.

Serves 4 to 6

ALL IN A PACKAGE STEAK SUPPER

1 ½ pounds chuck steak, 1-inch thick
1 envelope onion soup
3 medium carrots, quartered
2 stalks celery, cut into sticks
2 or 3 medium potatoes, peeled and halved
2 tablespoons butter or margarine
½ teaspoon salt
¼ teaspoon paprika

Tear off a 2½ foot length of 18-inch wide heavy-duty foil. Place meat in center, sprinkle with onion soup mix, cover with vegetables. Dot vegetables with butter and sprinkle with salt and paprika. Fold foil over and seal securely to hold in juices. Place on baking sheet. Bake in hot oven at 400 degrees, 1 to 1 ½ hours or until done.

This is so easy and so good. It will be one of your favorites when you are in a hurry.

Serves 4

DAD'S FAVORITE ROUND STEAK

2 pounds round steak
Flour
2 tablespoons butter
1 tablespoon olive oil
2 large onions, thinly sliced
1 clove garlic, minced
1 cup white wine
1 cup beef broth
1 teaspoon Worcestershire sauce
1 teaspoon soy sauce
⅛ teaspoon pepper
1 cup Cheddar cheese, grated
½ cup sour cream

Cut steak into 4 serving pieces. Dredge steak with flour seasoned with salt and pepper. Brown on both sides in butter and oil in a heavy pan. Remove steak from pan, add onions to the pan and saute until golden. Stir in garlic, wine, broth, Worcestershire sauce, soy sauce and pepper, being careful to get all the darling brown bits from the pan. Return steak to pan. Cover and simmer very slowly for 1 ½ hours or until meat is very tender. Remove meat to a platter and keep warm. Stir the cheese into the onions and pan juices until melted. Then stir in sour cream and heat. Do not boil. Pour the sauce over the meat and serve with fluffy mashed potatoes or noodles.

Serves 4

ROUND STEAK BRAISED IN BEER

3 pounds round steak
Flour
1 teaspoon salt
1 teaspoon pepper
3 tablespoons butter
6 onions, sliced
2 cups beer

Sprinkle meat heavily with flour and pound salt and pepper into both sides of meat using a pounder on a board. Cut meat into serving size pieces. Melt butter, add about half of the meat at a time and brown on both sides. Avoid crowding of the pan so meat browns rapidly. Add onions with last batch of meat and brown lightly. Add beer, cover tightly and simmer 1½ hours or until meat is tender.

This is down home wonderful . . . I serve with creamy mashed potatoes. It will only cost you about 25 more sit-ups.

Serves 6

MUSHROOMS AND STEAK

1½ pounds top sirloin steak
3 tablespoons butter or margarine
1 tablespoon Worcestershire sauce
1 teaspoon dried basil
½ teaspoon dried tarragon
3 cups mushrooms, sliced
½ cup dry vermouth
¼ teaspoon salt
⅛ teaspoon pepper
1 cup Jack cheese, shredded
1 tablespoon flour

Cut steak into 4 serving pieces. In a large skillet melt butter or margarine. Add Worcestershire sauce, basil and tarragon. Place steaks in skillet, cook 5 minutes on each side for medium. Remove to a warmed platter, cover with foil to keep warm. Place mushrooms in skillet. Add wine, salt and pepper. Saute until mushrooms are cooked. In a small bowl, toss cheese with flour, stir in mushrooms. Cook until cheese is melted. Pour mushroom sauce over steaks and serve.

This is sooo easy and wonderful.

Serves 4

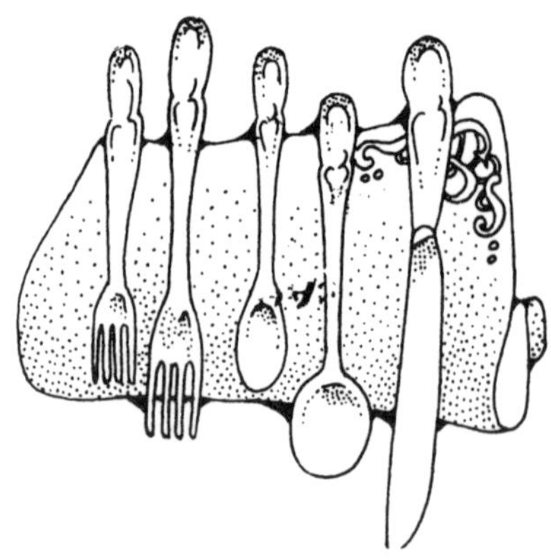

NO PEEKIE STEW

This is a great dish that smells and tastes as if you've been in the kitchen all afternoon and it takes only a few minutes. Serve this with some noodles and a green vegetable. Scrumptous!

2 pounds stew meat
1 package onion soup mix
1 can cream of mushroom soup
1 small can cooked mushrooms, drained
1 cup ginger ale

Throw all ingredients together in a pot with a tight fitting lid and bake at 350 degrees for 3 hours. NO PEEKIE.

Serves 6

TERI MAKI IN THE MICRO

1 pound round steak
½ cup pineapple juice
½ cup soy sauce
¼ cup sherry
1 teaspoon ginger root, minced
2 cloves garlic, crushed
1 (8½ ounce) can water chestnuts

Cut round steak into strips. Combine pineapple juice, soy sauce, sherry, ginger root and garlic together. Mix well. Marinate steak strips for 1 hour stirring occasionally. Cut water chestnuts in half crosswise. Drain steak strips and wrap each strip around chestnut halves. Secure with a wooden pick. Arrange on a shallow baking dish and microwave, uncovered, for 1½ to 2 minutes on HIGH. Repeat until all Teri Maki are cooked. This can be broiled or barbecued as well.

Makes about 2½ dozen

BEEF STROGANOFF *Microwave*

3 tablespoons butter or margarine
1½ pounds sirloin steak, sliced into thin strips
1 cup mushrooms, sliced
1 cup onion, sliced
1 teaspoon salt
2 teaspoons paprika
1 teaspoon Worcestershire sauce
1 cup sour cream

Preheat browning casserole dish 5 minutes on HIGH. Add butter and when melted stir in beef strips and brown on all sides on HIGH about 3 minutes. Add remaining ingredients, except sour cream, cover with glass lid and cook on HIGH 3 to 5 minutes. Stir in sour cream, reduce setting to MEDIUM and cook 15 to 18 minutes, or until meat is tender and sauce is bubbly. This is lovely with rice, a steamed green vegetable and a peach half with a teaspoon of chutney in the center.

Serves 4

HOW TO COOK A COUNTRY HAM

Weigh ham. When you are buying a ham try to get one from 20 to 22 pounds. Scrub in cold water with stiff brush. Soak overnight in cold water, making certain the ham is completely covered. Remove ham and place in large kettle, skin side down. Barely cover with fresh water and add:

1 cup pickle juice or ½ cup apple vinegar
1 red pepper pod (seeds removed)
1 lemon quartered
1 onion, halved
2 bay leaves

Let come to a boil and cut heat to medium. Ham is done when large flat bone can be removed with your fingers, a little less than 15 minutes a pound. When done, remove lid and cool ham in liquid which it was cooked in. When ham is cool, skin off rind and lightly pierce the fat side. Rub ham with prepared mustard, then pat on brown sugar. Sprinkle with sifted bread crumbs and pour ½ cup sherry over entire top of ham. Stick with cloves. Brown in a 350 degree oven. Let cool at least 12 hours before slicing.

Feeds the entire family with lots of good leftovers.

HONEY BASTED HAM

¼ cup dark corn syrup
1 pound honey
⅔ cup butter or margarine

In a small saucepan combine the 3 ingredients. Bring to a boil. Stir constantly over just enough heat to keep the mixture at a gentle boil for 15 minutes. For half of a semi-boneless fully cooked ham, approximately 4 to 5 pounds, place ham, cut side down in a shallow baking pan. Score the fatted sides of the ham in diamond shapes. Insert a whole clove in the center of each diamond. Baste surface of the ham with the simmering glaze, using about 3 tablespoons of the mixture, every 10 minutes for 1 hour and 15 minutes at 350 degrees, or until the glaze becomes candied but not overly browned. It will harden while cooling. Keep honey mixture warm over hot water in top of a double boiler. At the end of the baking period open the door, turning on the broiler just to candy the honey coating of the ham. Let stand 20 minutes before carving.

COCA COLA BASTED HAM

1 (10-pound) precooked ham (not cured or canned)
6 cups Coca-Cola
1 cup brown sugar
1 tablespoon dry mustard
2 tablespoons Dijon mustard
2 cups fine, dry bread crumbs

Preheat oven to 325 degrees. Place ham fat side down in a shallow pan. Pour cola into pan ½-inch deep. Bake 2 to 3 hours or until ham can easily be pierced with a fork, basting with Coca-Cola every 15 minutes. Center of ham will read 140 degrees on a meat thermometer. Remove ham from pan and cool. Cut away rind with a sharp knife. Combine sugar, mustard, bread crumbs and enough cola to form a thick paste. Place ham on roasting rack in pan and pat all over with paste. Add remaining cola to bottom of pan. With oven at 375 degrees bake 45 minutes longer, basting every 10 minutes, until mustard paste has melted into a dark glaze. Let stand at room temperature 30 minutes before slicing.

Serves 12 to 15

HOLIDAY CREAM CHEESE HAM

1 (5-pound) canned ham, chilled thoroughly
2 (8-ounce) packages cream cheese
1 (3-ounce) package Roquefort cheese
¼ cup parsley, chopped
¼ cup chives, chopped
2 tablespoons brandy

Remove ham from can and place on serving dish and chill. Combine remaining ingredients until smooth. Frost the ham with this mixture and chill again for at least 1 hour to set cheese frosting.

Serves 16 to 20

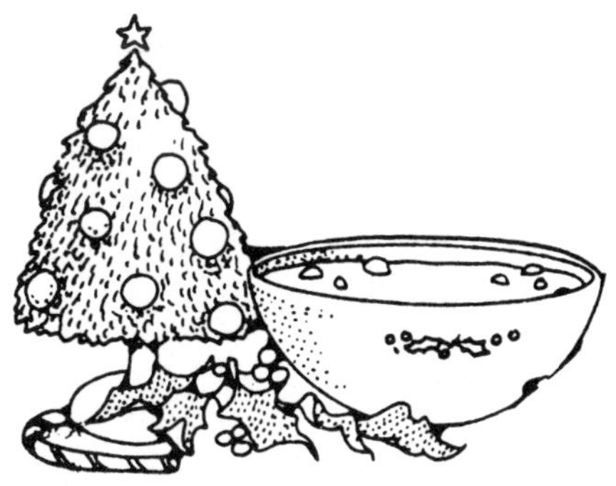

SHERRY GLAZED HAM FOR EASTER

1 (5 pound) canned ham
1½ cups cream sherry
½ cup apricot or peach jam
½ cup honey
Dash of nutmeg or cinnamon
1 tablespoon cornstarch

Place ham in a shallow baking pan and pour over ½ cup of the sherry. Bake 1 hour in a 325 degree oven. Meanwhile, combine jam with honey and a generous dash of nutmeg or cinnamon in a saucepan. Stir in cornstarch and remaining cup of sherry. Cook stirring constantly until thick. Spoon sauce over ham and bake about 20 minutes more until ham is glazed, basting occasionally.

Fabulous with candied sweet potatoes, hot fresh asparagus and a fruit salad, relishes, rolls and pineapple sherbert.

Serves 6 to 8

HAM HOCKS AND BEANS

1 pound package pinto beans
2 to 4 smoked ham hocks
1 large onion, chopped
3 cloves garlic, minced
1 teaspoon pepper
1 teaspoon oregano
1 teaspoon cumin
1 teaspoon crushed hot red peppers
2 (7-ounce) cans Ortega green chili salsa

Put the ham hocks in a large pot and cover with water. Cook slowly several hours until meat comes off the bone. Half way through cooking time, add onion, garlic, black pepper, oregano, & cumin. Remove ham hocks and cut meat into small cubes, return to pot. Add crushed red pepper and salsa. Continue simmering until beans are done. Serve with your favorite corn bread.

Serves 6 to 8

APPLE HAM CASSEROLE

¼ teaspoon cloves
½ teaspoon dry mustard
1 cup soft bread crumbs
3 cups cooked ham, ground
1 tablespoon onion, minced
1 egg, beaten
½ cup milk
Salt to taste
3 baking apples, peeled, cored and sliced
¼ cup honey
2 tablespoons butter

Mix the first 8 ingredients. Place in a greased baking dish. Spread apples over mixture. Sprinkle with honey and dot with butter. Bake at 375 degrees for about 40 minutes.

Serves 4 to 6

ASPARAGUS JAMBON WITH CURRY SAUCE

1 pound fresh asparagus, steamed al dente
4 thin slices cooked ham
¼ cup butter or margarine
½ onion, finely chopped
¼ cup flour
½ teaspoon curry powder
2 cups milk
¼ teaspoon salt
⅛ teaspoon pepper

Preheat broiler. Arrange asparagus in 4 piles and cut so all spears are approximately the same length. Wrap each bundle with a slice of ham and secure with a wooden pick. Place on a broiler pan and broil 5 minutes. Meanwhile, in a medium saucepan melt butter or margarine, add onion and saute until soft. Stir in flour and curry powder. Blend in milk. Stir over medium heat until thickened. Season with salt and pepper. Place asparagus Jambon on platter and pour sauce over. I serve this with a fruit salad and buttered noodles.

Terrific and easy!

Serves 4

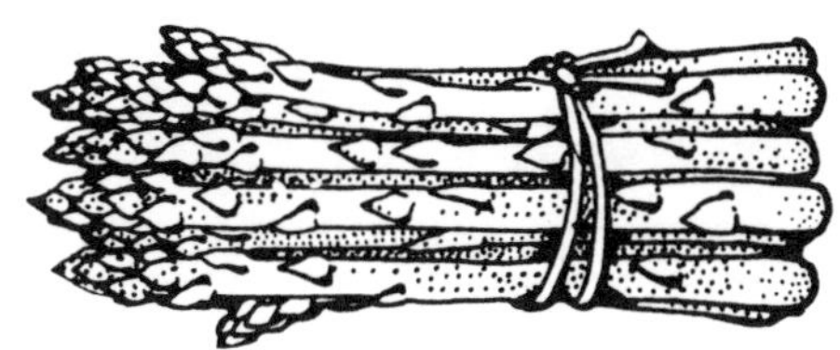

HAM LOAF *Microwave*

½ cup brown sugar
1 tablespoon lemon juice
1 tablespoon water
1 pound ground ham
½ pound ground beef
1 tablespoon minced onion
½ teaspoon dry mustard
½ cup evaporated milk
¼ cup catsup
½ cup bread crumbs
½ teaspoon salt
¼ teaspoon pepper

Combine brown sugar, lemon juice and water in a 2-cup measure. Cook on HIGH 2 to 3 minutes or until mixture forms a syrup. Combine remaining ingredients and shape into a loaf. Place in a 9x5-inch loaf pan. Cook on HIGH 5 minutes. Spoon syrup over meat. Cover with wax paper. Reduce setting to MEDIUM and cook 15 minutes or until firm.

Serves 4 to 6

SPICED HAM PATTIES

1 (1 pound) can ham patties
2 oranges, thinly sliced
1 (12-ounces) can orange-cranberry or raspberry-cranberry sauce

Spread ham patties out on the bottom of a baking dish and top each with a slice of orange. Stir cranberry sauce to soften and spoon over ham and orange slices, coating them evenly. Bake at 375 degrees for 30 minutes or until sauce is bubbly. Serve immediately.

Serves 4 to 6

HEAD CHEESE (SOUSE)

1 whole beef tongue
1 (3-pound) pork shoulder roast, bone in
2 pigs' feet or knuckles
1 ham hock
1 (1 ½ ounce) package pickling spice
3 tablespoons salt
½ cup vinegar
1 (12-ounce) jar stuffed green olives, drained
1 (2-ounce) jar sliced pimientos
6 envelopes unflavored gelatin

Place meat in a large kettle and cover with water. Simmer 1 ½ hours or until the tongue is tender. Remove tongue and continue cooking until pork meat falls from bones. Drain meat and bones, reserving liquid. Pick over bones saving all tender pieces of meat and skin. Return broth to heat adding water to make 1 ½ quarts, if necessary. Add pickling spice, salt and vinegar. Simmer 15 minutes. Strain broth to remove spices. Skin tongue and cut into ¾-inch cubes. Cut pork and ham hock meat into smaller pieces. Soften gelatin in ¼ cup cold water and stir into hot liquid. After gelatin has dissolved, stir in meat, olives and pimiento. Simmer mixture 5 minutes. Pour into loaf pans evenly dividing meat and broth. Cool to room temperature, then refrigerate overnight. Serve in ½-inch slices.

Serves 20

BACHELOR JAMBALAYA

¾ pound hot Italian sausage, casings removed
2 onions, chopped
1 green bell pepper, chopped
3 garlic cloves, minced
2 (16-ounce) cans tomatoes
2 cups chicken broth
1 cup raw rice
1 tablespoon Worchestershire sauce
½ teaspoon thyme
½ pound raw shrimp, shelled and deveined
1 cup cooked chicken or turkey, diced
¼ teaspoon Tabasco

In a large skillet, saute sausage and onions over medium heat until sausage is cooked. Drain off excess fat. Add the next seven ingredients, bring to a boil, cover and simmer 15 minutes. Add remaining ingredients and cook 5 minutes longer or until rice is tender and shrimp is pink.

Serves 4 to 6

SPICY PORK KEBOBS

1½ pounds pork, trimmed and cut into 1-inch cubes
1 (12-ounce) can beer
½ cup orange marmalade
¼ cup sugar
½ cup soy sauce
1 clove garlic, minced
16 large mushrooms
8 pearl onions, peeled and blanched
1 large green pepper, cut into eighths

Place pork in a deep bowl. Combine the next 5 ingredients and pour over pork. Refrigerate overnight. Stir several times. One hour before cooking add vegetables to the marinade. Thread pork and vegetables on skewers and barbecue on medium-hot charcoal fire, basting frequently with the marinade.

I serve this with cold rice salad and fruit. Just wonderful!

Serves 4

PIGS' KNUCKLES WITH SAUERKRAUT

3 pounds fresh pigs' knuckles or feet
1 tablespoon salt
½ teaspoon black pepper
2 carrots
1 stalk celery
1 parsnip
2 large onions
2 pounds sauerkraut
2 green apples, peeled and diced

Wash the knuckles or feet well and place them in a large kettle. Cover with warm water and add the salt, pepper, carrots, celery, parsnip and 1 onion. Bring to a boil, cover and cook over low heat 3 hours. While the knuckles are cooking, prepare the sauerkraut. Chop the remaining onion and combine with the sauerkraut and apples. Simmer covered over very low heat 2 hours, stirring often. Remove knuckles to a heated platter and surround with sauerkraut. Spoon vegetables from broth and puree in a blender. Return to broth, thicken if necessary and check for seasoning. Serve as gravy for the knuckles.

For a typical German pigs' knuckles and sauerkraut dinner, include boiled potatoes. If sausages are to be included, drop them into broth with the knuckles about 15 minutes before done.

Serves 6

PORK LOIN SAUTEED WITH PAPAYA

4 pounds pork loin roast
½ cup catsup
⅓ cup orange juice
1 teaspoon orange peel, grated
½ teaspoon ground ginger
1 papaya
1 tablespoon butter
Juice of ½ lime

Place roast on a rack in a shallow baking pan. Combine catsup, orange juice, orange peel and ground ginger. Brush meat with part of this sauce. Roast uncovered in a 325 degree oven for 3 hours or until meat thermometer registers 185 degrees. Baste several times with remaining sauce. Just before serving, peel papaya, half and scoop out seeds. Slice papaya lengthwise and saute slices in butter, turn to brown on all sides. Squeeze lime juice over papaya in pan. To serve, spoon hot rice onto platter. Place around meat. Pour any butter remaining over fruit.

This is to die for. Wonderful!

Serves 6

POLISH STYLE PORK LOIN ROASTED IN BEER

Slow roasting in beer keeps this loin of pork meltingly tender and juicy.

3 to 4 pounds pork loin roast
2 tablespoons flour
1 tablespoon dry mustard
1 teaspoon sage
Salt and pepper to taste
24-ounces beer
6 medium-sized yellow onions
12 soaked prunes, pitted
12 small carrots, peeled
3 medium-sized white rose potatoes with jackets, quartered

Trim excess fat from the roast leaving just a thin layer on the top. Mix the flour, mustard, sage and about 1 teaspoon of salt together on a large piece of wax paper. Roll the roast in the flour mixture until it is evenly coated. Put the roast into a deep covered roaster. Sprinkle with a bit more salt and pepper to taste. Pour the beer into the roaster (not directly on the roast). Cover and roast for 2 hours at 300 degrees, basting often. Meanwhile, prepare the vegetables. Peel the onions and slice off the ends. Push the centers out of each onion and stuff with pitted prunes that have been soaked in warm water for an hour (one or two prunes per onion, depending on their size). After the pork has roasted for 2 hours, add the vegetables to the pan and baste with the juices. Continue to cook uncovered for another 1½ hours, basting often. Cook until the internal temperature of the pork reaches 160 to 165 degrees, it's brown and tender, and the vegetables are fork-tender. Allow the roast to rest on a heated platter for about 10 minutes before carving. Using a slotted spoon, transfer the vegetables to a warm serving dish. Skim the fat off the pan juices and pass the juice at the table to accompany the meat and vegetables.

Yummers!

Serves 6

SPICY GLAZED PORK ROAST

1 (4 to 5-pound) pork loin roast
1 teaspoon salt
½ teaspoon allspice
½ cup apple jelly
¼ cup light corn syrup
3 tablespoons catsup
Canned or fresh pineapple slices, fresh orange slices, sprigs of parsley or watercress for garnish

Rub outside of the roast with salt and ¼ teaspoon allspice. Place roast on a rack in a shallow baking pan. Bake in a 325 degree oven 2¾ to 3 hours. If using a meat thermometer it should read 170 degrees. Prepare glaze while meat is baking. Combine jelly, syrup, catsup and remaining allspice in a saucepan. Simmer several minutes. Brush meat with sauce frequently during last half hour of cooking. Garnish with pineapple, orange and parsley or watercress.

This is a delightful holiday pork roast.

Serves 6 to 8

PORK CHOPS WITH APPLE-ONION SAUCE

4 center-cut pork chops, ¾-inch thick
¼ cup water
Salt and pepper
2 tablespoons butter
2 cups apple, diced
½ cup onion, chopped
½ cup sour cream
1 teaspoon lemon juice
½ teaspoon onion salt
Paprika
Chopped parsley

Brown chops in a heavy skillet on both sides. Drain off fat. Add water and season with salt and pepper. Cover and cook over low heat 45 minutes. Meanwhile, melt butter and saute apple and onion over low heat 15 minutes. Add sour cream, lemon juice, onion salt to the apple onion-mixture. Cook 5 minutes. Place chops on serving platter. Spoon sauce over chops and garnish with paprika and parsley.

Serves 4

PORK CHOP CASSEROLE

5 or 6 center-cut pork chops
2 bouillon cubes
2 cups boiling water
1 cup raw rice
1 onion, sliced
1 tomato, sliced
1 green pepper, sliced
Salt and pepper to taste

Brown pork chops in a skillet and then remove from skillet. Add bouillon cubes dissolved in boiling water. Stir in rice. Place pork chops back in skillet and top each with a slice of onion, a slice of tomato, and a slice of green pepper. Season to taste. Cover and simmer 30 minutes.

Serves 4

CHINESE PORK CHOPS *Microwave*

4 pork chops, ¾-inch thick (1½ pounds)
1 tablespoon flour
1 tablespoon oil
¼ cup soy sauce
¼ cup vinegar
½ teaspoon ginger
⅓ cup sugar
¼ cup water

Flour chops on both sides. Preheat casserole type browning dish on HIGH 5 minutes. Add oil. Brown chops on one side and turn. Cook on HIGH 5 minutes. Combine remaining ingredients and pour over chops. Cover with glass lid. Reduce setting to MEDIUM power and cook 25 to 30 minutes, or until meat is fork tender. (May be browned on top of the stove and transferred to a 9x11-inch glass baking dish. Cover with plastic wrap and cook on MEDIUM as above.)

Serves 4

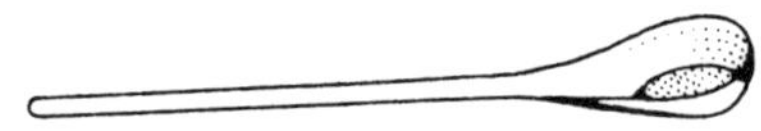

HUNGARIAN PORK CHOPS

6 pork chops, about ½-inch thick
Salt and pepper
1 medium onion, chopped
1 garlic clove, minced
3 tablespoons lard or butter
1 bay leaf
¾ cup chicken bouillon
1 cup dairy sour cream
2 tablespoons paprika

Trim excess fat from pork chops and sprinkle chops with salt and pepper. Saute onion and garlic in lard until soft and golden. Push aside or remove from skillet. Add pork chops and brown on all sides. Pour off fat. Lower heat and add bay leaf and bouillon. Cook, covered, over low heat for about 1 hour. Transfer chops to hot serving plate and keep hot. Reduce pan juices to half by cooking over high heat. Add sour cream, paprika and onions (if you removed them). Blend thoroughly with pan juices. Heat through but do not boil. Pour sauce over chops.

Serves 4 to 6

PORK CHOPS AND SAUERKRAUT

4 pork chops about 1-inch thick
Salt and pepper
2 tablespoons butter or margarine
1 medium-sized onion, diced
2 medium-sized green apples, pared and diced
1 pound fresh or canned sauerkraut, rinsed and drained
1 pound potatoes, peeled and sliced ¼ to ½-inch thick
1 cup hot meat stock
½ cup dry white wine

Sprinkle pork chops all over with salt and pepper. Heat butter in a casserole and brown pork chops slowly on both sides. Remove chops and add diced onions and apples to hot fat. Saute slowly until onions are soft and slightly yellow and apples have begun to take on color. Remove apple and onion mixture and reserve. Saute drained sauerkraut in fat 5 to 10 minutes then remove from pot. Put layer of kraut on bottom of casserole, then a layer of apple-onion mixture, all of the potatoes, then another of the kraut, apples and onions and finally chops. Pour hot stock over this and wine. Cover tightly and bake in 375 degree oven 45 minutes to 1 hour.

Serves 2 to 4

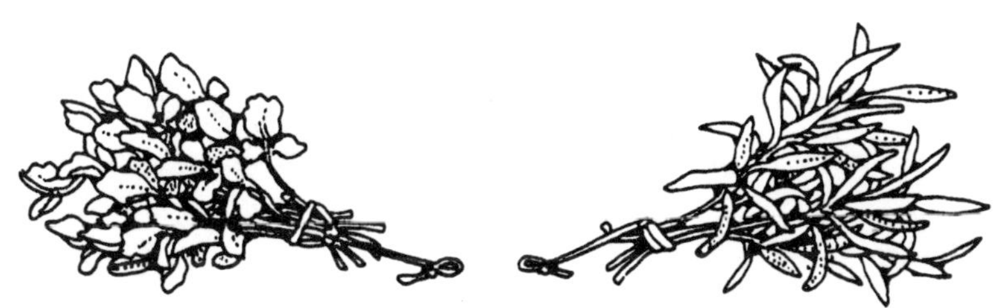

JAMES BEARD'S PORK WITH SAUERKRAUT NOODLES

2 tablespoons butter
1 tablespoon oil
2 to 2½ cups cooked pork, thinly sliced or 1½ to 2 pounds fresh pork
2 tablespoons hot Hungarian paprika
1½ cups white wine
3 cups sauerkraut, rinsed and drained
1 teaspoon caraway seeds
1 pound egg noodles
Salt and freshly ground black pepper
½ cup heavy cream

Heat 2 tablespoons butter with oil in a heavy skillet. Brown the pork slices on each side over fairly high heat, about 3 minutes to a side. Remove meat, add the paprika and cook in the fat for 1 minute. Pour in the wine and bring to a boil, stirring up the flavorful bits on the bottom of the pan. Cook until the wine is reduced slightly, then return the meat to the pan with the drained sauerkraut and caraway seeds. Simmer 10 to 12 minutes. Cook and drain the noodles. Stir them into the pork and sauerkraut mixture and then turn gently over medium heat, adding the heavy cream as you do so.

Serves 6

OCTOBERFEST PORK CHOPS AND SAUERKRAUT

½ pound bacon, diced
1 (19-ounce) jar sauerkraut, drained and rinsed
1 (15-ounce) jar applesauce
1 tablespoon brown sugar
½ teaspoon dry mustard
¼ teaspoon dry white wine
Dash pepper
¼ teaspoon paprika
6 medium shoulder pork chops
Bacon drippings

Saute bacon until crisp. Drain. To sauerkraut, add bacon, applesauce, brown sugar, mustard, white wine and pepper. Turn into a shallow dish. Sprinkle with paprika. Saute chops in bacon drippings until golden on both sides. Place on top of sauerkraut. Cover and bake at 350 degrees for 1 hour or until chops are tender.

A little German beer to complete the festivities, what could it hurt?

Serves 4

CAMPFIRE SAUSAGE AND BEANS

1 medium-sized onion, thinly sliced
1 medium-sized green pepper, cut into ½-inch squares
1 or 2 tablespoons vegetable oil
1 (15-ounce) can baked pork and beans
1 (15-ounce) can butter beans, drained
1 small can sliced mushrooms, drained
5-ounces ready-to-eat smoked sausage
½ cup catsup
¼ cup mustard
⅔ cup maple syrup
1 teaspoon oregano
5 whole cloves
2 small bay leaves

Heat the oil in a large saucepan over a low fire and gently saute the onion slices and pepper squares until the onion is slightly transparent, about 3 or 4 minutes. Add the baked beans, butter beans and sliced mushrooms and stir well. Cut the sausage into bite-size pieces and add to the beans, together with the catsup, mustard, maple syrup, oregano, cloves and bay leaves. Cook the beans, stirring occasionally, until all the ingredients are piping hot. Serve immediately.

Serves 4

ITALIAN SAUSAGE

2 pounds lean pork
3 teaspoons salt
2 cloves garlic, crushed
Dash of chopped red chili pepper
1 pound fat pork
2 teaspoons fennel seed
½ teaspoon fresh ground pepper

Grind meat twice using a fine blade. Combine seasoning ingredients. Add to meat and mix thoroughly. Use for patties or put into sausage casings.

Serves 4 to 6

ROSEMARY SAUSAGE

1 pound pork
1 pound beef
1 pound veal
1 pound suet
1 tablespoon salt
1 teaspoon freshly ground pepper
2 teaspoons ground rosemary
½ teaspoon thyme
½ teaspoon marjoram
½ teaspoon freshly grated nutmeg

Grind meat twice using a fine blade. Combine seasoning ingredients. Add to meat and mix thoroughly. Use for patties or put into sausage casings. To prepare sausage casing soak in warm water for about 2 hours. Then rinse thoroughly under running water. Pour a cup of vinegar through casing to help sausage hold longer. In order to handle casing cut into 2-foot lengths, tie ends and fill.

SCRAPPLE

6 cups water
2 large onions, finely chopped
1 pound lean pork, finely chopped
½ teaspoon each; thyme, sage and pepper
1½ teaspoons salt
1½ cups yellow corn meal

Combine water, meat, onion and seasonings. Bring to a boil and simmer a half hour. Very slowly stir in the corn meal and cook slowly, stirring constantly until mixture is thick. Add more salt and pepper if needed. Pour into a loaf pan. Cool. Unmold and cut in ½-inch slices. Saute in butter until brown on both sides. Serve with maple syrup or apple sauce.

Serves 6

APPLE STUFFED SPARERIBS

4 pounds spareribs in matching sides
Salt and pepper to taste
3 medium cooking apples, peeled, cored and cut into wedges
2 tablespoons brown sugar
2 cups apple juice, heated

Season spareribs with salt and pepper. Put one side of ribs fat side down on a foil-lined roasting pan. Cover with the apples, sprinkle with the brown sugar. Put second side of ribs on top, fat side up. Add apple juice. Bake in a 350 degree oven, basting now and then, for 2½ to 3 hours, or until very tender. Serve hot or cold.

Serves 6

BARBECUED SPARERIBS

6 pounds spareribs, cut up
1 tablespoon ground ginger
½ cup soy sauce
3 tablespoons lemon juice
2 cloves garlic, crushed

Put spareribs in a baking pan. Brown in a 425 degree oven for 15 minutes. Pour off fat. Combine remaining ingredients and pour over ribs. Cover and bake at 325 degrees about 1½ hours, basting several times with drippings in pan.

Serves 6 to 8

MEXICAN PORK STEW

3 pounds boneless pork cut into 2-inch cubes
2 tablespoons oil
1 medium onion, chopped
1 clove garlic
½ pound tomatoes, peeled, seeded and coarsly chopped
¾ can tomatillos verde (Mexican green tomatoes)
2 green hot chiles, seeded and chopped
½ teaspoon crumbled dried oregano
⅛ teaspoon sugar
½ teaspoon cumin
Salt and freshly ground pepper to taste
2 chorizo sausages, skinned, sliced, browned and drained
1 ripe avocado, sliced

In skillet brown pork on all sides in oil without allowing cubes to touch. Transfer to a large heatproof casserole, barely cover with water, sprinkle with a little salt and cook over medium heat for 1 hour or until tender. Strain off stock and reserve. Set casserole aside. In the same skillet in which meat was browned, saute onion and garlic until onion is transparent. Add tomatoes, tomatillos verde, chiles, oregano, sugar and cumin. Cook and stir for 5 minutes. Add 1 cup of the reserved stock and season to taste with salt and pepper. Continue cooking, stirring occasionally, for 15 minutes or until thickened. Add this mixture to the pork in the casserole along with the sausages and reheat. Garnish with avocado and serve with potatoes or rice.

Serves 6

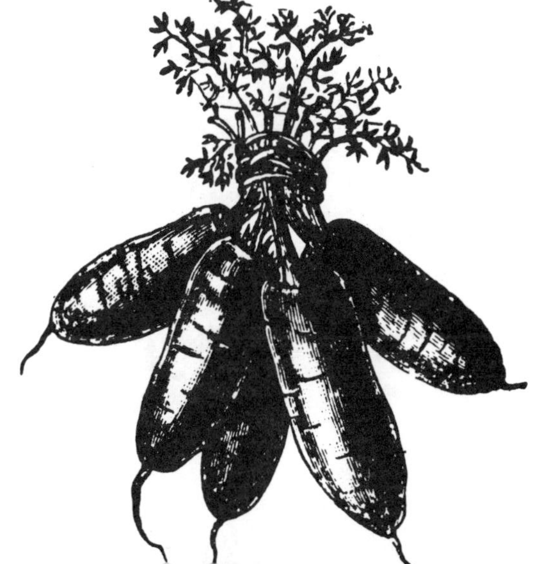

BARBECUED LEG OF LAMB

2 cups dry red wine
2 teaspoons poultry seasoning
2 teaspoons salt
3 cloves garlic, minced
1 leg of lamb, butterflied

Combine wine, poultry seasoning, salt and garlic. Pour over lamb in a glass dish. Marinate overnight in the refrigerator. Barbecue over medium heat skin side up for 30 minutes. Turn over and cook 30 minutes more. Baste the whole time with the marinade. When done, slice across the grain to serve.

I serve this with rice pilaf, green salad and strawberries in port. Simply a great dinner.

Serves 8

ROAST RACK OF LAMB

1 (14-chop) saddle of lamb
2 cups fresh bread crumbs
4 garlic cloves, crushed
1 cup parsley, chopped
½ cup olive oil
2 teaspoons salt
1 teaspoon rosemary
½ teaspoon pepper

Ask your butcher to cut saddle of lamb into 2 racks to "French" the bones and to crack the ribs at the backbone. Trim off all the fat. Combine bread crumbs, garlic, parsley, olive oil, salt, rosemary and pepper. Mix well. Firmly press half of this mixture across surface of each rack. Place meat in shallow roasting pan and bake at 400 degrees for 30 minutes for rare, for well—45 minutes.

Serves 6

GRILLED LEG OF LAMB WITH HERBS

1 (4 to 5-pound) leg of lamb, boned and butterflied
1 onion, sliced
1 clove garlic, minced
Juice of 1 lemon
½ cup red wine vinegar
¾ cup olive oil
¼ teaspoon oregano
¼ teaspoon thyme
½ teaspoon rosemary
½ teaspoon basil
1 teaspoon salt
Dash of pepper

Place lamb flattened in a glass dish just large enough to hold it. Combine remaining ingredients and pour over meat. Marinate for several hours in the refrigerator, turning occasionally. Barbecue meat over a hot charcoal fire for 25 to 35 minutes per side for medium rare.

This is absolutely fabulous with green vegetables and almonds, a little rice pilaf with dried fruit (I like apricots) and a simple green salad. Wonderful.

Serves 6

ROAST LEG OF LAMB WITH DIJON COATING

5 to 6-pound leg of lamb
½ cup Dijon mustard
2 tablespoons soy sauce
1 clove garlic, mashed
1 teaspoon ground rosemary or thyme
¼ teaspoon powdered ginger
2 tablespoons olive oil

Blend mustard, soy sauce, garlic and seasonings together in a bowl. Slowly beat in olive oil by droplets until the mixture has obtained a mayonnaise-like appearance. Coat the leg of lamb with this mixture several hours before roasting. Place lamb on rack in a shallow baking pan. Bake at 325 degrees for 2½ hours. Let stand 20 minutes before carving. Simply wonderful.

Serves 6 to 8

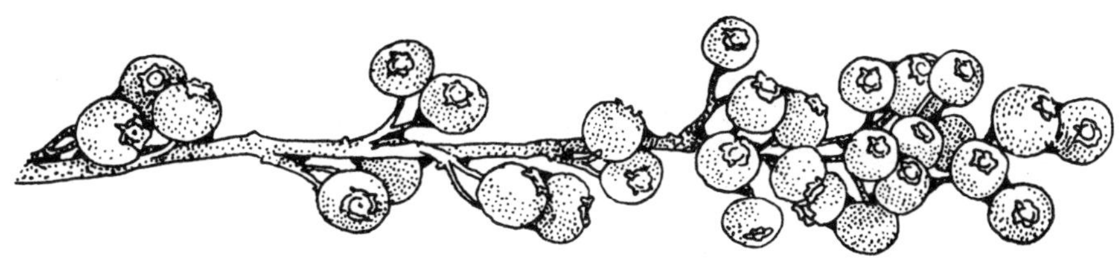

sauces

BASIC BARBECUE SAUCE

1 onion, minced
1 clove garlic, minced
2 tablespoons oil
1½ teaspoons chili powder
¼ teaspoon tumeric
½ teaspoon dry mustard
2 bay leaves
¼ teaspoon marjoram
¼ cup cider
2 (15-ounce) cans tomato sauce
2 tablespoons sugar
¼ teaspoon hot sauce or cayenne pepper

Saute onion and garlic in oil for 5 minutes. Add remaining ingredients and simmer 35 minutes. Remove bay leaves and cool. Store in covered containers and refrigerate. Sauce will keep several weeks.

Makes 1 quart

SEVILLE BARBECUE SAUCE

Rind of 1 orange, cut into small pieces
Juice of 2 oranges
½ cup cider vinegar
¼ cup brown sugar
1 tablespoon prepared mustard
¼ teaspoon tarragon

Blend orange juice, vinegar and brown sugar in saucepan over heat. Stir in remaining ingredients and heat almost to the boiling point (do not boil), stirring occasionally. Strain before using. Good for roast duck, barbecued ham or pork roast, as last minute basting or table sauce.

Makes about 2 cups

QUICK RED CHILI SAUCE

1 tablespoon chili powder
1 teaspoon sifted flour
1 cup condensed tomato soup
½ cup water
2 tablespoons lard 2 tablespoons onions, chopped
1 small garlic clove, minced
⅛ teaspoon oregano, minced
Salt to taste

Fry the onion and garlic in the lard until transparent. Add the chili powder, flour and oregano with the condensed tomato soup. Stir well. Add salt to taste. Let simmer until thickens. This sauce may be served on the side.

Makes 1½ cups

TOMATO & GREEN CHILI SAUCE

6 medium-size tomatoes, peeled and finely chopped
½ cup or more thinly sliced or diced canned California green chiles (seeds and pith removed) or fresh chiles
⅓ cup onion, minced
1 teaspoon salt
Jalapeno chiles, minced (or other hot chiles)

Mix tomatoes with green chiles, onion, salt and jalapeno chiles to taste (about 1 jalapeno to each cup of sauce will make it noticeably hot).

Makes about 3 cups

MARINADE CUCUMBER

1 tablespoon salt
2 large cucumbers
¾ cup vinegar
½ cup water
1 teaspoon salt
½ teaspoon salt
½ teaspoon chopped dill weed
1 tablespoon salad oil
Sliced onions, optional

Peel the cucumbers and slice them thin. Sprinkle with tablespoon of salt and toss. Put them in bowl with plate on top and a weight on top of plate for two hours. Drain juice and make a dressing by blending together the remaining ingredients. Pour over cucumbers and let stand two hours. Add sliced onions, if desired.

Serves 4

SOUR CREAM DILL SAUCE

1 cup dairy sour cream
1 teaspoon dill weed
1 tablespoon wine vinegar
¼ teaspoon sugar
½ teaspoon salt

Mix all ingredients and let blend several hours in refrigerator.

Makes 1 cup

ALMOST HOLLANDAISE SAUCE (MOCK)

½ cup sour cream
½ cup mayonnaise
1 teaspoon prepared mustard
2 teaspoons lemon juice

Combine all ingredients in a saucepan and cook over low heat just until heated through — but not boiling. Do not boil. Serve over vegetables, eggs or wherever Hollandaise sauce is required.

Makes 1 cup

MUSTARD SAUCE

½ onion, chopped
¼ pound butter
2 tablespoons flour
½ cup white wine
2 cups beef or chicken broth or stock
2 teaspoons prepared mustard

Cook onion in butter a few minutes. Blend in flour and stir until evenly mixed. Add wine and stock and stir until smooth. Simmer 10 minutes, stirring frequently. Add mustard and stir until smoothly mixed.

Makes about 3 cups sauce

SALSA BORRACHA

3 tomatoes, chopped
2 teaspoons oil
½ stalk celery, thinly sliced ¼ teaspoon oregano
1½ teaspoon salt
1 teaspoon (or more) ground red chiles
2 teaspoons vinegar
½ medium onion, finely chopped
¼ teaspoon cumin
½ teaspoon black pepper

Mix all ingredients together. This sauce should be mixed fresh. A milder sauce could be made with green chiles. This is good served over eggs or zucchini.

Serves 4 to 6

BASIC GREEN SAUCE (SALSA VERDE)

½ cup parsley, finely chopped
1 clove garlic, chopped
1 tablespoon capers, chopped
1 shallot or 1 tablespoon onion, chopped
½ teaspoon salt
½ teaspoon pepper
½ cup olive oil
2 tablespoons lemon juice or vinegar

Combine parsley, garlic, capers and shallot on a board and chop again together or quickly whirl together in a blender. Add remaining ingredients and stir together (do not blend). Chill sauce overnight to combine flavors. Serve over cold meats, seafood, poultry and eggs. Variations — Add a few anchovies before blending, or stir in ¼ cup finely chopped cooked potato or pimiento.

Makes 4 servings

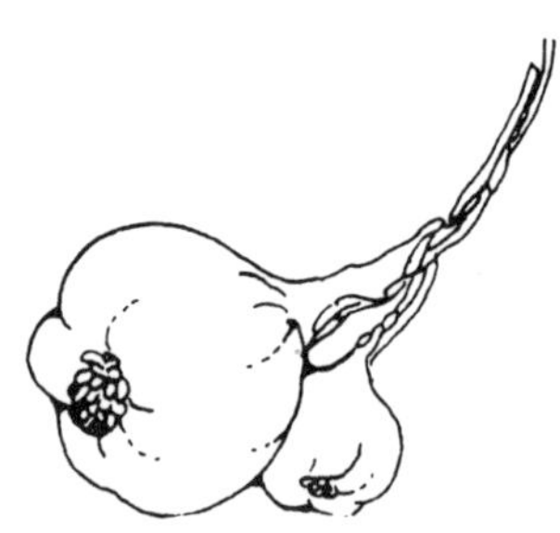

SALSA RANCHERO

1 cup tomato sauce
6 jalapenos chiles
1 tablespoon vinegar
1 teaspoon oregano
½ teaspoon cumin
½ teaspoon salt

Toast the peppers in a dry iron skillet — no grease. Crush them well and add them to the tomato sauce with the rest of the ingredients stir well. Store in a wide-mouth jar. Serve as a side dish whenever hot sauce is desired.

Makes 1 cup

SWEET & SOUR SAUCE

3 tablespoons corn starch
¼ cup pineapple juice
1 tablespoon soy sauce
3 tablespoons wine vinegar, white or red
⅓ cup water
½ cup brown sugar

Blend all ingredients in a saucepan and cook until it thickens.

Makes 1 cup

TERIYAKI SAUCE

½ cup soy sauce
½ cup sherry
2 tablespoons brown sugar
¼ teaspoon dry mustard
1 clove garlic, crushed
1 tablespoon fresh ginger or ¼ tablespoon powdered ginger

Mix all ingredients and cook until it boils and sugar dissolves. Cool and baste meat, poultry or fish.

Makes 1 cup

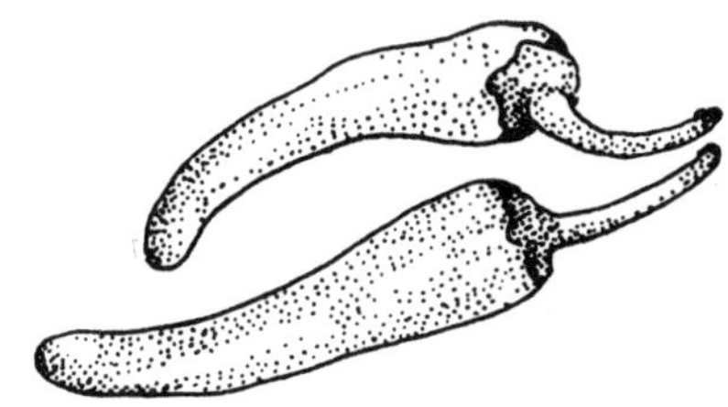

desserts & fruit

SPIKED APPLE CRISP

5 cups apples, peeled and sliced (Pippin, Jonathan or Winesap)
½ teaspoon cinnamon
1 teaspoon lemon rind, grated
1 teaspoon orange rind, grated
1 jigger Grand Marnier
1 jigger Amaretto
¾ cup granulated sugar
¼ cup light brown sugar, packed
¾ cup sifted flour
¼ teaspoon salt
½ cup butter
Cream, whipped cream or ice cream for topping

Arrange apple slices in greased 2-quart round casserole. Sprinkle cinnamon, lemon and orange rinds and both liqueurs on top of apples. In a separate bowl, mix sugars, flour, salt and butter with a pastry blender until crumbly. Spread mixture over top of apples. Bake uncovered at 350 degrees until apples are tender and the top is lightly browned, approximately 1 hour. Serve warm with cream, whipped cream or vanilla ice cream.

A wonderful way to welcome October.

Serves 8

STEWED APPLES IN WINE

2 pounds apples
¼ cup butter
2 tablespoons honey
½ cup water
½ cup dry white wine
½ teaspoon salt
1 teaspoon lemon peel, grated
¼ teaspoon ground nutmeg

Peel and core apples and cut into thick wedges. Melt butter in skillet which has a lid. Add apples and saute until golden, drizzle honey over apples. Add water, wine, salt, lemon peel and nutmeg. Cover and simmer until apples are just tender, about 20 minutes. Cool. Cover and refrigerate.

Makes 6 to 8 servings

BAKED BANANAS

4 medium-size bananas
1 tablespoon butter
1 tablespoon honey
1 teaspoon lemon

Preheat oven to 350 degrees and butter a shallow baking dish. Peel bananas and cut in half horizontally. Arrange in the prepared baking dish. Sprinkle with mixture of butter, honey and lemon juice. Bake in prepared oven for 15 to 20 minutes.

Baked bananas are very rich. They can be served at the end of the meal or as a side dish with chicken or pork.

Serves 4

BANANA FRITTERS

1 ½ cups sifted flour
1 ½ teaspoons baking powder
½ teaspoon salt
3 tablespoons sugar
2 eggs
2 tablespoons milk
2 tablespoons banana liqueur
2 tablespoons brandy
1 ripe banana, mashed
Solid vegetable shortening for deep fat frying

Sift first 4 ingredients together. Using electric mixer set at medium speed, individually add eggs, milk, liqueur, brandy and mashed banana in order given, mixing well after each is added. Preheat shortening in deep-fat fryer to 375 degrees. Form fritters with tablespoon. Fry 6 at a time until fork inserted in fritters comes out clean, about 4 minutes. Drain on paper towels and serve immediately.

Makes 16 to 18 fritters

BUTTER SAUTEED CHESTNUTS

1 pound fresh chestnuts
2 tablespoons butter
½ teaspoon salt

Cut a small cross in the chestnut skin on the flat side of the nut to prevent exploding. Spread nuts on a baking pan and roast 15 minutes at 400 degrees or until nuts are tender or drop into boiling salted water 10 to 15 minutes until tender. Peel shells and remove membranes from nuts. Melt butter in a saucepan and saute nuts 5 minutes or until edges are golden. Place on a paper towel and sprinkle with salt.

Serve hot or cold.

Variations — saute chestnuts as above and sprinkle with:

1. garlic or onion salt
2. sugar seasoned with cinnamon
3. roll in powdered sugar
4. drizzle with honey

Brandy Flamed Chestnuts

After chestnuts have been sauteed in butter; sprinkle with salt and add ¼ cup warmed brandy to the pan. Ignite and swirl chestnuts in the flame to coat all sides. When the flame dies, serve immediately.

Yields 1 pound

SPICED CRANBERRIES

4 cups fresh cranberries
⅔ cup cider vinegar
⅓ cup water
3 cups sugar
1 teaspoon cinnamon
1½ teaspoons cloves
1½ teaspoons allspice

Rinse cranberries and place in a large saucepan. Add remaining ingredients and bring to a boil. Lower heat and simmer slowly for 45 minutes. Chill before serving.

Yiels 4 cups

GEORGE WASHINGTON'S CHERRY CRUNCH SUPREME

1 cup oil
1 cup sugar
5 eggs
1½ cups flour
2 tablespoons baking powder
1 teaspoon almond extract
1 teaspoon vanilla extract
1 tablespoon dark rum
1 (21-ounce) can cherry pie filling
¼ cup ground nuts

Lightly grease a 9x13-inch pan. Mix all the ingredients except the pie filling and nuts together. Put half the dough on the bottom of the pan, add the cherry filling and cover with the rest of the dough. Top with ground nuts and bake at 350 degrees for 40 minutes.

Serves the family

DRIED FRUITS

This age old method is easily followed and with a few modern conveniences, brings even better results than in the old days. Generally, apricots, apples, pears and grapes lend themselves to drying. The fruit should be washed and the pits removed. The fruits that have a tendency to oxidize (turn black) should be dipped in a solution of 1 tablespoon of lemon juice and 1 cup of water. The fruit should be spread to dry on a wire screen, usually the screen is stretched on a wood frame, making a rack-like appliance. The fruit should be covered with cheesecloth and the racks may be placed outside in the sun to dry the fruit, but be sure to take them in at night so that they do not pick-up moisture from the night air. Actually, a well-ventilated attic is as good a place as any. The drying time will vary in ratio to the humidity, but somewhere between a week and two weeks should do it.

FRESH LEMON ICE CREAM

1 cup heavy cream
1 egg
1½ cups sugar
2 teaspoons lemon peel
⅓ cup fresh lemon juice
Pinch salt
1⅓ cups milk

Combine cream and egg. Beat until blended. Add sugar gradually and beat until mixture is almost stiff. Beat lemon juice, peel and salt. Stir in milk. Pour in an 8-inch square dish and freeze for 5 hours. Stir occasionally during the first hour. Especially good with frozen raspberries, just barely thawed, on top.

Serve 6

LEMON-PINEAPPLE WHIP

1 small package lemon jello
1 cup hot water
¼ cup pineapple juice, drained from crushed pineapple
4 tablespoons lemon juice
1 cup crushed pineapple, drained
½ cup heavy cream

Dissolve gelatin in hot water, add pineapple juice and 3 tablespoons of the lemon juice. Chill until the mixture is syrupy. Fold in crushed pineapple. Beat cream and add remaining 1 tablespoon of lemon juice to it. Fold into pudding. Pour into sherbert glasses and chill until firm.

Serves 6

NECTARINE ICE CREAM

2 pounds soft, ripe nectarines
(about 8 medium), peeled and sliced
1 tablespoon lemon juice
½ cup sugar
2 cups whipping cream
1 teaspoon vanilla

Coarsely puree nectarines in a food processor, with the lemon juice. Stir into sugar. Set aside. In a large, chilled bowl, mix whipping cream and vanilla until stiff. Fold in nectarine mixture. Turn into a 9x9-inch square pan. Freeze uncovered until set, about 1 hour. Beat until smooth. Freeze until firm, then cover airtight. Remove from freezer about 10 minutes before serving.

An easy ice cream to make early on in the day.

Serves 4 to 6

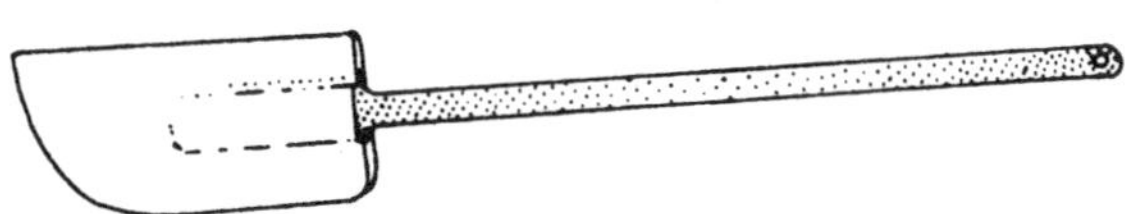

MINCEMEAT

¼ pound dates
¼ pound currants
¼ pound raisins
1-ounce candied orange peel
¼ pound apple, chopped
¾ ounce suet, finely chopped
4 tablespoons sugar
½ teaspoon mixed spice
Dash of grated nutmeg
2 teaspoons lemon extract

Chop dried fruits together with candied peel and apple (may use food processor). Add suet, sugar and spices. Stir in lemon extract and a dash of rum or whiskey if you have it. Stir every day for a week, then use as required.

Yield 1 pound mincemeat

BAKED PEARS WITH ALMONDS AND YOGURT

6 firm, ripe pears
¼ to ⅓ cup honey, depending on sweetness of pears
1 teaspoon vanilla
½ cup slivered almonds
2 tablespoons butter
1 cup yogurt

Preheat oven to 350 degrees and grease a 9-inch baking dish. Core and slice pears (do not peel unless skins are tough or if you want the dessert to be especially fancy). Arrange the slices of pears in attractive rows in prepared dish. Mix honey and vanilla and drizzle over pears, top with the almonds and dot with butter. Bake for 10 to 15 minutes or until pears are tender. Baste frequently during the baking using the accumulated juice. Serve hot or cold, topped with yogurt.

Serves 6

PINK LADY DESSERT

1½ pints whipping cream
1 cup peppermint candy, crushed in blender
½ cup broken pecans
2 cups miniature marshmallows
Vanilla wafers

Whip cream and carefully fold in remaining ingredients except the wafers. Crush wafers to make 2 cups. Place half crumbs in a 8x12-inch pan. Spread the whipped cream mixture evenly over crumbs. Sprinkle with remaining crumbs. Cover with foil and freeze until firm. Serve in small squares with chocolate syrup, whipped cream and a cherry.

Serves 12

BREAD PUDDING

1 (1-pound) loaf bread, coarsely broken
1 quart hot milk
3 eggs, beaten
2 cups sugar
2 tablespoons vanilla
1 cup golden raisins
3 tablespoons margarine

Pour hot milk over bread in a bowl. Blend eggs, sugar, and vanilla. Add to the bread mixture and blend well. Add raisins and combine. Melt the margarine in a 9x13-inch pan, pour bread mixture over margarine. Bake in a 350 degree oven for 40 minutes or until firm or golden brown. Serve hot or cold with a dollop of cinnamon flavored whipped cream.

Serves 8 to 10

CHRISTMAS BREAD PUDDING

1 cup sugar
1½ cups water
½ teaspoon cinnamon
Dash of cloves
1 teaspoon vanilla
6 slices bread, toasted and diced
1 cup raisins
1 cup pinion nuts or walnuts
1½ cups longhorn cheese, grated

Caramelize the sugar. Add the water, cinnamon and cloves. Bring to a boil, reduce heat, and simmer until the sugar remelts. Add the vanilla. Layer in a 2-quart greased casserole, half the toast, half the raisins and nuts, half the syrup and half the cheese. Repeat. Bake uncovered in a 350 degree oven for 30 minutes. Serve warm topped with cream or your favorite hard sauce.

Serves 6

RUMTOPF

First, take thoroughly washed strawberries and soak them in rum — they will probably float for a day or two before they sink. Then likewise take cherries, gooseberries, red currents, raspberries, apricots, peaches, plums and pears. For an extra delicious touch of flavor, use fresh pineapple. DO NOT USE apples, black currents, blueberries or blackberries. Use the same weight of sugar as the fruit. To avoid fermentation half the liquid should be rum. Make sure fruits are always covered and jar is air tight. When a new layer of fruit is added, add more rum. It takes six weeks for one layer to mature. Stir well before you serve Rumtopf. It can be used as a dessert, cocktail, with ice cream or in a fruit salad.

Alternative: Use arrak instead of rum and honey instead of sugar.

KIWI FRUIT SHERBET

1 cup water
1¾ cups sugar
2 cups kiwi fruit puree
1 tablespoon lemon juice
2 egg whites, beaten stiff
Green food coloring

Dissolve sugar in water and boil 5 minutes. Cool. Make puree by processing kiwi fruit in blender. Do not process long enough to crush seeds. Add puree and lemon juice to sugar syrup. Fold in egg whites. Pour into a shallow pan and freeze until firm around the edges. Remove from freezer and beat for 1 minute with mixer, or until smooth. Return to freezer until firm. Since sherbet will be very pale in color, add a little coloring to the sugar syrup if you would like a darker color.

Serves 6

PARISIAN STRAWBERRIES IN PORT WINE

2 boxes strawberries, washed and hulled

MARINADE:

Zest of 1 orange
¾ cup fresh orange juice
½ cup port wine
½ cup sugar

CREAM:

1 cup heavy cream
2 tablespoons sugar
2 tablespoons Grand Marnier

Mix together the marinade and pour over strawberries. Marinate 3 to 5 hours. When serving, whip cream and flavor with sugar and liquor. Drain berries and fold into cream. Serve in stemmed champagne glasses.

Serves 6

breads

CHEDDAR APPLE BREAD

½ cup butter
¾ cup sugar
2 eggs
1¾ cups all-purpose flour
1 teaspoon baking powder
1 teaspoon baking soda
¼ teaspoon salt
½ teaspoon cinnamon
½ teaspoon nutmeg
1 cup apple, cored and finely chopped
¾ cup sharp Cheddar cheese, shredded
½ cup pecans, chopped

Preheat oven to 350 degrees. Cream together butter and sugar then beat in eggs. Sift together flour, baking powder, soda, salt, cinnamon and nutmeg. Add to creamed mixture ⅓ at a time and blend well. Stir in apples, cheese and pecans. Pour into a greased 9x5x3-inch loaf pan and bake for 1 hour or until a wooden pick inserted in the center comes out clean. Cool a few minutes then remove from pan and cool on a rack.

This is a fabulous blend of everybody's favorite tastes. A great way to start any holiday event.

APRICOT-CRANBERRY LOAF

2 cups unsifted flour
¾ cup sugar
1 tablespoon baking powder
½ teaspoon salt
1 cup dried apricots, diced
1 cup cranberries, chopped
½ cup nuts, chopped
2 eggs
1 cup milk
¼ cup butter or margarine, melted
1 teaspoon lemon peel, grated

Stir together dry ingredients in a large bowl. Add apricots, cranberries and nuts. Toss lightly until fruits are coated. Beat eggs, milk, butter and lemon peel in a small bowl. Pour over dry ingredients. Stir until dry ingredients are moistened. Pour into a greased 9x5-inch loaf pan. Bake at 350 degrees for 60 to 65 minutes. Cool.

This makes a delightful bread for your family or as a hostess gift.

Makes 1 loaf

BANANA NUT BREAD

2 cups flour, sifted
¾ cup sugar
3 teaspoons baking powder
1 teaspoon salt
½ teaspoon soda
½ teaspoon cinnamon
1 cup chopped Hawaiian macadamia nuts (almonds or walnuts)
1 egg, beaten
1 cup mashed bananas
2 tablespoons shortening, melted

Sift all dry ingredients together. In separate bowl, beat egg. Stir in bananas and shortening. Stir into dry ingredients just enough to blend; add nuts. Pour into greased loaf pan (8 x 4 x 4 inches), and bake in a 350 degree oven for 1 hour. Cool on rack.

BANANA TEA BREAD

1¾ cups sifted flour
2 teaspoons baking powder
¼ teaspoon baking soda
½ teaspoon salt
⅓ cup shortening
⅔ cup sugar
2 eggs, well-beaten
1 cup mashed ripe bananas (2 to 3 bananas)

Sift together flour, baking powder, soda and salt. Beat shortening until creamy, in mixing bowl. Add sugar gradually and continue beating until light and fluffy. Add eggs and beat well. Add flour mixture alternately with bananas, a small amount at a time, beating after each addition until smooth. Turn into a well greased bread pan (8½x4½x3 inches) and bake in a 350 degree oven about 1 hour 10 minutes or until bread is done.

Makes 1 loaf

BREAKFAST PUFFS

½ cup shortening
½ cup sugar
1 egg
1½ cups sifted flour
1½ teaspoons baking powder
½ teaspoon salt
¼ teaspoon nutmeg
½ cup milk
⅓ cup butter, melted
½ cup sugar
1 teaspoon cinnamon

Blend shortening and ½ cup sugar thoroughly. Add egg, mixing well. Sift together the flour, baking powder, salt and nutmeg and add to shortening mixture alternately with milk. Fill greased muffin cups ⅔ full. Bake at 350 degrees for 20 to 25 minutes until golden brown. Immediately roll in melted butter, then mixture of ½ cup sugar and cinnamon. Serve hot.

Makes 12 to 16 muffins

BISCUIT NIBBLERS

Roll 1 can (8 ounce) refrigerated flaky buttermilk biscuits into 8x6 inch rectangle on floured surface. Brush with 2 tablespoons melted butter. Sprinkle with 1 teaspoon dill weed and 1 teaspoon celery seed. Fold into thirds, roll again into 8x6 inch rectangle. Cut into desired shapes. Place on ungreased baking sheet. Brush with melted butter and sprinkle with 1 tablespoon shredded Parmesan cheese. Bake at 375 degrees 10 to 12 minutes or until golden brown.

Makes about 1 dozen.

JACKIE'S CARROT BREAD MAGIC

2 cups flour
2 teaspoons baking soda
2 teaspoons cinnamon
½ teaspoon salt
½ cup nuts, chopped
1 cup oil
2 teaspoons vanilla
1 ½ cups sugar
2 cups carrots, grated
3 eggs
½ cup raisins
½ cup coconut, grated

Sift dry ingredients together in a large bowl. Add remaining ingredients and mix well. Pour into 2 greased and floured loaf pans or angel food cake pan. Let stand 20 minutes. Bake 1 hour at 375 degrees. Cool before slicing.

This will be a favorite, easy and so good. It only takes a minute if you have a food processor to grate the carrots.

CARROT COCONUT BREAD

2 eggs, beaten
1 cup sugar
¾ cup oil
1 ½ cups flour
½ teaspoon salt
1 teaspoon baking soda
1 teaspoon cinnamon
2 cups raw carrots, finely grated
½ cup coconut

Mix together the eggs and sugar. Add oil and beat well. Add the remaining ingredients, blending well. Pour into a greased loaf pan. Bake at 325 degrees for 45 minutes.

Makes 1 loaf

CHERRY NUT BREAD

2 ½ cups flour
1 cup sugar
4 teaspoons baking powder
1 teaspoon salt
1 cup walnuts, chopped
1 cup sweet cherries, diced
1 egg
1 ¼ cups milk
2 tablespoons oil

In a large bowl mix well flour, baking powder, salt, walnuts and cherries. In a small bowl beat egg, milk and oil until blended. Pour over flour mixture, stir until all the ingredients are just moistened. Turn into a greased 9x5x3-inch loaf pan. Bake in a 350 degree oven for 60 to 70 minutes or until pick inserted in the center comes out clean. Cool in pan on rack 10 minutes. Turn out on rack and cool.

Makes 1 loaf

QUICK CRANBERRY BREAD

1 ½ cups all-purpose flour
½ teaspoon salt
1 teaspoon soda 1 ½ cups whole grain flour
¼ cup shortening
½ cup sugar
1 egg
¾ cup unsweetened, mashed cranberry pulp, cooked
¼ cup cranberry juice
1 cup buttermilk
1 cup broken nut meats
Grated rind of 1 orange

Preheat oven to 350 degrees. Sift before measuring the all-purpose flour. Resift with salt and soda. Add whole grain flour. Cream shortening with sugar. Beat in the egg. Add mashed cranberry pulp and cranberry juice. Add the sifted ingredients alternately to the creamed mixture with buttermilk. Stir the batter with a few swift strokes, until just blended. Fold in nut meats and grated rind. Place the dough in a greased loaf pan. Bake the bread for about 1 ¼ hours. Let it cool in the pan.

CRUMPETS

1 cup warm milk
1 package yeast
½ cup butter
½ teaspoon salt
2 cups all-purpose flour

Dissolve yeast in warm milk. Let stand 5 minutes. Stir in butter and salt. Beat with a rotary beater until the ingredients are thoroughly blended. Add flour and continue to beat as long as possible with a beater. Then finish beating with a wooden spoon. Cover the bowl and let it set in a warm place for about 45 minutes. Stir down the batter and fill buttered muffin rings. Place rings on a hot greased griddle. Cook slowly until well risen and browned underneath. Turn the rings over and brown the crumpets on the other side. Watch heat carefully so that they do not brown too fast.

CINNAMON DOUGHNUTS

¾ cup sugar
2 teaspoons shortening
2 eggs, well-beaten
¾ cup milk
3½ cups flour
5 teaspoons baking powder
1 teaspoon salt
1 teaspoon cinnamon
½ teaspoon nutmeg
1 teaspoon vanilla

Cream shortening, eggs and sugar. Add remaining ingredients. Roll out and let stand about 15 minutes. Roll dough out to ¼ to ½-inch thick. Cut with a floured doughnut cutter. Fry in deep fat until browned on both sides.

Makes 2 to 3 dozen doughnuts

NORWEGIAN FLATTBROD

2 cups rye flour
2 cups whole wheat flour
½ teaspoon salt
1½ cups lukewarm water

Sift the flours and salt into a bowl. Stir in enough lukewarm water with a wooden spoon to mix to a fairly soft dough. Turn out onto a floured surface and knead well for about 15 minutes or until a little of the dough rolled into half will not crack. Place the dough in a greased bowl, cover with a folded damp dish towel and leave for at least 2 hours. Divide the rested dough into 8 equal pieces and roll out each piece into a round approximately 10-inches in diameter. Heat a griddle or a large frying pan and when it is very hot, place one of the rounds on the heated griddle. Cook the bread until it is starting to brown in spots on the underside, then turn it over and brown the other side. Now reduce heat and keep turning the bread until it becomes crisp. Repeat this process with all the rounds. If preferred, the rolled dough rounds may be placed on baking sheets, pricked well and baked in a 425 degree oven for about 20 minutes until slightly brown and crisp.

Makes 8 large flattbrod

GARLIC FRENCH BREAD

1 loaf French bread
½ cup mayonnaise
¼ cup butter or margarine, softened
½ cup Parmesan cheese
½ cup onion, finely chopped
1 clove garlic, crushed
½ teaspoon Worcestershire sauce
Paprika

Cut loaf of French bread in half lengthwise. Spread cut surfaces with butter. Mix remaining ingredients, except paprika and spread on bread. Put crusty sides of bread back to back and wrap securely in foil. To bake place in a 375 degree oven for about 8 minutes a side. To barbecue place butter side down on grill over medium heat and turn over every 5 minutes until hot and steamy. Garnish with paprika before serving.

Serves 8 to 10

GARLIC BREAD

1 (1-pound) loaf frozen bread dough
¼ cup (½ stick) unsalted butter
1 tablespoon fresh parsley, finely chopped
1 tablespoon egg, beaten
1 teaspoon garlic salt

Thaw bread dough just until it can be sliced, about 20 minutes. Cut into 15 pieces. Melt butter in small saucepan over low heat. Remove from heat. Stir in parsley, egg and salt. Roll bread pieces into balls. Dip each into butter mixture, coating completely. Arrange in single layer in buttered 9x5-inch loaf pan. Let rise in warm draft-free area until doubled, about 2½ hours. Preheat oven to 350 degrees. Bake until top is golden brown, about 25 minutes. Let cool slightly in pan before serving.

Makes 1 loaf

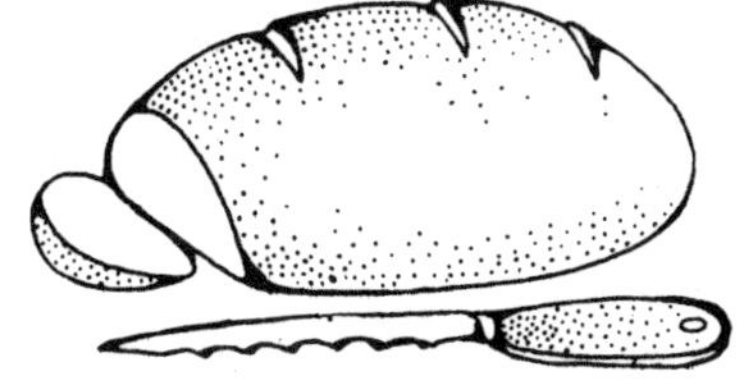

JACKIE'S FABULOUS GARLIC LOAF

1 (1-pound) loaf sweet French bread
½ cup butter
6 cloves fresh garlic, crushed
2 tablespoons sesame seed
1½ cups sour cream
2 cups Monterey Jack cheese, cubed
¼ cup Parmesan cheese, grated
2 tablespoons dried parsley flakes
2 teaspoons lemon pepper seasoning
1 (14-ounce) can artichoke hearts, drained
1 cup Cheddar cheese, shredded
1 (6-ounce) can pitted ripe olives
Tomato slices and parsley sprigs for garnish

Cut French bread in halves lengthwise. Place halves on aluminum foil covered baking sheet. Tear out soft inner portion of bread in large chunks, leaving crusts intact. Melt butter in a large skillet and stir in garlic and sesame seeds. Add bread chunks and fry until bread is golden and butter is absorbed. Remove from heat. Combine sour cream, Jack cheese, Parmesan cheese, parsley flakes and lemon pepper seasoning. Stir in drained artichoke hearts and toasted bread mixture. Mix well. Spoon into bread crust shells and sprinkle with Cheddar cheese. Bake at 350 degrees for 30 minutes. Meanwhile drain olives. Remove bread from oven and arrange olives around edges of bread and tomato slices and parsley strips down the center.

Makes 8 servings of cheesy, garlic goodness

JACKIE'S GINGERBREAD

1 cup sugar
½ cup Crisco or lard
2 cups flour
2 teaspoons ginger
⅓ teaspoon ground cloves
1 egg
½ cup molasses
1¼ cups buttermilk
1 teaspoon baking soda

Cream together the sugar and shortening. Add the flour and spices and crumble together. Reserve ½ cup for the topping. Combine the egg, molases, buttermilk and baking soda. Add to the flour mixture and pour into a greased and floured 9x13-inch pan. Sprinkle with reserved topping. Bake 30 to 40 minutes in a 350 degree oven. Serve with whipped cream or applesauce.

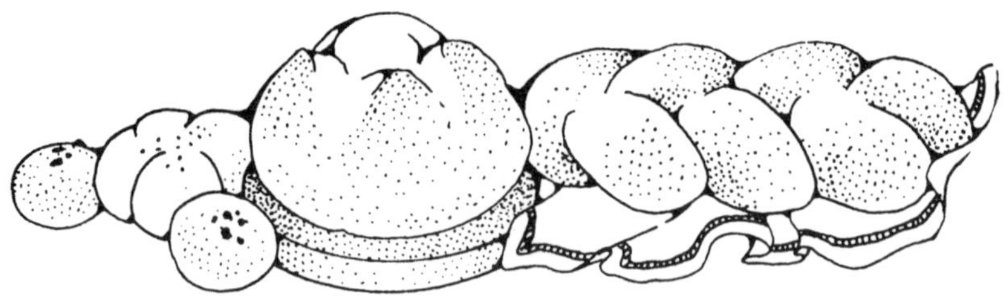

HERB BREAD

1 loaf unsliced white bread
Brown wrapping paper
1 recipe herb butter, as follows:
¼ pound soft butter
2 tablespoons parsley, chopped
2 tablespoons chives, chopped (or green onion tops)
1 tablespoon celery leaves, chopped
1 teaspoon herbs (use sweet basil, oregano or thyme)
½ teaspoon lemon juice

Blend herb butter ingredients well. Trim off the ends, side and top crusts of the bread loaf, leaving the bottom crust. Slice bread in 1-inch slices down to the bottom crust. Spread the slices thickly with the herb butter. Wrap in a double thickness of the plain brown wrapping paper and tie with a string. If possible, let the wrapped loaf stand overnight in the refrigerator. Bake in a 350 degree oven for 30 minutes. Unwrap and serve.

CANADIAN HOVIS BREAD

1 tablespoon sugar
¼ teaspoon ground ginger
2 cups warm water
2 packages dry yeast
⅓ cup molasses
2 tablespoons softened butter
3½ cups whole wheat flour
1 cup whole or flaked bran
½ cup wheat germ
½ cup powdered skim milk
2 teaspoons salt

Combine sugar, ginger, water and yeast and let stand 10 minutes in a warm place. With mixer blend molasses, butter and yeast mixture. Combine remaining ingredients and gradually mix in to form dough. Do not knead. Let dough rise to double size, then punch down. Place in a greased loaf pan and let rise again to double size. Bake at 375 degrees 45 to 50 minutes.

Makes 1 loaf

LAVOSH

2 cups milk
2 whole eggs
3 cups bread flour
½ teaspoon salt
½ teaspoon sugar
4 tablespoons shortening
Poppy seeds
Sesame seeds

Work all ingredients into a firm dough. Let stand for one hour. Divide dough into two equal parts. Roll dough out very thinly on floured surface. Sprinkle with poppy seeds and sesame seeds and roll again. Place on floured sheet pan. Place a pan of hot water on shelf below bread for first 5 minutes of baking at 475 degrees. Turn down heat to 275 degrees, remove water, and bake for 15 minutes more.

Makes 2 sheets

LEMON DREAM LOAF

2½ cups flour
1 tablespoon baking powder
1 teaspoon salt
1⅔ cups sugar
½ cup shortening
2 eggs
1 (8-ounce) package cream cheese, cut into ¼-inch cubes
1 cup milk
½ cup nuts
2 tablespoons lemon peel, grated
¼ cup lemon juice

Sift flour with baking powder and salt. Add 1⅓ cups sugar to shortening. Cream with electric mixer at high speed. Blend in eggs. Add dry ingredients. Fold in cream cheese, milk, nuts, and lemon peel. Pour into 5x9-inch loaf pan lined with wax paper. Bake at 375 degrees for 50 minutes. Combine remaining sugar and lemon juice. Brush over hot loaf. Cool 30 minutes.

Makes 1 large loaf

SALLY LUNN (English Bread)

1 cup milk
1 package dry yeast or 1 cake compressed yeast
½ cup butter (1 stick)
⅓ cup sugar
3 eggs
4 cups sifted flour
1 teaspoon salt

Scald milk and skim. Cool to lukewarm and stir in yeast. Beat butter and sugar together until creamy, then add eggs and beat thoroughly. Sift flour and salt together. Beat flour and milk mixture together alternately. Cover dough with a towel and set in a warm place until it doubles in size. Beat dough again and pour into a greased 10-inch tube pan. Let rise again until double in size. Bake in 350 degree oven for 40 to 50 minutes or until browned on top.

BANANA OATMEAL MUFFINS

1 cup rolled oats
¼ cup evaporated milk
1 cup bananas (3-medium), mashed
¼ cup brown sugar
1 egg
¼ cup oil
1 cup flour
2½ teaspoons baking powder
½ teaspoon salt
Raspberry jam (for centers)

Mix all ingredients together just until moistened. Fill greased muffin tins ½ full. Place ½ teaspoon jam on top of each muffin. Cover jam with remaining batter. Bake 25 minutes at 375 degrees. Wonderful with cream cheese.

This is a wonderful way to use ripe bananas.

Makes 11 muffins

BANANA WHOLEWHEAT MUFFINS

1 cup stone ground whole wheat flour
1 teaspoon baking powder
1 teaspoon baking soda
¼ teaspoon salt
½ teaspoon cinnamon or nutmeg
1 tablespoon safflower oil
3 tablespoons dark molasses (or honey)
7 tablespoons yogurt
2 mashed bananas
White raisins

Mix dry ingredients. Add remaining ingredients. Mix well but do not beat. Bake at 425 degrees for 15 to 20 minutes.

Makes approximately 10 muffins

BLUEBERRY MUFFINS

¾ cup unsweetened blueberries, fresh or frozen
2 cups all-purpose flour
½ cup sugar
1 tablespoon baking powder
½ teaspoon salt
1 egg
1 cup milk
¼ cup salad oil

Heat oven to 400 degrees. Grease 12 (2½ inch) muffin pan cups. In a large bowl, mix flour and next 3 ingredients with a fork. In a small bowl, with fork, beat egg slightly. Stir in milk, blueberries and oil. Add egg mixture all at once. With spoon stir just until flour is moistened. (Batter will be lumpy.) Spoon batter into muffin pan cups. Bake for 20 to 25 minutes.

Makes 12 muffins

SESAME CHEESE MUFFINS

1½ cups Bisquick
¾ cup mild Cheddar cheese
¼ cup onion, minced
1 egg, well beaten
½ cup milk
1 tablespoon sesame seeds, toasted

Saute onions in 1 tablespoon butter or margarine until transparent. Mix Bisquick and ½ cup cheese together. Combine egg, milk and onion. Add all at once to Bisquick mixture and beat vigorously for 30 seconds. Fill well greased muffin tins two-thirds full. Sprinkle tops with remaining cheese and sesame seeds. Bake at 400 degrees for 12 to 15 minutes.

Great for brunch.

Makes 1 dozen muffins

FABULOUS BRAN MUFFINS

1 cup whole wheat flour
1 teaspoon baking soda
½ teaspoon salt
1½ cups bran
3 tablespoons oil
2 tablespoons brown sugar
2 tablespoons molasses
1 egg
1½ cups buttermilk

Sift flour, soda and salt together and stir in bran. Beat oil, sugar and molasses together then add egg and buttermilk. Mix dry ingredients into liquids. Place in greased muffin tins. Bake in a preheated 375 degree oven for 15 to 20 minutes. If you like raisins or currants you may add ½ cup.

Makes 12

ENGLISH MUFFINS

½ envelope dry yeast
1½ cups milk, scalded and cooled
1 tablespoon sugar
1 teaspoon salt
3 cups pre-sifted flour
1 egg, beaten
⅛ teaspoon baking soda

Soften yeast in milk. Stir in sugar and salt. Beat in enough flour to make a drop batter. Beat well. Let batter rise for about 2 hours, or light and doubled in bulk. Stir down. Add egg and baking soda. Beat again thoroughly. Drop in cakes on a hot greased griddle, using about ¼ cup batter per muffin. Bake until browned on both sides, turning once.

RHUBARB STICKY MUFFINS

1 cup finely chopped rhubarb
¼ cup butter
1 cup firmly packed brown sugar
⅓ cup butter
⅓ cup sugar
1 egg
1½ cups flour
2 teaspoons baking powder
½ teaspoon salt
½ teaspoon nutmeg
½ cup milk

Combine rhubarb, butter and brown sugar in a small bowl and mix with a fork until blended. Put in the bottom of 12 large greased muffin cups. Beat ⅓ cup butter, sugar and egg until fluffy. Sift flour, baking powder, salt and nutmeg. Add to butter-sugar mixture alternately with milk. Stir just to blend. Spoon on top of rhubarb. Bake in a 350 oven for 20 to 25 minutes. Invert pan on rack and let stand for a few minutes. Remove pan. Serve warm.

Makes 12 large muffins

RICE MUFFINS

2 cups cooked rice
3 cups sour milk
½ cup melted butter
2 teaspoons salt
2 tablespoons sugar
3 eggs, well beaten
1 teaspoon soda dissolved in 1 tablespoon hot water
2 cups flour

Mix all together. Pour into greased muffin pans. Bake at 350 degrees for 25 minutes.

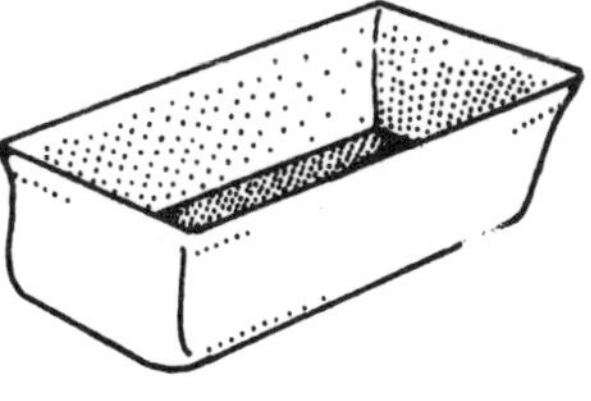

OATMEAL BREAD

1 cup rolled oats
2 cups boiling water
2 tablespoons shortening
1 package dry yeast
¼ cup lukewarm water
1 teaspoon sugar
1 tablespoon salt
½ cup brown sugar
½ cup lukewarm milk
5 cups flour

Place rolled oats in a large mixing bowl. Add boiling water and shortening. Soften the yeast in the ¼ cup of lukewarm water and add 1 teaspoon sugar. When oats and water are lukewarm add yeast, salt, brown sugar and lukewarm milk. Mix in flour. Knead if not too soft. Place in an oiled bowl and allow to double in bulk. Form into 2 small loaves. Let rise again until doubled. Bake 8 to 10 minutes at 400 degrees then lower the temperature to 375 degrees and continue baking for 40 minutes. Watch, the bread browns easily.

Makes 2 small loaves

PINEAPPLE MACADAMIA NUT BREAD

4 eggs
1 cup sugar
½ cup oil
¾ cup pineapple juice
½ cup crushed pineapple with juice
1 tablespoon baking powder
3 cups flour
½ cup coconut
½ cup macadamia nuts, chopped

Combine eggs, sugar, oil, juice, pineapple and mix well. Sift flour and baking powder together and stir into pineapple mixture. Fold in coconut and nuts. Pour into a greased loaf pan and bake at 350 degrees for 50 minutes or until done.

Makes 1 large loaf

PITA BREAD

6 cups flour
1 cup milk or water
2 tablespoons shortening or butter, melted
1 tablespoon salt
2 tablespoons sugar
1 yeast cake
½ cup lukewarm water

Dissolve yeast in lukewarm water. Warm milk or water and add it to the sugar, melted shortening and salt. Sift flour into a large bowl and work into it the liquids until it reaches the consistency of bread dough. Cover the bowl with a damp towel and let dough rise for 2 hours. Turn out onto a floured board and knead down. Cover again and let rise for about an hour. Now pinch off pieces the size of a lemon. Roll out to oblong pieces ½-inch thick. Place side by side in a baking pan. You can make the loaves any size or shape you like, for individual or larger servings. Brush tops with melted butter. Bake in 400 degree oven for 10 minutes, then lower temperature to 350 degrees. Bake until nicely browned all over. Serve hot. Bread may be reheated in oven for later use.

APPLESAUCE PUMPKIN BREAD

⅔ cup shortening
2½ cups sugar
4 eggs
1 cup applesauce
1 cup pumpkin, canned or fresh
3⅓ cups flour
½ teaspoon baking powder
2 teaspoons baking powder
1½ teaspoons salt
1 teaspoon cinnamon
½ teaspoon mace
⅔ cups apple juice
1 cup walnuts or pecans, chopped

Cream together sugar and shortening. Add eggs one at a time, beating well after each addition. Stir in applesauce and pumpkin. Sift together the dry ingredients and add alternately with the apple juice. Stir in nuts. Turn batter into 2 greased loaf pans. Bake at 350 degrees for 1 hour or until done.

Makes 2 large loaves

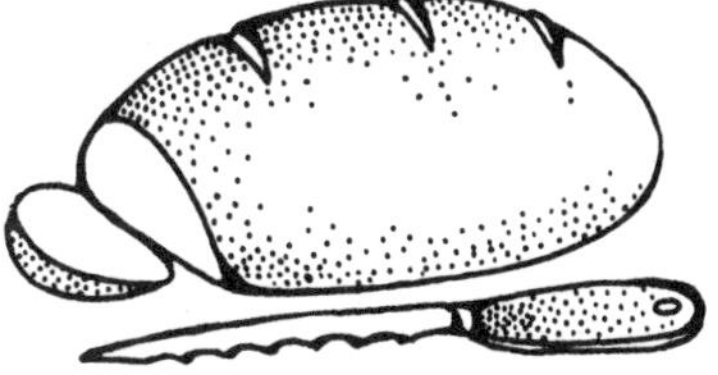

QUICK CINNAMON ROLLS

½ cup hot milk
3 tablespoons shortening
3 tablespoons granulated sugar
1½ teaspoons salt
1 envelope active dry yeast
½ cup warm water
1 egg, lightly beaten
3¼ cups presifted flour
Softened butter, brown sugar and cinnamon

In a mixing bowl combine milk, shortening, sugar and salt. Soften yeast in water. Add to milk mixture. Add egg. Stir in flour to make a soft dough. Turn onto lightly floured board. Knead lightly until smooth. Grease 13x9x2-inch baking pan. Roll out dough into a rectangle. Spread with butter, sprinkle with brown sugar and cinnamon. Roll up lengthwise like a jelly roll. Cut into 1-inch thick slices. Arrange in pan. Let rise for about 1 hour. Preheat oven to 350 degrees. Bake for about 30 minutes.

Makes 24 rolls

HOLIDAY PECAN ROLLS

1 cup butter
2 tablespoons sugar
¼ cup light molasses
2 cups flour, sifted
½ teaspoon salt
2 cups pecans, chopped
Powdered sugar

Cream butter and sugar together. Add molasses. Gradually add flour and salt. Mix well. Stir in nuts. Shape dough into small balls and palce on greased cookie sheets. Bake at 350 degrees for 20 to 25 minutes. Roll in powdered sugar.

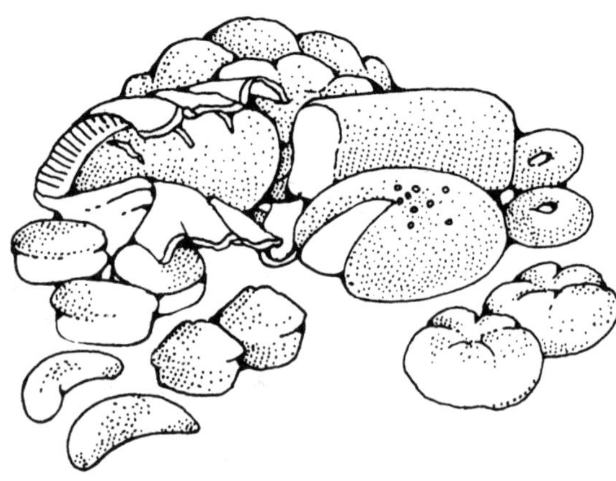

KUMMELWECK ROLLS

4½ to 5½ cups flour
2 tablespoons sugar
2 teaspoons salt
1 package active dry yeast
3 tablespoons margarine
1½ cups hot tap water
1 egg white (room temperature)

In a large bowl, thoroughly mix 1⅓ cups of the flour, the sugar, salt and undissolved yeast. Add margarine. Gradually add tap water to dry ingredients and beat 2 minutes at medium speed of electric mixer, scraping bowl occasionally. Add egg white and another cup of flour (enough to make a thick batter). Beat at high speed 2 minutes, scraping bowl occasionally. Stir in enough additional flour to make a soft dough. Turn out on a lightly floured board. Knead dough until smooth and elastic, about 8 to 10 minutes. Place in greased bowl, turning dough to grease the top. Cover bowl, let dough rise in a warm place free of drafts until double in bulk, about 45 minutes punch down dough. Place on floured board. Knead gently for a minute or two. Break dough into 2-ounce pieces (a little less than ¼ cup.) Form the pieces into balls. Let them stand, covered on the board for 15 minutes. To shape the rolls: Swab a small amount of melted butter on the top of each round. Using a ½-inch dowel, press across each round firmly then make another indentation at right angles to the first crease forming 4 equal segments. Pickup each creased round. Gently squeeze it together with the hand, compressing the quarters somewhat. Turn face down on greased baking sheet. Repeat with each roll. Then cover rolls and let them rise again until double, about 35 minutes. Mix coarse or kosher salt with caraway seed (proportion according to taste). Rub through the fingers to combine the flavors. Turn each risen roll face up. With a pastry brush, lightly brush the top of the roll with water, sprinkle well with caraway mixture. Bake on cookie sheet for about 30 minutes at 375 degrees.

Makes 1½ dozen

MASHED POTATO DINNER ROLLS

½ cup shortening
1 cup hot mashed potatoes
1 teaspoon salt
⅔ cup sugar
2 cups lukewarm milk
1 package dry yeast
2 eggs
6 cups flour (or there abouts)

Mix shortening, potatoes, salt and sugar. Dissolve yeast in milk. Add to potatoes. Beat eggs in a large bowl. Pour in potato mixture and stir well with a spoon. Add enough flour to make a soft dough. Rub surface with a little oil. Cover with dish towel and leave in a warm place until doubled in bulk. Use hands to form rolls about the size of a large egg. Place in large greased muffin tins. Let rise again and bake in a 450 degree oven for 10 minutes.

Makes 5 dozen rolls

OLD COUNTRY SOFT RYE PRETZEL STICKS

1 tablespoon dry yeast
1 ¼ cups lukewarm water
1 tablespoon honey
4 cups rye flour
1 teaspoon salt
½ cup rye flour
1 egg, beaten with ½ teaspoon water
1 medium-sized chopped onion, sauteed and drained on paper towel (you may substitute caraway seeds, unhulled sesame seeds or poppy seeds for the onion)

Soften yeast in lukewarm water. Add honey and set mixture aside for 5 minutes. Combine 4 cups rye flour with salt. Stir in yeast mixture. Turn dough onto lightly floured board and knead with ½ cup rye flour until smooth. Divide dough into 48 pieces and roll each into a rope about 5 inches long. Place on a buttered baking sheet. Brush with egg and water glaze and sprinkle with onion. Let rise for 20 to 30 minutes. Preheat oven to 425 degrees and bake for 15 to 20 minutes. Cool on rack.

Makes 4 dozen

RYE BREAD

1 package dry yeast
½ cup warm water
¾ cup molasses
⅓ cup margarine
2 teaspoons salt
2 cups boiling water
3 cups rye flour
5 cups white flour
3 tablespoons caraway seeds (optional)

Dissolve the yeast in warm water and set aside. Combine molasses, margarine, salt and boiling water; cool to lukewarm and add to the yeast mixture. Stir in rye flour, white flour and caraway seeds then turn out onto a floured board and knead for 10 minutes. You may need ½ to 1 cup additional flour to keep dough from sticking. Let rise, in an oiled bowl, until doubled in bulk. Divide dough into 3 round balls. Put in pans on a cookie sheet. Let rise until almost doubled then bake at 375 degrees for 40 minutes.

Makes 3 loaves

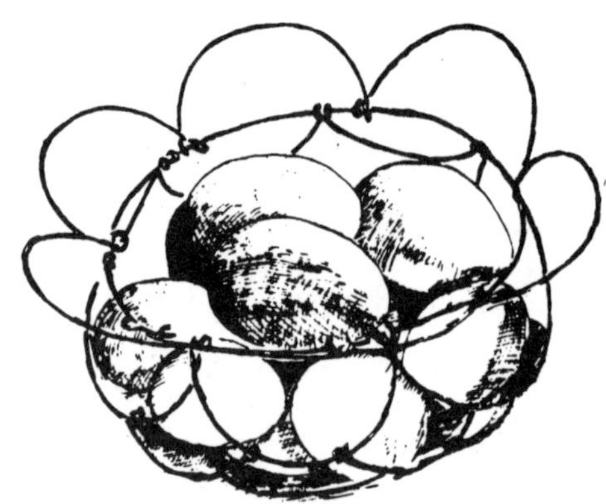

SWEDISH ORANGE-RYE BREAD

1 package yeast
⅓ cup sugar
¼ cup molasses
2 tablespoons shortening
Grated rind of 2 oranges
1⅛ teaspoons salt
2½ cups (about) unsifted rye flour
2½ cups (about) all-purpose flour

Sprinkle yeast into ¼ cup lukewarm water, stir to dissolve. Combine 1½ cups lukewarm water, sugar, molasses, shortening, orange rind, salt and yeast in a large bowl. Add flours gradually, beating until smooth. Knead dough lightly on a lightly floured board. Turn into greased bowl. Cover. Let rise in warm place until almost doubled in bulk. Punch down and shape into 2 loaves. Place loaves into greased 9x5x3-inch loaf pans. Let rise again until almost doubled in bulk. Bake at 375 degrees for 40 minutes.

Makes 2 loaves

CORNBREAD

1 cup flour
3½ teaspoons baking powder
1 teaspoon salt
3 tablespoons sugar
1 cup yellow cornmeal
1 egg, slightly beaten
1 cup milk
¼ cup cooking oil

Sift together flour, baking powder, salt, sugar and cornmeal. Add remaining ingredients and stir until flour is moistened (do not beat). Bake at 425 degrees for 20 to 25 minutes.

Serves 6 to 8

UKRAINIAN RYE BREAD

8 cups rye flour
1 ¼ cups very hot water (not boiling)
¾ cup milk
1 cake compressed yeast or 1 tablespoon active dry yeast
¾ cup lukewarm water
2 teaspoons sugar
1 tablespoon salt
2 tablespoons butter, melted
1 tablespoon vegetable oil

Place ½ cup rye flour in a bowl then beat in the very hot water, stirring continuously to prevent lumps forming. Cover and leave for about 1½ hours. Bring the milk to a boil, let it cool slightly then stir it into the above mixture. Beat well. Blend the yeast into the lukewarm water with 2 teaspoons sugar. Leave the yeast liquid for 10 minutes then add to the flour paste. Mix well and then add the salt, melted butter and oil. Work in the remaining flour to give a firm dough, rather stiffer than an ordinary bread dough. Shape the dough into a ball, place in an oiled plastic bag and leave to rise until doubled in size. Punch down and then let rise again for about 1 hour. Divide the dough into 2 pieces and shape into two large loaves. Place in greased large 9 X 5 X 3-inch loaf pans and let rise until the dough reaches the top of the pans. Brush the tops of the loaves with beaten egg and bake toward the top of a 425 degree oven for 40 to 50 minutes until the loaves sound hollow when the bottoms are tapped. Cool on a cake rack.

Makes 2 large loaves.

OLD COUNTRY SODA BREAD

5 cups flour (3 cups white flour, 2 cups wheat
or brown flour)
1 teaspoon salt
1 teaspoon baking soda
2 heaping teaspoons baking powder
4 ounces butter
2 tablespoons honey
½ cup buttermilk
2 eggs, beaten

Melt butter and honey together over heat. When hot, combine with buttermilk. Mix all dry ingredients together. Add to liquid mixture and knead. Cut dough in quarters and place on floured cookie or pizza pan. Bake in 325 degree oven for 55 minutes.

SQUAWBREAD

2½ cups wheat flour
2½ cups white flour
2 tablespoons baking powder
1 teaspoon salt
2 cups milk
1 tablespoon butter, margarine or lard
Oil or lard for frying

Sift the flours with baking powder and salt. Combine 4 cups of the flour mixture with milk and melted shortening, a little at a time, beating them in at first with an egg beater. Work into a soft dough. Lightly flour board with part of the remaining 1 cup flour. Turn dough out onto board and knead lightly, working in the rest of the flour. Divide the dough into three parts and shape each into a round about ⅛ inch thick and the size of the frying pan in diameter. Heat ¼ inch deep oil in skillet and add dough patty. Quickly brown until golden on both sides. Spread with any meat mixture, jam or stewed dry fruits. Cut into wedges and serve at once.

SALT-RISING BREAD

2 medium-size potatoes, sliced
4 tablespoons corn meal, yellow or white
3 tablespoons plus ½ cup sugar
½ teaspoon baking soda
1 teaspoon baking powder
½ teaspoon plus 1 tablespoon salt 7½ to 8½ cups flour
2 cups warm water
½ cup melted butter or oil

In a plastic container or ceramic bowl place the potatoes, corn meal, 3 tablespoons sugar, baking soda, baking powder and ½ teaspoon of the salt. Pour boiling water over to cover. Stir and set in a warm place overnight. The next day, pour off the liquid. It should measure about 1½ cups. Stir in 1½ cups flour to make a thick, creamy batter. Cover and set in a warm place until it doubles in bulk, about 2 hours. Add warm water, butter or oil, the remaining salt and sugar. Stir in enough flour to make a soft dough. Knead on a lightly floured board until smooth and elastic, about 15 minutes. Divide the dough in half and from each half form a loaf, either round or oblong and place in greased 9 x 5 x 3 inch loaf pans or deep 8-inch cake pans. Cover and let rise until doubled in bulk, 2 or 3 hours. Preheat oven to 350 degrees. Bake the loaves about 45 minutes or until they test done. Cool on a rack.

Makes 2 loaves

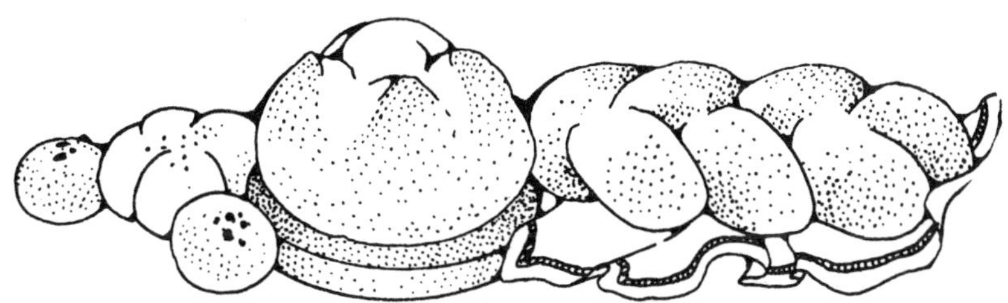

SALT STIX NIBBLERS

⅔ cup butter or margarine
⅔ cup vegetable shortening
2 cups unsifted flour
2 egg yolks
1 teaspoon salt
2 tablespoons water
2 eggs
4 teaspoons milk
Coarse salt (Kosher variety is best)
Caraway seeds

Cut the butter and vegetable shortening into the flour, add the egg yolks and one teaspoon of salt. With a fork, mix in the water. Chill the dough. Roll out the dough and cut it into pencil thick sticks about three inches long. Beat the eggs lightly with the milk and brush the sticks. Place on a cookie sheet, sprinkle with the coarse salt and caraway seeds and bake in a 425 degree oven until brown, about 10 to 12 minutes.

Makes about 5 dozen sticks.

GRANDMA'S IRISH SODA BREAD

¼ cup margarine, softened
¼ cup sugar
1 egg
1 teaspoon baking soda
1 teaspoon salt
1 teaspoon baking powder
4 cups flour
1½ cups buttermilk
2 cups raisins
2 tablespoons caraway seeds

Cream margarine and sugar, beat in egg. Combine soda, salt, baking powder and flour. Add alternately with buttermilk to egg mixture. Add raisins and caraway seeds. Do Not Overmix. Place in 2 (8-inch) round baking dishes. Cut an X in the top of each loaf. Bake at 350 degrees for 65 minutes.

Makes 2 loaves

SHORT'NIN' BREAD

1½ cups flour
¼ cup light brown sugar
¼ pound butter, softened

Cream the butter and sugar. Add the flour and mix thoroughly. Roll out quickly on floured board about ½ inch thick. Cut shapes with small biscuit cutter. Bake on lightly greased and floured shallow pan at 350 degrees for about 20 minutes.

STRAWBERRY BREAD

½ cup butter
1 cup sugar
1 teaspoon vanilla
1 tablespoon lemon juice
3 eggs
2 cups all-purpose flour
½ teaspoon salt
¾ teaspoon cream of tartar
½ teaspoon baking soda
½ cup sour cream
1 cup pureed strawberries

Preheat oven to 350 degrees. Cream butter and sugar. Add vanilla and lemon and beat until fluffy. Add eggs one at a time. Sift together flour, salt, cream of tartar and baking soda. Mix together sour cream and strawberries. Alternately fold flour mixture and strawberry mixture into egg mixture. Pour into a greased 9x5-inch loaf pan and bake for 1 hour.

This is so much fun to make when strawberries are in season. Love to bake this for brunches or the church bazaar.

Makes 1 loaf

STRAWBERRY BREAD

½ cup butter
1 cup sugar
½ teaspoon almond extract
2 eggs, separated
2 cups flour
1 teaspoon baking powder
1 teaspoon baking soda
1 teaspoon salt
1 cup crushed fresh strawberries or 10-ounce package
frozen, undrained

Cream together the butter, sugar and almond extract. Beat in the egg yolks one at a time. Sift together the flour, baking powder, baking soda and salt. Add alternately with the crushed strawberries. Fold in egg whites that have been beaten stiff. Line pan with wax paper. Bake at 325 degrees for 50 minutes to one hour. Very good toasted for breakfast.

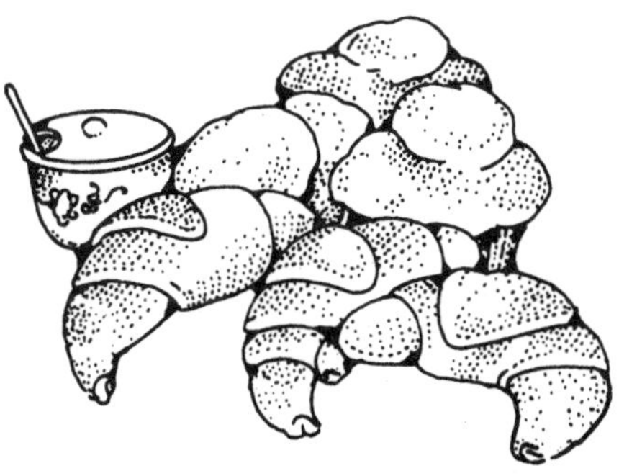

FOOLPROOF WHOLE WHEAT BREAD

2 packages dry yeast
⅔ cup honey or molasses
½ cup warm water
⅔ cup cooking oil
5 cups hot tap water
2 tablespoons salt
7 cups whole wheat flour
5 to 6 additional cups whole wheat flour

Dissolve yeast in warm water, set aside. Combine hot tap water and the 7 cups of flour in a large mixing bowl and beat until smooth. Add honey or molasses, oil and salt and the dissolved yeast, blending thoroughly. Add remaining flour to make a dough stiff enough to knead. Knead about 10 minutes. Divide into four loaves (do not let rise first). Place in greased 9 x 5-inch loaf pans. Allow to rise but not until double in bulk. Bake at 350 degrees for 40-50 minutes.

QUICK WHOLE WHEAT BREAD

1 egg, beaten
2 cups buttermilk
3 tablespoons molasses or honey
1½ tablespoons butter, melted
2 cups whole wheat flour
1 teaspoon baking soda
1 teaspoon salt
1 teaspoon baking powder
½ cup nuts
½ cup raisins

Combine egg, buttermilk, molasses and butter. Stir in dry ingredients that have been mixed together. Stir in nuts and raisins. Spoon batter into 2 greased loaf pans. Bake at 400 degrees for 1 hour.

Makes 2 loaves

cakes

BETTER THAN ANGEL FOOD CAKE

Buy or make a 10-inch angel food cake. Place it upside down on a piece of wax paper. Slice entire top from cake about 1 inch down. Lift off top and set aside. Cut into the cake about 1 inch from outer edge and 1 inch from center, leaving a wall of 1 inch and a 1 inch base at bottom. Remove center. Place on serving plate. Fill cavity with filling. Replace top and frost with remaining filling.

Filling

2 cups whipping cream, whipped
4 tablespoons powdered sugar
¾ cups crushed pineapple, well drained
1 cup strawberries, halved
6 marshmallows cut in quarters or 16 small marshmallows

Chill cake 4 to 6 hours after filling.

EASY APPLE CAKE

3 eggs
1 package yellow cake mix
1 (20-ounce) can apple pie filling

Beat eggs, add cake mix and combine thoroughly. Add pie filling and mix. Pour into a 13x9x1½-inch greased pan. Sprinkle topping on batter. Bake at 350 degrees for 30 to 35 minutes.

TOPPING

⅓ cup brown sugar
1 tablespoon flour
1 tablespoon butter
1 teaspoon cinnamon
1 cup chopped nuts

Combine sugar, flour, butter and cinnamon. Add nuts.

SPICE CARROT CAKE

Spice cake mix
4 eggs
½ cup cooking oil
½ to ¾ cup grated carrots
½ cup water
½ to 1 cup crushed pineapple, drained
Nuts and raisins (optional)

Beat all ingredients thoroughly. Bake in a 10-inch fluted tube pan in 350 degree oven for 55 minutes.

FROSTING

1 small package cream cheese, powdered sugar and a little pineapple juice. Mix until spreadable.

CHOCOLATE CHIP RUM CAKE

1 yellow cake mix
1 small package instant vanilla pudding
1 cup sour cream
½ cup oil
1 tablespoon vanilla
2 tablespoons dark rum
2 tablespoons water
4 eggs

Combine all ingredients and beat for 7 minutes.

Add:

1 (12-ounce) package chocolate chips
1 cup pecans

Spray a fluted tube pan with Pam. Bake 1 hour at 350 degrees. Invert immediately. A hit every time.

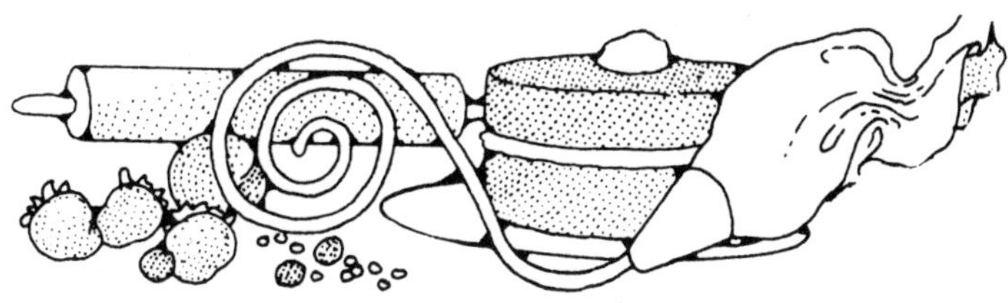

GERMAN CHOCOLATE CHEESECAKE

1 package German chocolate cake mix
⅔ cup shredded coconut
⅓ cup soft butter
3 eggs
16-ounces cream cheese, softened
2 teaspoons vanilla
¾ cup sugar

Mix cake mix, coconut, butter and 1 egg and put into bottom of a 9 x 13-inch ungreased pan. Beat cream cheese with remaining 2 eggs, vanilla and sugar until smooth. Spread over cake mix in pan and bake at 350 degrees for 20 to 25 minutes. Remove from oven and spread Sour Cream Frosting over top. Allow cake to cool. Refrigerate at least 8 hours before cutting.

SOUR CREAM FROSTING

¼ cup sugar
1 tablespoon vanilla
2 cups sour cream

Add sugar and vanilla to sour cream and stir until the sugar is dissolved.

Serves 15

OLD FASHIONED CHOCOLATE CAKE

3 squares baking chocolate
5 tablespoons hot water
½ cup butter
1½ cups granulated sugar
4 eggs, separated
1¾ cups sifted cake flour
2 teaspoons baking powder
½ teaspoon salt
½ cup milk
1 teaspoon vanilla

Melt the baking chocolate cut into small pieces with the hot water in top of double boiler over simmering water. Cream the butter and sugar together well, add the egg yolks, which have been beaten, and combine thoroughly. Add chocolate mixture that has been cooled. Add flour, baking powder, salt and milk. Cream the butter and sugar together well, add the egg yolks, which have been beaten, and combine thoroughly. Add chocolate mixture that has been cooled. Add flour, baking powder, salt and milk. Beat the egg whites until stiff. Fold into cake mixture and add vanilla. Pour into a well-greased and floured 13x9x2-inch baking pan. Bake at 350 degrees 40 to 45 minutes.

Serves 8 to 10.

RED CHOCOLATE CAKE

2 eggs
¾ cup margarine or butter
1½ cups sugar
2 tablespoons vinegar
2 cups flour
½ cup cocoa
½ cup buttermilk or sour milk
1 teaspoon soda
1 teaspoon vanilla
½ cup boiling water
Red food coloring, (optional)

Beat eggs, add margarine or butter and sugar, blend well. Add vinegar, mix well. Sift flour and cocoa together. Add to creamed mixture alternately with buttermilk and soda that have been mixed together. Blend in vanilla. Stir in boiling water and food coloring. Pour into 2 buttered and lightly floured 8-inch cake pans. Bake at 375 degrees for 25 minutes. Cool and frost as desired.

CHOCOLATE VINEGAR CAKE

1½ cups sifted all-purpose flour
1 cup sugar
3 tablespoons cocoa
½ teaspoon salt
1 teaspoon soda
6 tablespoons melted butter
1 teaspoon vanilla
1 cup cold water
1 tablespoon vinegar

Preheat oven to 350 degrees. Sift all dry ingredients together into an ungreased 8x8x2-inch cake pan. Melt butter on warm or simmer. Make three depressions with spoon in the dry ingredients and add one of the three liquids to each depression. Pour the water over all and mix well. Bake for 30 to 35 minutes. Frost in cake pan and serve warm.

QUICK CHOCOLATE FROSTING

1 (6 to 7-ounce) package chocolate morsels
2 tablespoons butter
1 to 1¼ cups sifted powdered sugar
¼ cup sweetened evaporated milk

Melt chocolate and butter on warm or simmer. Beat in powdered sugar alternately with milk. Spread on top of cake. If desired, sprinkle nut meats on top of cake.

COCONUT CAKE

⅔ cup cake flour
1 teaspoon baking powder
Dash salt
3 tablespoons butter
½ cup sugar
3 tablespoons milk
½ teaspoon vanilla
2 eggs, separated
½ cup flaked coconut

Preheat oven to 350 degrees. Grease and flour lightly an 8-inch baking pan. Sift together flour, baking powder and salt. In bowl cream together the butter and sugar until fluffy. Add flour mixture with milk to this beating all the time. Stir in vanilla. In a separate bowl, beat egg whites until soft but not dry. Combine everything. Spoon into pan. Bake 25 to 30 minutes, remove from pan and cool 5 minutes. Sprinkle with powdered sugar and coconut or make white icing and put that on and sprinkle with coconut.

Serves 6

FRESH GRAPEFRUIT COFFEE CAKE

1 grapefruit
2 cups biscuit mix
½ cup raisins
⅓ cup plus 2 tablespoons sugar
⅓ cup plus 1 tablespoon butter or margarine, melted
⅓ cup milk
1 egg, slightly beaten
½ teaspoon ground cinnamon

Over bowl, peel and section grapefruit, reserving sections and ¼ cup juice. In large bowl, combine biscuit mix, raisins and ⅓ cup sugar. Add ⅓ cup butter, milk, egg and reserved grapefruit juice. Mix just until blended. Spoon into lightly greased 8-inch square baking pan. Arrange grapefruit sections on top. Drizzle with 1 tablespoon butter. Combine 2 tablespoons sugar and cinnamon, sprinkle over cake. Bake at 400 degrees for 30 minutes or until toothpick inserted in center comes out clean. Serve warm.

Makes 8 servings

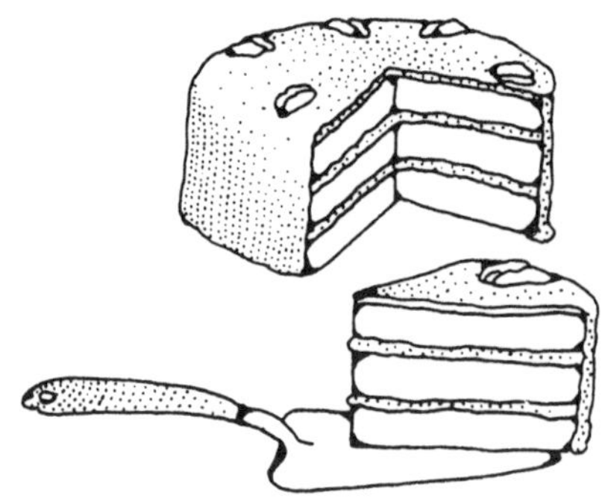

SOUR CREAM COFFEE CAKE

1 cup butter
1¼ cups sugar
2 eggs
2 cups flour
½ teaspoon soda
Dash of salt
1½ teaspoons baking powder
1 cup sour cream
1 teaspoon vanilla

TOPPING

¾ cup nuts, chopped
1 teaspoon cinnamon
2 tablespoons sugar

Combine butter, sugar and eggs. Beat until light and fluffy. Sift flour, soda, baking powder and salt. Add alternately to creamed mixture with sour cream and vanilla. Mix well. Grease and flour a fluted tube pan or tube pan. Spoon ½ batter into pan. Sprinkle ½ topping mixture over this. Add remaining batter. Sprinkle on remainder of topping. Swirl spoon or spatula through batter so topping will be striped through coffee cake. Place in cold oven. Bake at 350 degrees for 50 to 55 minutes. Let cool and remove from pan.

PECAN SOUR CREAM COFFEE CAKE

½ cup (¼ pound) butter or margarine
1 cup granulated sugar
3 eggs
2 cups regular all-purpose flour (sift before measuring)
1 teaspoon baking powder
1 teaspoon soda
¼ teaspoon salt
1 cup sour cream
½ cup golden raisins

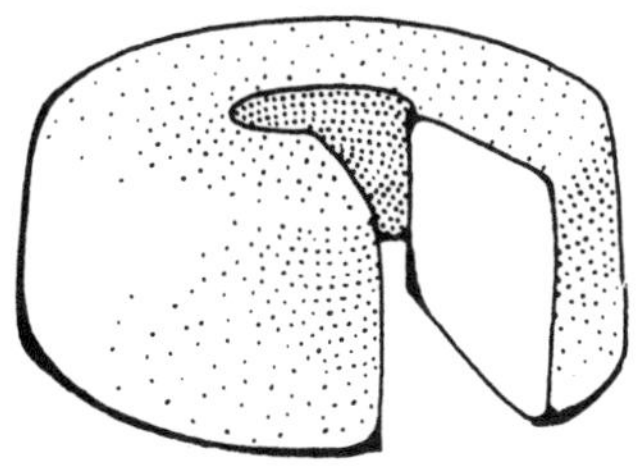

PECAN TOPPING

¾ cup brown sugar, firmly packed
1 tablespoon flour
1 teaspoon cinnamon
2 tablespoons butter
1 cup pecans, chopped

In the large bowl of your electric mixer, cream together butter and sugar. Add eggs, one at a time, beating well after each addition. Sift flour again with baking powder, soda and salt. Add to creamed mixture alternately with sour cream, making about 3 equal additions of each and blending after each addition. Sprinkle raisins over the top and stir in. Spread mixture in a 13x9x2-inch greased baking pan. Sprinkle with pecan topping, made as follows: Combine the brown sugar, flour and cinnamon. Mix together. Cut in butter until the consistency of corn meal. Mix in the pecans. Bake in a 350 degree oven (325 degree for a glass pan) about 30 minutes or until it tests done. Cut in squares and serve either warm or cold.

Makes 12 servings.

COTTAGE CHEESE CAKE

½ pound graham crackers, crushed
½ cup powdered sugar
⅓ cup melted butter
4 eggs
2 pounds cottage cheese
1 cup sour cream
1 teaspoon vanilla
1 tablespoon flour
1½ cups sugar
¼ teaspoon salt

Stir together cracker crumbs, sugar and butter. Spread in the bottom of a 10-inch baking pan. Save a few crumbs for topping. Beat eggs until light. Add remaining ingredients and beat until cottage cheese is crumbled and batter is almost smooth. Pour over crumb crust and bake 1 hour at 350 degrees or until cake is set. Refrigerate and serve chilled.

Makes one 10-inch cake

DATE CAKE

2 eggs
¾ cup powdered sugar
1 cup dates, chopped
1 cup nuts, chopped
3 heaping tablespoons flour
1 teaspoon baking powder
1 teaspoon vanilla

Mix all ingredients together. Bake in shallow pan for 30 minutes at 350 degrees. Serve with whipped cream on top.

JELLO CAKE

1 package white or yellow cake mix
1 (3-ounce) package jello, any fruit flavor
¾ cup water
½ cup salad oil
4 eggs

Empty cake mix into large bowl. Add remaining ingredients. Beat 3 minutes or until smooth and creamy. Pour mixture into a 10-inch tube pan which has been lined on the bottom with wax paper. Bake at 350 degrees for 50 to 55 minutes. Cool in pan 15 minutes, then remove from pan and continue to cool on rack.

Cake may also be baked in any of the following pans:

One 13 x 9-inch pan 40 to 45 minutes
Two 9-inch layer pans 30 to 35 minutes
Two 8-inch layer pans 35 to 40 minutes

FOR NUT CAKE: Prepare as directed above, adding ¾ cup finely chopped walnuts to batter.

FOR COCONUT CAKE: Prepare as directed above, adding 1 cup Bakers angel flake coconut to batter.

FOR STRAWBERRY CAKE: Prepare as directed above, adding 1 cup whole strawberries to batter.

LEGENDARY MAYONNAISE CAKE

1 cup sugar
1 cup water
1 cup mayonnaise
1 teaspoon vanilla
2¼ cups sifted flour
1½ teaspoons baking soda
¼ cup unsweetened cocoa
⅛ teaspoon salt
¼ teaspoon red food coloring

In a large bowl mix together the sugar, water, mayonnaise and vanilla and mix well. Gently fold in all other ingredients (which have been sifted together except for the coloring!) Add coloring last and divide between two 8-inch layer pans that have been well-greased. Bake in a 375 degree oven for 20 to 25 minutes.

Frost with your favorite chocolate frosting.

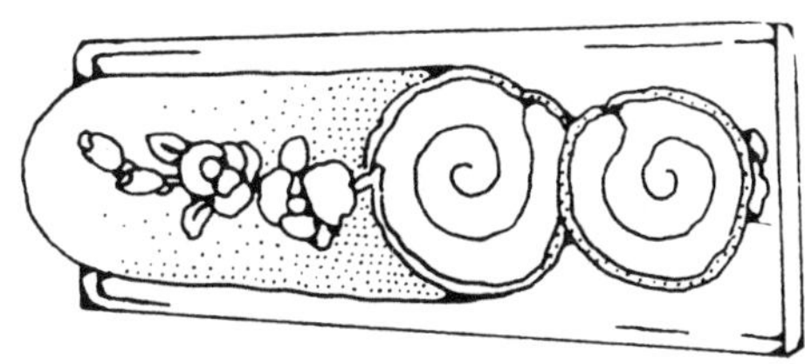

HICKORY NUT CAKE

1 cup butter or margarine
2 cups sugar
3 cups sifted all-purpose flour
1 tablespoon baking powder
1 cup milk
½ teaspoon vanilla
½ teaspoon orange extract
1 tablespoon grated lemon rind
7 egg whites, beaten until very stiff
1 cup hickory nuts, chopped

Cream butter until soft. Gradually beat in sugar, a little at a time. Beat until fluffy. Sift together flour and baking powder. Add flour and milk alternately with butter mixture, beginning and ending with flour. Stir in vanilla and orange extracts with grated lemon rind. Fold in beaten egg whites. Pour into greased 9-inch angel food cake pan, scatter hickory nuts on top of batter. Bake in preheated oven at 350 degrees for 1 hour.

Makes 1 9-inch cake

LAZY DAISY OATMEAL CAKE

1½ cups boiling water
1 cup oats, uncooked
½ cup butter, soft
1 cup granulated sugar
1 cup firmly packed brown sugar
1 teaspoon vanilla
2 eggs
1½ cups sifted all-purpose flour
1 teaspoon soda
½ teaspoon salt
¾ teaspoon cinnamon
¼ teaspoon nutmeg

Pour water over oats, cover and let stand 20 minutes. Beat butter until creamy. Gradually beat in sugars, blend in vanilla and eggs. Stir in oats. Sift together flour, soda, salt and spices, and add to cream mixture, blending well. Pour batter into greased and floured 9-inch square baking pan. Bake in oven 350 degrees for 55 minutes.

Frosting:

¼ cup butter, melted
½ cup brown sugar, firmly packed
3 tablespoons light cream
½ cup chopped nutmeats
¾ cup coconut

Do not remove cake from pan for frosting. Combine melted butter, brown sugar, cream, nutmeats and coconut. Spread over cake. Broil until bubbly.

Makes one 9-inch cake

PERSIMMON CAKE

2 cups sifted flour
1 teaspoon baking powder
1 teaspoon baking soda
¾ teaspoon salt
1 cup dates, sliced
½ cup raisins
¾ cup nuts, chopped
½ cup shortening
½ teaspoon cinnamon
½ teaspoon nutmeg
½ teaspoon allspice
1½ cups sugar
2 eggs
1 tablespoon lemon juice
1½ cups persimmon pulp

Sift together flour, baking powder, soda and salt Mix dates, raisins and nuts, add ¼ cup of the flour mixture and toss to coat fruit and nuts well. Cream together shortening, cinnamon, nutmeg and allspice. Gradually add sugar and continue to cream until fluffy. Beat in eggs one at a time. Combine lemon juice and persimmon pulp and add to creamed mixture alternately with flour mixture. Stir in fruits and nuts. Turn into a greased 9x5-inch loaf pan and bake at 350 degrees 1 hour or until cake tester inserted in center comes out clean. Cool 5 minutes in pan then turn out onto wire rack to cool. Serve with whipped cream or frost with orange butter cream.

PISTACHIO CAKE

1 (16-ounce) box almond flavored cake mix or use
white cake mix and 1 teaspoon almond extract
1 (3-ounce) package pistachio instant pudding
¾ cup cold water
Green food coloring (optional)
¾ cup cooking oil
1 teaspoon almond extract (optional)
4 eggs

Stir cake mix with pudding. If more color is desired, add a few drops of green food coloring to the water. Add water and oil to the mix, then add extract. Add the eggs, one at a time, using low speed of mixer. Beat 5 minutes. Grease a large angel food cake or fluted tube pan. Bake at 350 degrees for 45 to 50 minutes. Cool, then remove from pan. This cake freezes well.

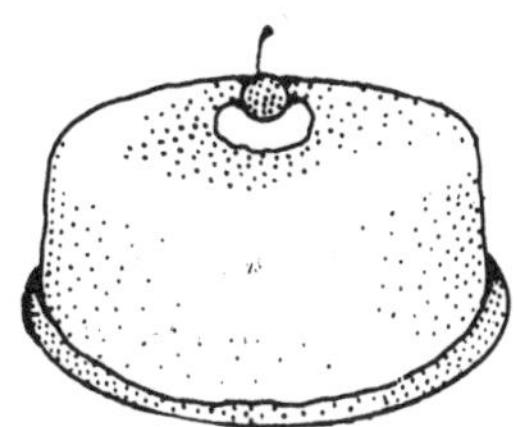

POPPY SEED CAKE

½ pound butter
1½ cups sugar
4 eggs, separated
½ pint sour cream with 1 teaspoon soda
2 cups flour
3 teaspoons vanilla
2 ounces poppy seeds

Cream butter, sugar and egg yolks. Add sour cream soda, flour, vanilla and poppy seeds. Fold in beaten egg whites. Make in an ungreased fluted tube pan for 1 hour at 350 degrees.

Serves 10 to 20

SWEET POTATO CAKE

½ cup butter, melted
1¼ cups all-purpose flour
1 cup sugar
1 egg
1 cup chopped nuts
2 teaspoons cinnamon
1 teaspoon soda
1 teaspoon vanilla
½ teaspoon salt
½ cup strained baby food sweet potatoes
1 (8½ ounce) can crushed pineapple

Combine all ingredients. Pour into a 9 x 9-inch cake pan and bake at 350 degrees for approximately 30 minutes.

COCONUT POUND CAKE

6 eggs, separated
1 cup vegetable shortening
½ cup sugar
½ cup margarine or butter
1 tablespoon almond extract
3 cups flour plus 2 tablespoons of cornstarch sifted together, or 3 cups plus 2 tablespoons cake flour
1 cup milk
2 cups flaked coconut (14-ounce package)

To egg yolks add shortening, sugar, margarine or butter and almond extract. Beat at high speed until smooth and fluffy. Add flour and milk gradually at low speed until smooth then add coconut flakes. Beat egg whites and fold into mixture. Bake at 300 degrees in a 10-inch tube pan for 2½ hours.

NOTE: This cake is better aged than fresh. No need for frosting.

PUMPKIN PIE CAKE

1 package yellow cake mix (reserve 1 cup for top)
½ cup butter or margarine, melted
1 egg
Combine mix with butter and egg and press into bottom and sides of 9-inch pie pan.
1 (14-ounce) can pumpkin pie mix
2 eggs
⅔ cup milk
Mix and pour over cake mix.
In a bowl with the 1 cup of the reserved cake mix, add:
¼ cup sugar
1 teaspoon cinnamon
¼ cup margarine (cut up)
¼ cup walnuts or pecans, chopped (optional)
Sprinkle over top of filling and bake at 350 degrees for 45 to 50 minutes.

7-UP CAKE

1½ cups butter or margarine
3 cups sugar
5 eggs
3 cups flour
2 tablespoon lemon extract
¾ cup 7-UP
Cream butter. Add sugar and beat for 20 minutes. Add eggs, one at a time, beating well after each addition. Stir in flour and lemon extract. Fold in 7-UP. Pour into well-greased fluted tube pan. Bake at 325 degrees for 1¼ hours.

GOLDEN SPONGE LAYER CAKE

1½ cups sifted cake flour
2 teaspoons baking powder
¼ teaspoon salt
6 egg yolks
1 cup sugar, sifted
1 teaspoon lemon extract
½ cup boiling water
Sift flour and baking powder together three times. Add salt to egg yolks and beat with egg beater until light. Gradually add sugar to yolks, beating all the time. Add flour mixture. Stir well, and at once turn into two 8-inch greased layer cake pans. Bake in 325 degree oven for 30 minutes.
Serves 8

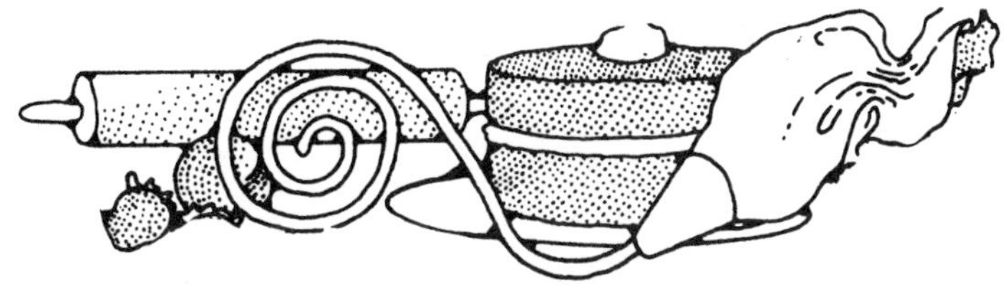

STOLLEN

1½ cups milk
¼ cup butter (and more)
⅓ cup sugar
2 teaspoons salt
2 cakes yeast
2 eggs, beaten
5 cups flour (or more)
½ cup slivered citron
½ cup quartered candied cherries
½ cup halved blanched raisins
1 tablespoon chopped candied orange peel

Scald milk and to it add ¼ cup butter, sugar and salt. When it is lukewarm, crumble in yeast cakes and stir until dissolved, then add eggs, 3 cups of flour, citron, cherries, raisins and orange peel. Beat well, then add rest of flour (or more) to make a soft dough, and knead until smooth. Cover and let rise until double in bulk, then knead again and divide into 3 portions. Roll each portion into a round shape, brush the top with melted butter and fold as you would a Parker House Roll—not quite double. Do not press the edges together. Place on a buttered baking sheet, let rise until double in size and bake at 350 degrees for a half hour or until done. Serve sprinkled with powdered sugar or iced with a thin sugar icing.

EASY ENGLISH TRIFLE

Trifle is a traditional English dessert usually made with leftover sponge cake or pound cake. Since there is no such thing as leftovers in my house, I usually buy ladyfingers or if I am in a big hurry, I just use frozen pound cake. It is also traditional to use jam, but my family thinks this dessert is more luscious with fruit so I use frozen blackberries or raspberries.

When I was a little girl in Nebraska, the dear little old lady that lived next door made this with fresh raspberries out of her garden and lots of thick clotted cream. She served this with homemade elder berry wine. Wonderful!

1 frozen pound cake (10¾ ounces) or 2 packages ladyfingers
½ cup cream sherry
2 packages frozen blackberries, raspberries or other berries
2 packages (5½ ounces each) instant vanilla pudding made according to package instructions
2 cups whipping cream for topping
Sliced toasted almonds for garnish

Slice cake. Line large glass bowl with half the sliced cake or ladyfingers. (I use a beautiful cut glass punch bowl.) Sprinkle half the sherry over the cake. Spread 1 package of berries over the cake. Top berries with half of the vanilla pudding. Repeat layers with other half of the ingredients. Top all of this with whipped cream and sprinkle almonds over the top.

A beautiful way to serve dessert on a hot summer evening.

Serves 12

ITALIAN WINE CAKE

¾ cup butter, at room temperature
⅞ cup sugar
3 eggs
½ teaspoon grated orange peel
1 cup chopped candied orange and lemon peel
2 jiggers rum or sherry
1 cup pastry flour
¾ cup potato flour

Cream butter, add sugar and mix until smooth and creamy. Add eggs, one at time, mixing well. Add orange peel. Steep candied fruits in rum 1 hour and add to batter. Sift together the two flours and add to other ingredients, mixing until smooth. Line a deep cake form with greased paper and pour batter over it. Bake in a 400 degree oven for 45 minutes.

WHOLE WHEAT 'N HONEY ZUCCHINI CAKE

2½ cups whole wheat flour
½ teaspoon baking powder
2 teaspoons baking soda
1 teaspoon salt
2 teaspoons cinnamon
1 teaspoon nutmeg
3 eggs
¾ cup salad oil
1 cup honey
2 teaspoons vanilla
1 small whole orange, chopped in processor or blender
2 tablespoons water
2 cups grated zucchini
2 cups coarsely chopped walnuts

Into a large mixing bowl, sift together dry ingredients. Add eggs, oil, honey, vanilla, orange and water. Stir until well blended. Stir in zucchini and nuts. Pour into greased and floured fluted tube pan or spoon into paper lined muffin pan cups. Bake at 350 degrees 50 to 60 minutes for cake or 20 to 25 minutes for muffins.

Hint: Substitute 2 cups finely grated carrots for zucchini for Whole Wheat 'N Honey Carrot Cake.

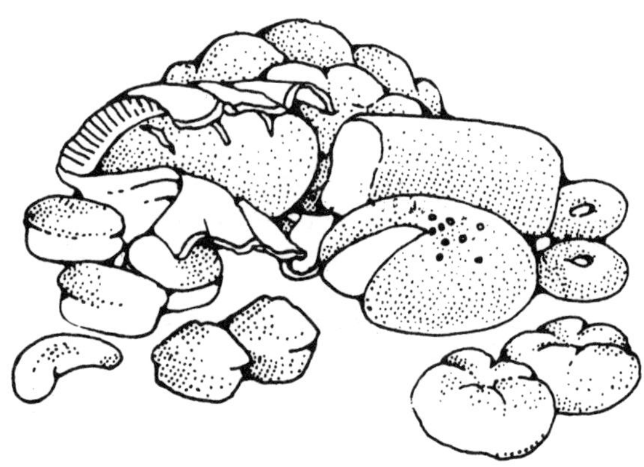

pies

BRANDIED APPLE MINCE PIE

PASTRY

2 cups flour
1 teaspoon salt
¾ cup shortening
Ice water
1 cup American or Cheddar cheese, grated

Mix and sift flour and salt. Cut in shortening with knife. Add cheese. Add only enough water to hold ingredients together. Divide dough into 2 parts and roll out on thin, slightly floured board. Line pie pan with ½ pastry.

FILLING

1 pint brandied mincemeat
3 apples, diced
⅔ cups sugar
2 tablespoons flour
½ teaspoon salt
Juice from ½ lemon
2 tablespoons butter
1 teaspoon cinnamon
1 teaspoon nutmeg

Spread mincemeat over pastry. Dice apples and pour lemon juice over them. Mix dry ingredients and pour over apples. Place on top of mincemeat. Dot with butter and add crust. Sprinkle with sugar and melted butter and a dash of cinnamon. Bake at 400 degrees for 30 to 40 minutes. After cooking, decorate with cheese slices cut into apple shapes and sprinkle with nutmeg. Make leaves from green candied fruit and stems from golden candied fruit.

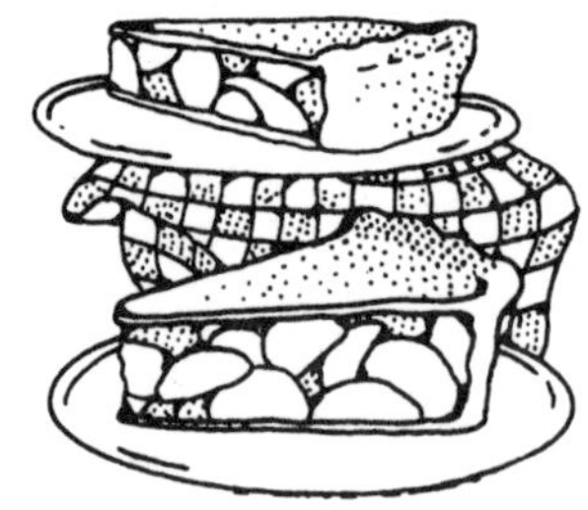

UPSIDE-DOWN APPLE PIE

1 tablespoon butter
4 tablespoons brown sugar
8 pecan halves
Pastry for 2-crust pie
6 large baking apples, peeled and sliced
1 tablespoon lemon juice
1 cup sugar
1 teaspoon cinnamon
¼ teaspoon nutmeg
3 tablespoons flour
1 tablespoon butter

Line a 9-inch pie plate with aluminum foil, turning down foil on the edges. Rub bottom with butter and spread evenly with brown sugar. Arrange pecan halves on top in pinwheel design, flat side up. Top with half the pastry, trimming along the outside edge to fit. In large bowl, combine sliced apples and lemon juice, stirring to coat. Add sugar, cinnamon, nutmeg and flour. Empty into bottom crust. Dot with butter. Cover with top pastry, trim and flute. Do not prick. Turn up foil edges to catch the brown sugar syrup during baking. Bake for 1¼ hours at 375 degrees or until the juices are bubbling all around the pie and crust is browned. Remove from oven. Cool 10 minutes. Invert into another 9-inch plate. Immediately peel off foil. Serve warm or chilled.

Fabulous!

Serves 8

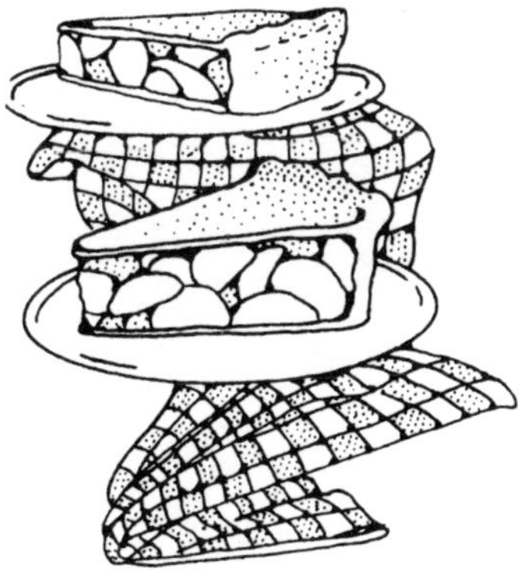

OCTOBERFEST APPLE PIE

CHEESE PASTRY

½ cup shortening
2 cups flour
¾ teaspoon salt
1 cup New York State Cheddar cheese, shredded
6 to 8 teaspoons cold water
Melted fat

Cut shortening into sifted flour and salt until mixture resembles peas in size. Mix in cheese lightly with fork. Add enough water to hold together. Roll lightly and put into a 9-inch pie pan. Brush bottom crust with melted fat to prevent soaking.

APPLE FILLING

5 to 6 large tart apples
¾ cup sugar
2 teaspoons flour
⅛ teaspoon salt
1 teaspoon cinnamon
1 teaspoon nutmeg
2 tablespoons butter

Pare, core and slice apples. Lay slices in pie plate lined with cheese pastry. Mix sugar, flour, salt, cinnamon and nutmeg. Sprinkle over each layer of apples, dot with butter, and cover with crust. Press edges together and slash top. Bake at 450 degrees for 10 minutes or until edges are brown. Reduce oven to 350 degrees and bake about 30 minutes longer.

Serves 6 to 8.

DOUBLE CRUST BANANA PIE

From "A Taste of Aloha," a cookbook issued by the Junior Assistance League of Hawaii. (September 1983)

2 (9-inch) unbaked pie shells (regular crust)
2½ cups bananas, cut in ¼-inch slices
1 cup pineapple juice
½ cup sugar
3 tablespoons flour
1 teaspoon cinnamon
½ teaspoon nutmeg
Pinch of salt
1 tablespoon butter
2 teaspoons milk

Preheat oven to 400 degrees. Soak bananas in pineapple juice for 20 to 30 minutes and then drain. Combine dry ingredients and mix with bananas. Pour filling into pastry shell and dot with butter. Place top crust over filling, seal and flute edges. Brush top with milk and cut slits on top crust. Bake for 30 to 35 minutes. Serve warm or cold.

Serves 8

CHERRY BERRY PEACH PIE

3 cups peaches, peeled and sliced
1 cup fresh blueberries
1 cup fresh sweet cherries, halved and pitted
1 tablespoon fresh lemon juice
¼ cup brown sugar, firmly packed
½ cup granulated sugar
3 tablespoons flour
⅛ teaspoon salt
¼ teaspoon cinnamon
Pastry for 2 crust pie
Milk
Granulated sugar

In a large bowl mix together peaches, blueberries and cherries, sprinkle with lemon juice. Gently stir in brown sugar, ½ cup granulated sugar, flour, salt and cinnamon. Line a 9-inch pie plate with half of pastry, trim overhang to 1-inch. Turn fruit into pie. Roll out remaining pastry and cut into ¾-inch wide strips. Arrange strips over fruit in lattice fashion. Fold under edge of pastry, make rim and flute edges. Brush lattice crust with milk and sprinkle with sugar. Bake at 450 degrees for 10 minutes then reduce heat to 350 degrees and bake 45 to 60 minutes longer until pastry is brown and fruit is tender. Serve warm or cold.

CHOCOLATE PIE

1 (4-ounce) package sweet chocolate
⅓ cup milk
2 tablespoons sugar
1 (3-ounce) package cream cheese
1 (8-ounce) container non-dairy whipped topping, thawed
1 (8-ounce) graham cracker crust

Melt chocolate with 2 tablespoons milk over low heat, stirring until chocolate is melted. Beat in sugar and cream cheese and add remaining milk. Stir until smooth. Fold in whipped topping. Spoon into crust. Freeze until firm, at least 4 hours. Garnish with chocolate curls.

Serves 6

CHOCOLATE CHIP PIE

1 chocolate cookie crust
1 cup powdered sugar
1 cube butter
6 ounces chocolate chips, melted
1 teaspoon vanilla
4 eggs

To make piecrust, crush one package of chocolate wafers. (I usually put them in a blender.) Blend in 1 cube of melted butter, then pat into the bottom and sides of a pan. To make the filling, cream sugar and butter then add melted chocolate chips. Beat well and add vanilla. Add egg one at a time, beating well after each addition. Pour into prepared pie crust and freeze. Top with whipped cream and toasted almonds.

CHOCOLATE MINT PIE

2 squares unsweetened chocolate
½ cup butter
1 cup powdered sugar
2 eggs
¼ teaspoon essence of peppermint
Chocolate Cookie Pie crust
Sweetened whipped cream
Grated chocolate

Melt chocolate in top of double boiler over hot water, set aside to cool. Cream butter and powdered sugar until light and fluffy. Add unbeaten eggs, one at a time, beating until smooth. Add melted chocolate and mint flavoring. Spread in Chocolate Cookie Pie crust. Chill for several hours or overnight. Just before serving, top with sweetened whipped cream and garnish with grated chocolate.

CHOCOLATE COOKIE CRUMB CRUST

1 cup finely crushed chocolate cookie crumbs
3 tablespoons sugar
¼ cup butter, melted

Combine cookie crumbs and sugar. Add butter and blend until all crumbs are evenly moist. Pat over bottom and side of 9-inch pie pan. Bake at 350 degrees for 6 minutes. Cool.

CHOCOLATE MINT ICE CREAM PIE

1½ quarts chocolate mint ice cream
16 cream filled chocolate sandwich cookies
¼ cup butter or margarine, melted
½ cup whipping cream
1 (9-ounce) jar fudge sauce

Prepare chocolate cookie pie crust in a 9-inch pie plate. Preheat oven to 350 degrees. Roll cookie crumbs between sheets of wax paper to measure 1¼ cups. Mix with butter. Press over bottom of pie plate to form a crust. Bake in center of oven for 8 minutes. Cool thoroughly and freeze. Remove ice cream from freezer and let soften slightly. Spoon ice cream into frozen crust. Freeze 1 hour. Meanwhile whip cream to soft peaks. Decorate border around pie platter with pastry tube or dollops of whipped cream. Freeze 3 hours. Spoon warmed fudge sauce over individual servings.

This takes only 25 more sit-ups 2 times a week, but it is really delicious.

Serves 6

DAQUIRI PIE

CRUST

1½ cups (16) graham cracker crumbs
6 tablespoons melted butter
3 tablespoons sugar

Combine and press to sides and bottom of 9-inch pie pan reserving a few crumbs for topping. Refrigerate 2½ hours or put in freezer for 10 minutes.

FILLING

1 large can (15-ounce) sweetened condensed milk
1 teaspoon grated lemon rind
1 package Island Inn Cocktail Mix
¼ teaspoon red food coloring
2 egg yolks
1 teaspoon vanilla

Put egg yolks in large bowl of mixer and beat well. Beat in Island Inn Cocktail Mix, rind and vanilla. Add milk slowly. Blend in coloring. Pour into shell and bake in 325 degree oven 20 minutes and top with the following which have been blended together:

½ pint sour cream
1 tablespoon sugar

Sprinkle remaining crumbs on top. Return to oven for 5 more minutes. Chill.

EGGNOG PIE

1 (9-inch) pie shell or crumb crust shell
2 cups prepared eggnog mix
2 tablespoons (2 envelopes) unflavored gelatin
½ cup milk
2 tablespoons rum
2 tablespoons brandy
½ teaspoon grated nutmeg
½ teaspoon cinnamon
1 teaspoon vanilla
1 cup whipping cream, whipped
1 cup mixed candied fruitcake fruits, diced

Soften gelatin in milk and melt over hot water in a double boiler until gelatin is dissolved. Let cool and add to eggnog mix, along with spices, brandy, rum and vanilla. Fold in whipped cream and fruits. Pour the whole mixture into the baked pie shell and refrigerate 3 hours to allow pie to set up. Garnish with nuts or pieces of fruit.

FRESH FIG CHIFFON PIE

2 teaspoons plain unflavored gelatin
3 tablespoons cold water
¾ cup milk
2 eggs, separated
6 tablespoons sugar
⅓ teaspoon vanilla
1½ cups fresh figs, diced
1 cup heavy cream, whipped
1 (9-inch) pie shell, baked

Soften gelatin in cold water. Scald milk in double boiler. Beat egg yolks slightly and add 4 tablespoons sugar. Stir in scalded milk. Return mixture to double boiler, cook over hot water, stirring constantly, until mixture coats metal spoon. Remove from heat and stir in softened gelatin and stir until dissolved. Add vanilla. Let mixture cool thoroughly, then fold in figs and whipped cream. Gradually beat remaining 2 tablespoons sugar into stiffly beaten egg whites and fold into fig mixture. Turn into baked pie shell and chill until firm. Before serving dust top of pie lightly with nutmeg.

SHAMROCK GRASSHOPPER PIE

1 (8½ ounce) package chocolate wafers
¼ cup butter or margarine, melted
1 (6½ ounce) package miniature marshmallows
½ cup milk
¼ cup creme de menthe
3 tablespoons creme de cocoa
1½ cups heavy cream
Green food coloring

Crumble wafers and mix well with the butter. Press crumb mixture into 9-inch pie pan. Bake at 350 degrees until firm. Cool. Melt marshmallows with milk in double boiler. Pour into bowl and chill until thickened. Blend creme de menthe and creme de cocoa into marshmallow mixture. Beat cream until stiff and fold in marshmallow mixture. Add coloring. Pour filling into pie shell. Chill until firm. Garnish with paper shamrocks.

Serves 6

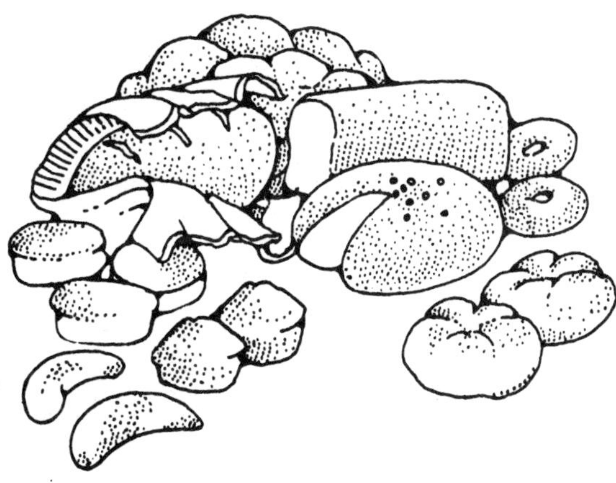

LEMON RIBBON-LAYERED MERINGUE PIE

6 tablespoons butter
Grated peel of 1 lemon
⅓ cup lemon juice
⅛ teaspoon salt
1 cup sugar
2 eggs
2 egg yolks
1 quart French vanilla ice cream
Lemon cream crust
3 egg whites
6 tablespoons sugar

Melt butter. Add lemon peel, lemon juice, salt and 1 cup sugar. Slightly beat whole eggs with egg yolks and combine with lemon-butter mixture. Cook over boiling water, beating constantly with a whisk, until thick and smooth. Cool. Spoon half of the ice cream in pastry shell and freeze. Spread half the cooled lemon butter over the ice cream, freeze. Cover with the other half of the ice cream, freeze. Top with remaining lemon butter, freeze. Beat egg whites until soft peaks form. Gradually beat in the 6 tablespoons of sugar. Continue beating to stiff peaks. Spread meringue on pie. Place on board, lightly brown in 475 degree oven. Serve immediately or freeze.

LEMON CREAM CRUST

1 cup sifted flour
½ teaspoon salt
1 tablespoon powdered sugar
⅓ cup vegetable shortening
¼ cup minus 1 teaspoon cream
1 teaspoon fresh lemon juice
1 tablespoon butter, melted

Sift flour, salt and sugar together. Cut in ½ the shortening until mixture is the size of very fine particles. Cut in remaining shortening to the size of peas. Combine cream and lemon juice and sprinkle over mixture. Stir only until mixture clings together. Form into ball. Chill 10 to 15 minutes. Roll out on lightly floured board. Fit into 9-inch pie plate, trim and flute. Brush with melted butter. Prick generously. Bake at 475 degrees for 8 to 10 minutes.

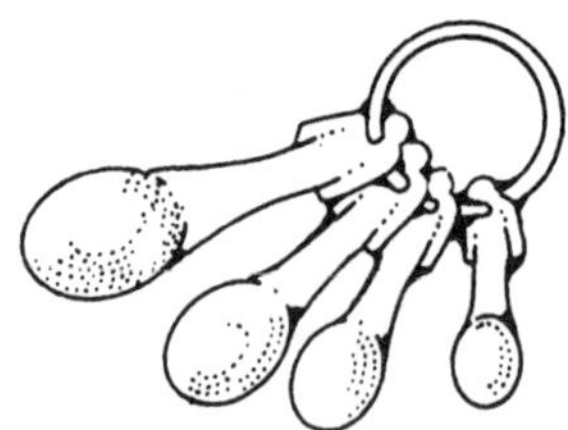

LEMONADE PIE AND STRAWBERRIES

1 can sweetened condensed milk
1 (6-ounce) can frozen concentrated lemonade, thawed
Rind of 1 lemon, grated
4 teaspoons lemon juice
1 (9-ounce) carton non-dairy whipped topping
Pastry shell
Sweetened fresh strawberries

Blend milk, lemonade, rind and lemon juice. Fold in non-dairy topping. Pour into pastry shell, chill. Serve in wedges and top with strawberries.

LIME PIE FOR MOM

1 (14-ounce) can sweetened condensed milk
¾ cup fresh lime juice (must be fresh)
1 (13½ ounce) can crushed pineapple, drained
2 to 3 drops green food coloring
½ pint whipping cream
1 tablespoon powdered sugar
1 teaspoon vanilla
1 (9-inch) pie shell

Combine milk, juice, pineapple and enough food coloring to make a pale green. Set aside. In a separate bowl, whip cream and add sugar and vanilla. Pour lime mixture into baked pie shell and top with whipped cream. Add a sprinkling of shaved chocolate over the top. Chill several hours before serving.

This is a very easy pie to make for the beginning cook and it is simply fabulous . . . your Mom will love it.

MILLIONAIRE PIE

2 eggs
½ cup flour
½ cup sugar
½ cup brown sugar
1 stick butter, melted
1 (6-ounce) package chocolate chips
1 teaspoon vanilla
1 cup pecans, coarsely chopped
1 (9-inch) pie shell, unbaked

Preheat oven to 325 degrees. In a large bowl, beat eggs until foamy. Beat in sugars, melted butter and flour. Stir in vanilla, chips and nuts. Pour into pie shell and bake for 1 hour until set. Serve with vanilla ice cream.

PEACH-CREAM PIE

1 (3-ounce) package peach jello
1 ¼ cups boiling water
1 pint peach ice cream
2 medium peaches, peeled and diced
¼ teaspoon almond extract
1 (9-inch) pie shell, baked

In a bowl dissolve gelatin in the boiling water. Add ice cream and stir until melted. Chill until mixture is thickened, but not set, about 20 minutes. Fold in peaches and almond extract. Spoon into pie shell. Chill until firm, about 2 hours.

Serve with whipped cream — This is so fast and so good, a great summer hurry up . . .

PEACH UPSIDE DOWN PIE

1 (12-inch) square aluminum foil
2 tablespoons butter, softened
⅔ cup toasted almonds or pecan halves
9 tablespoons brown sugar
Pastry for a double crust 9-inch pie, unbaked
5 cups fresh peaches (about 8 medium-sized), peeled and sliced
¾ cup granulated sugar
2 tablespoons quick-cooking tapioca
½ teaspoon nutmeg
¼ teaspoon cinnamon
1 egg white, slightly beaten

Line a 9-inch pie pan with foil. Let excess foil overhang edge. Spread butter on bottom of foil, press nuts and 5 tablespoons brown sugar into butter. Fit a layer of pastry over nuts and brown sugar in pie pan. Mix peaches with sugar, 4 tablespoons brown sugar, tapioca, spices and pour into pastry shell. Cover with another layer of pastry, prick to allow steam to escape, seal and flute edges. Brush with egg white. Bake in a 450 degree oven for 10 minutes then lower heat to 375 degrees and bake 35 to 40 minutes longer or until done. Turn out upside down.

FROZEN PEANUT BUTTER PIE

4 ounces cream cheese
1 cup powdered sugar
⅓ cup peanut butter
½ cup milk
1 (9-ounce) package frozen non-dairy whipped topping
1 (9-inch) graham cracker crust or regular pie crust, baked and cooled
¾ cup peanuts, finely chopped

In a large bowl, whip the cheese until soft and fluffy. Beat in the sugar and peanut butter. Slowly add the milk, blending thoroughly into mixture. Fold whipped topping into mixture. Pour into baked pie shell. Sprinkle with chopped peanuts. Freeze until firm. If not used the same day, wrap in transparent food wrap after the pie is frozen. Remove from freezer about ½ hour before serving.

Makes 6 servings.

BUTTERMILK PECAN PIE

½ cup butter
2 cups sugar
2 teaspoons vanilla
3 eggs
3 tablespoons flour
¼ teaspoon salt
1 cup buttermilk
¾ to 1 cup pecans, chopped
1 (9-inch) pie shell, unbaked
Sweetened whipped cream

Cream butter and sugar, adding ½ cup sugar at a time. Blend in vanilla. Stir in eggs, one at a time. Combine flour and salt and add to creamed mixture a little at a time. Stir in buttermilk. Sprinkle pecans in bottom of pie crust and pour custard mixture over pecans. Bake at 300 degrees for 1 hour and 30 minutes. Best served at room temperature with sweetened whipped cream.

DIETER'S DOWNFALL PECAN PIE

Pastry for 9-inch pie
3 eggs, well beaten
⅔ cup sugar
1 teaspoon vanilla
2 tablespoons butter, melted
1 cup dark corn syrup
½ cup Vermont maple syrup
1¼ cups pecans

Beat eggs and sugar together. Add vanilla to butter and add to sugar mixture. Add syrups and pour over pecans in pie shell. Bake at 350 degrees for 40 to 45 minutes, or until filling is set. Serve chilled with whipped cream

SOUTHERN PECAN PIE

2 cups light corn syrup
3 eggs
1 cup whole pecans
Cinnamon
¼ teaspoon salt
1 teaspoon vanilla
1 (9-inch) pastry shell, unbaked

Beat corn syrup and eggs together very slowly until blended. Add salt and vanilla. Roll pecans in cinnamon coating well. Arrange in bottom of pastry shell. Pour egg mixture over pecans. Bake at 375 degrees for 30 minutes, reduce heat to 300 degrees and bake for 15 minutes longer. Cool. Delicious served with vanilla ice cream.

PERSIMMON MERINGUE PIE

2 cups persimmon pulp
½ cup sugar
½ teaspoon mace
1 teaspoon lemon peel, grated
⅛ teaspoon salt
2 teaspoons butter
2 egg yolks
1 (9-inch) pastry shell, baked

The persimmons should be sweet and very ripe. Peel. Press enough through a colander or food mill to make 2 cups of pulp. Add sugar, mace, lemon peel, salt and cook slowly for 5 minutes. Add a small amount to butter and beaten egg yolks. Return to persimmon mixture and stir until mixture is slightly thickened. Pour into pastry shell and cool. Cover with meringue.

MERINGUE

2 egg whites
4 teaspoons sugar
½ teaspoon vanilla or other flavoring

Beat eggs until frothy. Add sugar gradually and continue beating until stiff. Add flavoring. Pile on pie and bake in a 325 degree oven 15 to 18 minutes. Cool before serving.

PINEAPPLE CHEESE PIE

1 (20-ounce) can crushed pineapple, drained
4 tablespoons white shortening
4 tablespoons sugar
1 cup flour
½ teaspoon baking powder
1 large egg

Blend shortening, sugar, flour and baking powder well. Add egg and blend. Shape dough into ball and press into bottom and sides of a 10-inch pie plate, fluting the crust. Line crust with pineapple.

FILLING

8-ounces cream cheese
¾ cup sugar
2 eggs
1 tablespoon lemon juice
1 tablespoon flour
1 cup milk
1 cup cream
1½ teaspoons vanilla

Place filling ingredients in a blender and blend well. Pour into crust. Sprinkle top with cinnamon. Bake in a preheated oven at 350 degrees for 60 minutes.

SOUR CREAM-PINEAPPLE PIE

2 cups sour cream
1 large package vanilla instant pudding
1 small can crushed pineapple, undrained
2 teaspoons sugar (optional)

Mix above ingredients together and pour immediately into your pie crust. May be topped with chopped nuts, toasted coconut, or your favorite topping.

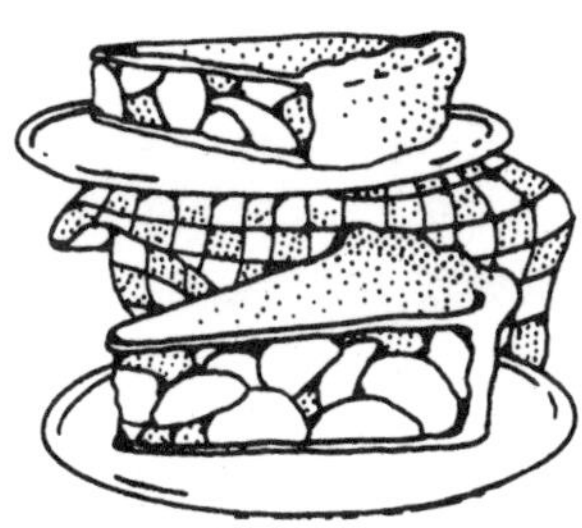

FROZEN PUMPKIN PIE

1 cup pumpkin, mashed
1 cup brown sugar
½ teaspoon cinnamon
½ teaspoon nutmeg
½ teaspoon ginger
¼ teaspoon salt
1 cup whipping cream
1 pint vanilla ice cream
1 (9-inch) pre-baked pie shell

Combine the first six ingredients. Whip the cream and fold into the first mixture. Spread slightly softened ice cream into bottom of pie shell and cover with the pumpkin mixture. Freeze. Remove from the freezer 10 minutes before serving for easier cutting.

This one is a winner for the whole family!

PUMPKIN ICE CREAM PIE

1 (8 or 9-ounce) box of ginger snaps
1 cup pumpkin
¼ cup brown sugar
½ teaspoon salt
½ teaspoon cinnamon
¼ teaspoon nutmeg
1 teaspoon cloves, ground
½ teaspoon allspice
1 tablespoon bourbon
½ cup pecans, chopped
1 quart vanilla ice cream, softened

Line the bottom and sides of a 9-inch pie plate with ginger snaps. Combine all ingredients except ice cream and mix well. Fold into softened ice cream. To assemble pie, pour half the ice cream mixture into prepared pie plate. Cover with a layer of ginger snaps, add remaining ice cream and freeze until firm.

What a wonderful delight at Thanksgiving and a little different from the traditional Pumpkin Pie.

Serves 8

WHISKEY PUMPKIN PIE

1 single crust for a 9-inch pie
2 cups pumpkin
¼ teaspoon salt
1 cup sugar
4 eggs, separated
½ teaspoon cinnamon
⅓ cup cream
1 cup whiskey
¼ cup butter
1 tablespoon corn starch

Beat egg whites until stiff. Sprinkle corn starch over egg whites and fold in. Set aside. Combine remaining ingredients and beat 5 minutes. Fold in egg whites. Pour into pastry shell. Bake at 450 degrees for 10 minutes, reduce heat to 350 degrees and bake for 30 minutes or until knife inserted in center comes out clean.

RAISIN PIE

1 pie shell, baked
1 cup seedless or seeded white raisins
1 cup water
½ cup white or brown sugar
2 tablespoons butter
2 tablespoons all-purpose flour
2 egg yolks
1 teaspoon lemon rind, grated
3 tablespoons lemon juice

Put raisins in cup of water and cook to the boiling point. Add the sugar. Cool ½ cup of this mixture and gently stir in butter and flour. Return it to the saucepan. Cook and stir these ingredients over low heat until the flour has thickened. Remove the pan from the heat and beat in the egg yolks, lemon rind and lemon juice. Cool the filling. Fill the pie shell with the mixture. Cover with meringue and bake in preheated oven at 325 degrees to 350 degrees for 10 to 15 minutes or until lightly browned.

RHUBARB CUSTARD PIE

Pastry for 2 crust pie
1 ½ cups sugar
3 tablespoons flour
½ teaspoon nutmeg
1 tablespoon butter, softened
2 eggs
3 cups rhubarb, cut into 1-inch pieces
Powdered sugar

Preheat oven to 450 degrees. Line 9-inch pie plate with half of pastry. Combine sugar, flour, nutmeg, butter and eggs. Beat until smooth. Put rhubarb in pastry-lined plate, pour egg mixture on top. Cover with lattice topping, flute edge. Bake in preheated oven for 10 minutes, reduce temperature to 350 degrees and bake for 30 minutes longer. Before serving dust with powdered sugar.

RICOTTA PIE

1 ¼ pounds Ricotta cheese
Very small pinch of salt
1 tablespoon flour
4 tablespoons sugar
4 egg yolks
1 teaspoon orange rind, grated
1 tablespoon seedless raisins
1 tablespoon candied orange peel
2 egg whites, stiffly beaten
2 tablespoons powdered sugar
1 teaspoon cinnamon

Mix together well the Ricotta, salt, flour, sugar, egg yolks and orange rind. Mix for at least 5 minutes. Add raisins and candied orange peel. Gently fold in the beaten egg whites. Butter and flour a deep cake pan and pour in batter, taking care not to fill the pan more than half full. Bake in 375 degree oven for 35 minutes, or until firm. Remove from oven, turn onto dish and sprinkle with powdered sugar and cinnamon.

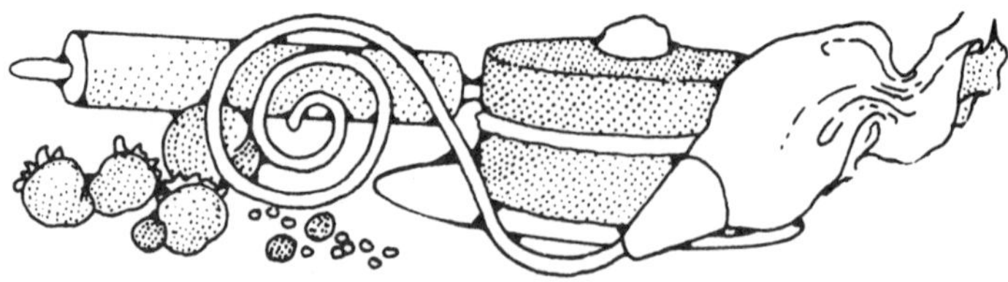

STRAWBERRY CREAM PIE

A beautiful pie! Glazed fresh strawberries are set on a snowy layer of soft cream cheese and whipping cream.

GRAHAM CRACKER CRUST

1¼ cups graham cracker crumbs
¼ cup sugar
6 tablespoons butter, melted

SPARKLING GLAZE

1 cup strawberries
¼ cup sugar
1 tablespoon cornstarch
¼ cup water
Red food coloring

CREAMY FILLING

6 ounces cream cheese, softened
½ cup powdered sugar
1 teaspoon vanilla
1 cup heavy cream, whipped
4 cups whole strawberries

Combine graham cracker crumbs and sugar, stir in butter. Mix well and press firmly into a 9-inch pie plate. Bake at 375 degrees for 5 to 8 minutes or until the edges are lightly browned, then cool. Blend cream cheese and powdered sugar. Stir in vanilla. Fold in whipped cream. Spread evenly in cooled crust. Refrigerate. Crush 1 cup strawberries. Combine ¼ cup sugar and cornstarch in small saucepan. Add water and crushed strawberries. Cook and stir over medium heat until clear and slightly thickened. Strain through sieve. Tint with food coloring and cool. Place whole strawberries, stem side down, on top of cream filling pressing slightly. Spoon glaze over berries and chill 3 hours.

ELEGANT STRAWBERRY PIE

½ tablespoon unflavored gelatin
¼ cup water
⅓ cup cream cheese, softened
6 tablespoons powdered sugar
1 teaspoon vanilla
1 cup heavy cream
¾ cup plain yogurt
1 (9-inch) pie shell, cooked and cooled
2 cups strawberries, hulled and halved
¼ cup strawberry jelly, melted

In a saucepan, combine gelatin with water and dissolve over low heat. Set aside. In a large mixing bowl, beat cream cheese with powdered sugar and vanilla until smooth and creamy. Add cream and beat until soft peaks form. Add dissolved gelatin and yogurt and beat until stiff. Pour into cooked pie shell and chill 3 hours. Before serving arrange berries on top and drizzle melted jelly over berries.

This is so good that you just can't eat one piece. My grandchildren always ask for this pie first.

cookies

GINGER ALMOND COOKIES

1 ½ cups butter or margarine
1 ½ cups granulated sugar
¾ cup honey
4 cups flour, unsifted
1 ½ teaspoons soda
1 ½ teaspoons salt
4 teaspoons ginger
1 tablespoon cinnamon
1 tablespoon cloves
1 ½ cups almonds, finely chopped

Cream butter and sugar until fluffy. Add honey in a fine stream. Mix dry ingredients and stir into creamed mixture. Add almonds. Shape in two thick rolls, each 2 inches in diameter. Wrap in wax paper and refrigerate several hours until very firm. Cut cookies in ¼-inch slices. Bake on lightly greased baking sheet at 350 degrees for 12 to 15 minutes.

Makes about 7 ½ dozen cookies

ANISE COOKIE STICKS

¾ cup butter
1 cup sugar
4 eggs
3 cups flour
3 teaspoons baking powder
½ teaspoon salt
1 teaspoon anise seed
1 cup nuts, chopped
Milk
Granulated sugar

Cream butter and sugar until light. Add eggs, one at a time, beating very well after each addition. Continue beating until very light and fluffy. Sift flour, baking powder, salt and anise seed together. Mix into creamed mixture. Stir in nuts. Divide dough into fourths. Place on greased cookie sheet. Form into 4 rolls 1 ½ inches wide and the length of the baking sheet. Bake at 350 degrees for 30 to 35 minutes. Remove from oven. Cut diagonally into ¾-inch slices. Place cut side down on cookie sheet, brush with milk and sprinkle with granulated sugar. Return to oven, bake 10 minutes longer until toasted and crisp.

APRICOT COCONUT CHEWS

1 box dried apricots (size is not that important)
2½ cups flaked coconut
1 (15-ounce) can sweetened condensed milk

Put apricots through a grinder. Combine with remaining ingredients. Mix well. Drop by scant teaspoonfuls onto greased cookie sheets. Bake at 375 degrees for 10 to 12 minutes, or until lightly browned on top and bottom.

Makes about 75 cookies

GRANDMA'S BUTTER BALLS

1 cup butter
2¼ cups flour
½ cup powdered sugar
½ cup chopped pecans
1 teaspoon vanilla
Pinch of salt

Mix all ingredients together in a bowl. Roll into small balls. Place on cookie sheets and bake at 325 degrees for 25 minutes. When cool, roll in powdered sugar.

JAM-FILLED BUTTER COOKIES

Blend until creamy:

½ cup butter
⅓ cup sugar or ½ cup brown sugar

Beat in:

1 egg
½ teaspoon vanilla
¼ teaspoon lemon rind, grated
1 cup all-purpose flour, sifted
⅓ teaspoon salt

Roll the dough into a ball. You may chill it briefly for easier handling. Pinch off pieces to roll into 1-inch balls. Roll the balls in sugar. Place them on a lightly greased and floured cookie sheet. Bake for 5 minutes. Depress the center of each cookie with your thumb. Continue baking until done, for about 8 minutes. When cool, fill the pits with a bit of jam or jelly, a preserved strawberry, a candied cherry, or pecan half or a dab of icing.

CARROT COOKIES

1 cup margarine
¾ cup sugar
1 cup cooked carrots, mashed
2 eggs
2 cups flour
2 teaspoons baking powder
½ teaspoon salt
¾ cup finely shredded coconut

Thoroughly combine the first 4 ingredients. Sift dry ingredients and add to mixture. Add coconut. Mix well. Drop by spoonfuls 2 inches apart on a lightly greased baking sheet. Bake in a 350 degree oven for 10 minutes or until lightly browned. While cookies are still warm, frost with orange icing.

ORANGE ICING

Powdered sugar, orange juice, 1 tablespoon butter, grated orange rind. Mix together until desired consistency.

Makes approximately 4 to 6 dozen

CHINESE CHEWS

1 cup dates, chopped
1 cup walnuts, chopped
1 cup granulated sugar
¾ cup flour
1 teaspoon baking powder
2 eggs, lightly beaten
¼ teaspoon salt
Powdered sugar

Mix dry ingredients together. Add dates, nuts, and eggs. Mix well. Spread out thinly on a greased cookie sheet. Bake in 325 degree oven for 20 minutes. Cut into squares and roll in powdered sugar.

HALLOWEEN CHOCOLATE BARS

½ cup margarine or butter
1 cup sugar
4 eggs
1 (1-pound) can chocolate syrup
1 teaspoon vanilla
1 cup flour
1 teaspoon baking powder
1 (10½-ounce) bag miniature marshmallows
1 cup pecans, chopped

Preheat oven to 350 degrees. Cream butter and sugar. Add eggs, one at a time, beating well after each addition. Add chocolate syrup and vanilla. Sift together flour and baking powder. Add to mixture beating well. Line a 9x13 pan with aluminum foil. Pour batter into pan and bake for 30 minutes. Remove from oven and immediately cover with marshmallows and pecans. Set aside for about 1 hour. Spoon topping onto cake and place in freezer about 20 minutes then refrigerate until serving time. Cut into 48 bars.

TOPPING

3 (1-ounce) squares unsweetened chocolate
1 cup margarine or butter
1 teaspoon vanilla
2 eggs
3 cups powdered sugar

Melt chocolate and butter. Let cool. Add vanilla, eggs and powdered sugar beating until smooth.

This is my husband's favorite excuse to have a Halloween party. He always says, "Jackie, you know Halloween is for big kids, too." In fact, these bars will be served all year long if your figure can take it.

Makes 48 bars

CHOCOLATE MINT PATTY COOKIE

¼ cup butter
¼ cup shortening
½ cup sugar
¼ cup brown sugar
1 egg
2 teaspoons water
1 teaspoon vanilla
1½ cups plus 2 tablespoons flour
½ teaspoon baking soda
¼ teaspoon salt
Approximately 3 dozen chocolate mint patties

Cream butter, shortening and sugars. Stir in egg, water and vanilla and beat well. Sift flour, soda and salt and stir into sugar mixture. Chill dough. Preheat oven to 400 degrees. Shape cookies by enclosing each chocolate mint patty in about 1 tablespoon of dough. Place 2 inches apart on a greased baking sheet. Bake 8 to 10 minutes, or until no imprint remains when touched lightly.

The grandkids love these and they will make any holiday table very festive . . .

Makes 3 dozen wonderful cookies

CRISPY CORNFLAKE COOKIES

1 cup sweet butter
1 cup sugar
1 egg
1 teaspoon vanilla
1½ cups flour
1 teaspoon baking powder
1 teaspoon baking soda
1¼ cups quick oatmeal
2 cups corn flakes, crushed

Cream butter and sugar; add egg and vanilla and beat well. Mix flour, soda, baking powder and add to sugar mixture. Beat well. Add oatmeal and corn flakes. Mix with a spoon. Roll dough into small balls and place 2 inches apart on a cookie sheet. Bake at 375 degrees for 10 to 12 minutes or until lightly browned.

Makes 4 dozen

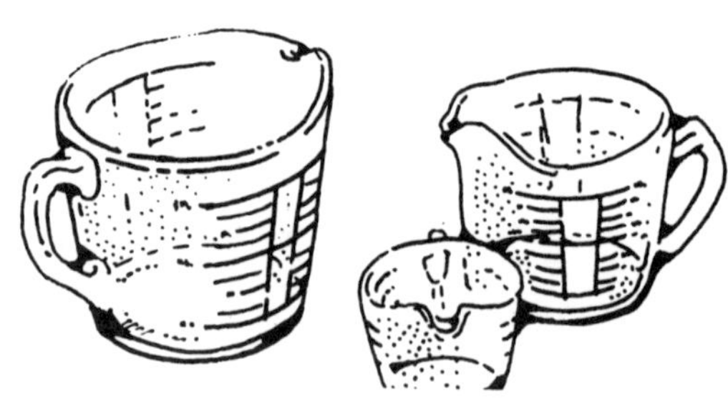

MOIST CRANBERRY APPLE COOKIES

½ cup butter or margarine
1 cup brown sugar
¾ cup sugar
1 egg
¼ cup milk
2 cups flour
1 teaspoon baking powder
1 teaspoon cinnamon
½ teaspoon salt
1 teaspoon orange rind, grated
1½ cups apples, pared and chopped
1 cup cranberries, chopped

Cream butter and sugars, beat in egg and milk. Sift together dry ingredients. Stir into butter mixture until well-blended. Stir in orange rind, apples and cranberries. Drop by teaspoonfuls onto greased cookie sheets. Bake at 375 degrees for 12 to 15 minutes.

Giving gifts of Christmas cookies is not a new idea or even an American tradition. According to an old Danish legend, no Christmas visitor is allowed to leave the house without taking a bag of Christmas cookies. Otherwise the host and hostess could run the risk of the holiday visitor carrying away the Christmas spirit in his empty hands. You needn't worry when you make these fabulous cookies.

Makes about 4 dozen

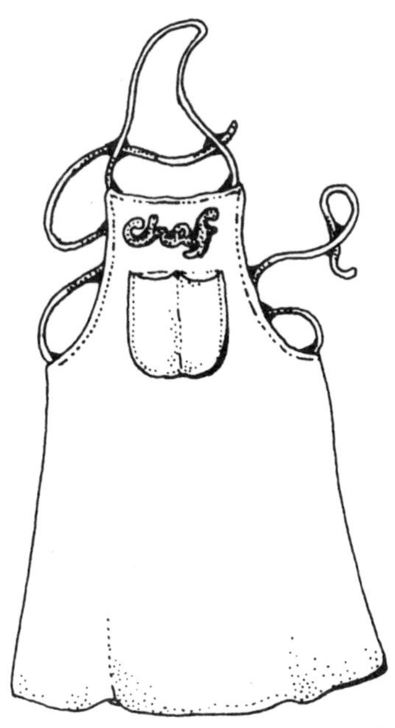

FIG FILLED COOKIES

½ cup shortening or butter
1 cup sugar
2 eggs
3½ cups flour
1 teaspoon soda
½ teaspoon salt
1 cup sour cream or buttermilk
1 teaspoon vanilla

Cream sugar and shortening and add vanilla. Add eggs and beat until fluffy. Sift together flour, soda and salt. Add dry ingredients alternately with egg-shortening mixture with sour milk beating after each addition. Set dough aside and prepare filling.

½ cup figs, chopped
½ cup sugar
2 tablespoons flour
1 cup water
½ cup nuts, chopped (optional)

Combine ingredients and stir until smooth. Cook until thickened, stirring constantly. Cool filling.

Roll out dough on a floured board to ⅛-inch thick and cut into 2-inch rounds. Put a teaspoon of the fig filling onto half the cookies. Cover with the remaining cookies and crimp edges together with a fork. Place 1-inch apart on a greased baking sheet. Bake 15 minutes at 375 degrees or until golden brown.

Makes 30

GRANDMA'S DEEP FRIED COOKIES

3 eggs
2 cups flour
3 tablespoons sugar
2 tablespoons butter, melted
¼ teaspoon salt
1 teaspoon vanilla
Powdered sugar
Oil for deep frying

Beat the eggs to blend whites and yolks. Add sugar, salt, butter and vanilla. Mix well. Add flour until dough is smooth and not sticky. Knead until well-blended and elastic. Wrap with wax paper and place in a bowl. Cover with a towel and let stand 1 hour. Pinch off pieces of dough and roll out very thin — then slit the center and slip one end through the slit. Fry in very hot oil until golden brown. Take from oil and dust with powdered sugar. These cookies are very fragile and must be handled with care.

GOOD 'N RICH COOKIES

½ cup butter
½ cup oil
½ cup powdered sugar
½ cup granulated sugar
Rind of 1 lemon, grated
1 egg yolk
2 cups flour
½ teaspoon soda
½ teaspoon cream of tartar
½ teaspoon salt
Almond or vanilla flavoring

Combine first 6 ingredients and beat well with an electric mixer. Sift dry ingredients together and stir into creamed mixture. Add flavoring and blend well. Form into small balls and place ½-inch apart on cookie sheet. Using a spring form wire whisk press down on each cookie to flatten and make a fancy design. Bake at 350 degrees for 15 minutes or until golden.

HALLOWEEN GUMDROP COOKIE BARS

1 cup brown sugar
1 pound orange and black gumdrops
⅓ cup shortening
1 cup nuts, finely chopped
2 cups flour
1 teaspoon baking soda
Pinch of salt
1 cup buttermilk
1 teaspoon vanilla
2 eggs, separated
Orange juice

Beat egg whites until stiff, set aside. Cut the gumdrops into small pieces and combine with remaining ingredients. Fold in beaten egg whites. Spoon mixture into a well-greased 12x8-inch cookie sheet. Bake in a 375 degree oven for 15 minutes. Cool and frost with 3 tablespoons of orange juice mixed to desired consistency with powdered sugar. Tint with a little orange food coloring to favorite shade for Halloween. Cut into squares.

Makes 2 to 3 dozen

PRUNE-FILLED HAMANTASHEN

½ pound butter or margarine
2 (8-ounce) packages cream cheese
2 cups flour
1 (12-ounce) package prunes, pitted
½ cup almond, chopped
½ cup orange marmalade
½ teaspoon cinnamon
2 tablespoons lemon juice
Powdered sugar

Have butter and cheese at room temperature. Cream butter, add cheese and beat together until light and fluffy. Stir in flour and mix to blend. Wrap in plastic wrap or foil and chill for three hours. Meanwhile, prepare filling. Snip prunes, combine with almonds, marmalade, cinnamon and lemon juice and cook over low heat a few minutes, just until thickened. Roll chilled pastry out on a board well sprinkled with powdered sugar. Cut into 3-inch circles. Place a spoonful of filling in center of each circle. Fold dough over from both sides and pinch together in point at base. Fold 2 top corners to form triangle with filling at center. Place on greased baking sheet and bake at 375 degrees about 30 minutes, until golden brown.

ITALIAN DEAD BONE COOKIES

3 egg whites
1¾ cups sugar
½ teaspoon lemon peel
½ teaspoon baking powder
1½ cups almonds, coarsely chopped
1¾ cups all-purpose flour, unsifted

With an electric mixer beat egg whites, sugar, lemon peel and baking powder until smoothly blended. With a heavy spoon work nuts into egg white mixture then flour. Lightly flour hands and pinch off a tablespoon of dough. Shape into a bone. Bake on a greased cookie sheet in a preheated oven at 375 degrees for 10 to 12 minutes. Cool on a wire rack.

Makes 2½ dozen

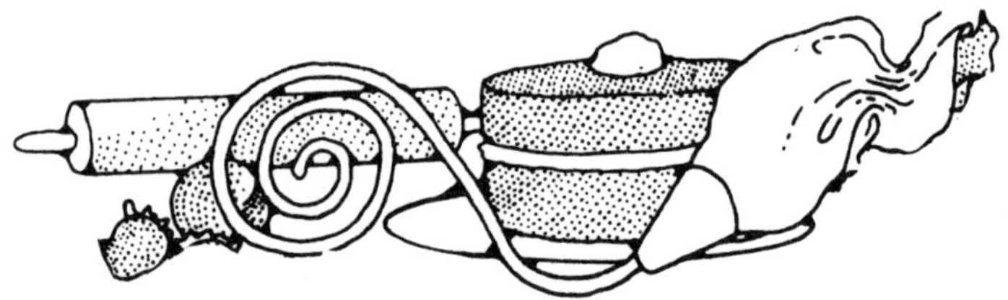

KRUSTI

1½ cups flour
2 eggs
½ teaspoon salt
¼ cup water
1 tablespoon rum
Oil for frying
Powdered sugar

Sift flour and salt. Add eggs, water and rum. Beat well to make a stiff dough, adding more flour if necessary. Knead well until dough becomes elastic. Roll out dough to paper thin. Cut in strips 6-inches long by 1½ inches wide. Put a slit in the center of the Krusti and twist an end through the slit. Fry in moderately hot oil until brown, about 2 to 3 minutes. Drain on paper towels. Dust with powdered sugar.

LACE COOKIES

½ cup light corn syrup
½ cup brown sugar
½ cup margarine (1 cube)
¾ cup flour, unsifted
½ cup nuts, chopped
1 teaspoon vanilla

Melt margarine, sugar and syrup over low heat. Stir flour, nuts and vanilla into this mixture. Mix well and drop by small teaspoonfuls onto a lightly greased cookie sheet 5 to 6 inches apart, as they spread very thin and crispy. Bake at 350 degrees 8 to 10 minutes. Don't let them get too dark. Wait a few minutes before removing from pan.

HOLIDAY LIQUEUR BARS

1½ cups graham cracker crumbs
1 cup toasted almonds
½ cup butter or margarine
¼ cup granulated sugar
⅓ cup cocoa
1 egg, lightly beaten
2 teaspoons vanilla
6 teaspoons of your favorite liqueur
6 tablespoons sweet butter
1 tablespoon milk or cream
1¾ cups powdered sugar
4-ounces semi-sweet chocolate

Combine graham cracker crumbs and almonds, put in the bottom of a 7x11x12-inch baking pan and set aside. In a small saucepan combine butter, sugar, cocoa, egg and vanilla. Cook over low heat about 4 minutes stirring constantly. Pour over crumb mixture and mix together well. Now press layer onto bottom of pan. Drizzle with 3 tablespoons of your liqueur and place pan in freezer. Cream sweet butter, milk and 3 tablespoons liqueur. Gradually add powdered sugar. Mix until smooth and creamy. Spread on graham cracker mixture and return to freezer until firm. Melt 1½ tablespoons butter with chocolate over low heat. Spread quickly over chilled layers. Chocolate will harden quickly so you must work fast.

These will keep well refrigerated or may be frozen.

Makes 36 bars

LUNCH BOX FAVORITES

2 cups all-purpose flour
2 cups mashed potato flakes
1 cup granulated sugar
1 cup brown sugar, firmly packed
1 cup nuts, finely chopped
1 cup butter or margarine, melted
1 teaspoon baking soda
1 teaspoon lemon peel, grated
2 eggs

Combine all ingredients in a large bowl and mix well. Form into 1-inch balls pressing firmly. Roll in granulated sugar. Place balls about 2 inches apart on an ungreased cookie sheet. Bake at 375 degrees for 10 minutes. Cool 1 minute before removing from cookie sheet.

Makes about 5 dozen

MACAROONS

5 egg whites
1½ pounds powdered sugar (approximately 4 cups)
1 pound blanched almonds, finely ground or use
½ pound almonds and ½ pound coconut, grated
4 tablespoons matzo meal
Rind of 2 lemons, grated

Beat egg whites stiff. Fold in ingredients in the order given. Drop mixture from tip of teaspoon onto cookie sheet covered with brown or parchment paper. Leave about 1-inch between cookies. Bake 15 minutes at 300 degrees then raise to 350 degrees and bake 15 minutes more until browned. Cool before removing to serving plate.

OATMEAL FUDGE COOKIES

½ cup butter
2 cups sugar
½ cup cocoa
½ cup evaporated milk
1 cup miniature marshmallows
1 teaspoon vanilla
3 cups quick cooking oats
1 cup nuts, chopped

In a saucepan combine sugar, cocoa, milk and butter. Boil 1 minute. Add miniature marshmallows and vanilla. Stir until dissolved. Place nuts and oats in a large bowl. Pour chocolate mixture over all. Mix and drop by spoonful onto wax paper.

Makes about 4 dozen

OLD FASHIONED OATMEAL HERMITS

1 cup brown sugar
1 cup butter or margarine
2 eggs
1 cup sour milk
1 teaspoon baking soda
1 teaspoon vanilla
2 cups rolled oats
2 cups flour
1 cup nuts, chopped
1 cup raisins
2 teaspoons cinnamon

Cream sugar and butter. Add eggs, beat well. Add milk mixed with soda and vanilla. Add oatmeal, flour, cinnamon, nuts and raisins. Drop from teaspoon onto cookie sheet. Bake at 375 degrees for about 20 minutes.

Wonderful for lunch.

Makes about 5 dozen

NO BAKE PEANUT BUTTER BARS

2 cups graham cracker crumbs
1 box powdered sugar
2 cubes butter or margarine, melted
1 teaspoon vanilla
1 cup peanut butter (whichever type you prefer)
1 (12-ounce) bag of chocolate chips

Mix together the first 5 ingredients. Press into a 9x13-inch pan. Melt chocolate chips and spread over batter. Chill. When set remove from the fridge and when at room temperature cut into small bars.

Makes 24 bars

PEANUT BUTTER BARS

2 sticks margarine
2⅓ cups powdered sugar
1 cup peanut butter
1¾ cups graham crackers, crushed
1 large package milk chocolate chips

Melt margarine, add powdered sugar, peanut butter and graham cracker crumbs. Spread in a buttered 9x13-inch dish. Melt chocolate chips and spread over peanut butter mixture and chill.

PEANUT BRITTLE COOKIES

1 cup flour
¼ teaspoon baking soda
½ teaspoon cinnamon
½ cup butter
½ cup brown sugar
1 egg plus 2 tablespoons beaten egg
1 teaspoon vanilla
1 cup peanuts, finely chopped

Sift together flour, soda and cinnamon. Gradually add brown sugar to butter. Cream well. Blend in the 2 tablespoons of beaten egg and vanilla. Add dry ingredients and ½ cup of the peanuts. Mix thoroughly. Spread or pat dough on a 15x10x2-inch greased baking sheet. Brush with remaining egg and top with remaining peanuts. Bake in a 325 degree oven 20 to 25 minutes. Do not overbake. Cut or break into pieces while warm.

Crispy, crunchy, peanutty, wonderful! Make extra batches - they don't last.

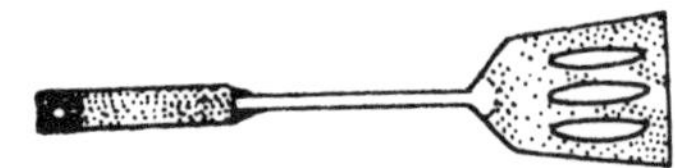

PINE NUT COOKIES

4 eggs
1½ cups granulated sugar
½ teaspoon lemon rind, grated
Few drops oil of anise
2¼ cups all-purpose flour
¼ teaspoon salt
Powdered sugar
Pine nuts

Put eggs and granulated sugar in top part of double boiler over hot water. Beat with rotary beater until mixture is lukewarm. Remove from water, beat until foaming and cool. Add flavorings and fold in flour and salt. Drop by teaspoonful onto greased and floured cookie sheets. Sprinkle with powdered sugar and nuts. Let stand for 10 minutes. Bake in preheated 375 degree oven for about 10 minutes.

Makes about 5 dozen

POINSETTIA COOKIES

2 cups powdered sugar
1 cup butter
2 eggs
1 teaspoon vanilla
½ teaspoon rum extract
3 cups flour
1 teaspoon salt
1 cup coconut, shredded
1 cup butterscotch chips
Granulated sugar
½ cup candied red cherries cut into wedges

Beat together powdered sugar and butter. Add eggs and extracts. Sift together flour and salt and stir into butter mixture. Add coconut and ¾ cup of the butterscotch morsels. Chill dough until firm. Roll into 1-inch balls. Place on ungreased cookie sheets. Flatten cookie with bottom of a glass dipped in granulated sugar. Place a butterscotch morsel in the center of each cookie. Place cherry wedges in a circle to resemble a poinsettia. Bake at 375 degrees about 12 minutes.

These are not only beautiful on your holiday table but they are delicious as well.

Makes about 5 dozen

RASPBERRY FINGERS

LAYER 1

1 cup flour
1 teaspoon baking powder
½ cup butter
1 egg, beaten
1 tablespoon milk
1 (10-ounce) jar raspberry preserves

LAYER 2

1 cup sugar
1 tablespoon butter
1 egg, beaten
2 cups fine coconut
1 teaspoon vanilla

Mix first 5 ingredients of layer 1 together and press in a 9x13-inch pan. Spread with preserves. Mix all ingredients of layer 2 together. Spread on top of preserves. Bake at 275 degrees for 25 to 30 minutes. Refrigerate before serving.

Makes 2 dozen bars

RUGELAHS

1 cup flour
½ cup sweet butter, softened to room temperature
¼ pound cream cheese, softened to room temperature
Sugar
Cinnamon
Chopped nuts
Raisins (optional)
Jam

In a bowl cream butter, cream cheese and flour forming a dough. Cover tightly with wax paper and refrigerate overnight. The next day, divide the dough into thirds, then roll each third out into a circle. Spread each dough circle with jam and sprinkle with any desired mixture of sugar, cinnamon, nuts and raisins. Cut into pie wedges then roll each wedge up from the outer side in. Shape into crescents. In an ungreased shallow baking dish in a 375 degree oven, bake rugelahs for 30 minutes.

RUMPOT COOKIES

1 cup butter or margarine
1 cup brown sugar
2 eggs
⅔ cup liquid from any of the rumpots
4 cups flour, sifted
1 teaspoon soda
½ teaspoon salt
½ teaspoon nutmeg
½ teaspoon cinnamon
1 cup dates, chopped
1 cup white raisins
3 cups brandied fruits, well-drained
1 cup nut meats, broken (optional)

Cream butter and sugar well then add unbeaten eggs. Mix fruit with 1 cup flour to prevent sticking together. Sift remaining ingredients together, add alternately with rumpot liquid. Add floured fruits and nuts if desired. Mix well. Chill dough overnight. Drop by generous teaspoons onto greased cookie sheets. Bake at 300 degrees for 10 to 20 minutes.

SNOWBALLS

¼ cup butter
4 cups miniature marshmallows
5 cups crisp rice cereal
1⅓ cups flaked coconut
½ cup crushed hard peppermint candy or other hard flavored candy (optional)

Melt butter in a large saucepan. Add marshmallows. Cook over low heat until marshmallows are melted and the mixture resembles syrup. Remove from heat. Add cereal. Stir until well-coated. With buttered hands shape into 24 balls about 2 inches in diameter. Roll in coconut and hard candy. Cool. May be frozen in an airtight container.

Makes about 2 dozen

FAVORITE SOFT COOKIES

½ cup sour cream
2 eggs
1 cup sugar
2 teaspoons vanilla
½ teaspoon nutmeg
4 cups Bisquick
1 cup semi-sweet mini chocolate chips

In a 2-quart mixing bowl beat with an electric mixer on high speed the sour cream and eggs until smooth. Beat in sugar, the vanilla and nutmeg. Beat in half of the Bisquick till very smooth. Remove beaters and using a large mixing spoon work in the rest of the Bisquick and then the mini chips. Preheat oven to 400 degrees and spray cookie sheet with Pam. Place empty cookie sheet in oven for 2 minutes or until the Pam turns brown. Wipe off with a paper towel. Drop cookie dough onto hot cookie sheet by level tablespoons 2 inches apart. Grease a flat bottomed glass and dip into sugar then slightly flatten each cookie before baking. Dip glass into the sugar for each cookie but do not regrease glass. Bake at 400 degrees for exactly 6 minutes. Cookies will appear slightly cracked on the surface and white in color with only a light brown around the edges. DO NOT OVERBAKE. Let cookies cool an baking sheet 2 minutes before carefully removing them to continue cooling on paper towels.

Makes 6 dozen

ROLLED SPICED CHRISTMAS COOKIES

4 cups flour
1¾ cups sugar
1 teaspoon allspice
1 teaspoon cinnamon
1½ cups butter
2 eggs, lightly beaten
3 tablespoons cold water

Sift together first 4 ingredients. Cut in butter until mixture resembles coarse meal. Stir in eggs and water mixing well. Dough will be stiff but do not add more water. Chill until dough can be handled easily, at least an hour. Roll out ⅛ inch thickness on a lightly floured board. Cut with assorted cookie cutters. Bake on an ungreased cookie sheet in a 400 degree oven 7 to 8 minutes or until lightly browned around the edges. Cool on racks. Frost as desired or decorate with colored sugars, cinnamon drops or bits of candied fruits.

This makes your whole house smell like Christmas and all the children love to help decorate these cookies. Merry Christmas from my kitchen to yours.

Makes about 9 dozen of assorted shapes and sizes

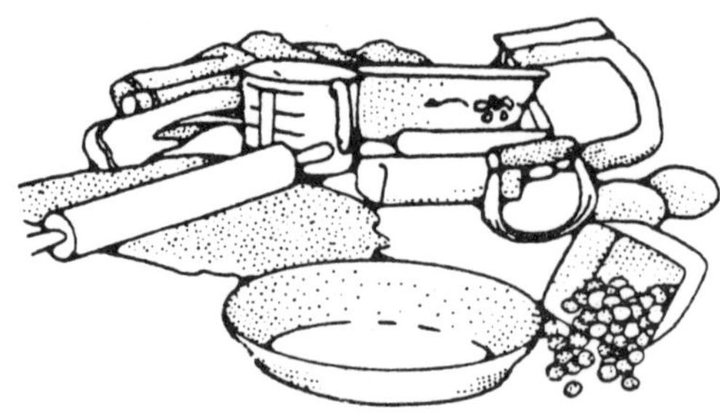

EASY SUGAR COOKIES

1 ½ cups sugar
1 cup butter, softened
3 egg yolks
½ teaspoon baking soda
1 teaspoon cream of tartar
½ teaspoon vanilla
½ teaspoon lemon juice
2½ cups flour

Mix in the order given and roll into small balls. Roll in granulated sugar. Place on ungreased cookie sheet and flatten with a fork. Bake at 350 degrees 10 to 12 minutes.

Makes about 3 dozen

candy & nuts

CHRISTMAS CHERRY BON-BONS

1 can cherry pie filling
1 large can pineapple, crushed and drained
1 can sweetened condensed milk
1 medium-size carton whipped topping
¼ teaspoon salt
1 teaspoon vanilla
1 teaspoon almond extract
Pecans, finely chopped
Maraschino cherries

Mix the first 7 ingredients together in a large bowl. Spoon into individual paper baking cups and place in muffin tins. Sprinkle with pecans and place a cherry in the center of each cup. Freeze. Remove paper cup and put in dessert dish when serving.

Makes 24 to 30

NEW YORK FRENCH CHOCOLATE BALLS

1 (14-ounce) can sweetened condensed milk
2 squares unsweetened chocolate

Heat milk in double boiler. Melt chocolate in milk then chill until workable. Use ½ to 1 teaspoonful to make balls. Roll in chopped nuts, multi-colored sprinkles, coconut or chocolate sprinkles or any other coating or leave plain.

Makes 1 dozen

CRACKY-JACKS

2 cups sugar
2 tablespoons white corn syrup
½ stick butter
½ cup water
¼ teaspoon salt
1 teaspoon vanilla
½ teaspoon baking soda
1 cup salted peanuts
1 gallon popped corn

Combine sugar, syrup, butter, water and salt in a saucepan. Cook until brown spots appear or to the hard-cooked stage. Add vanilla, soda and nuts. Stir and pour over the popped corn. Turn out on wax paper and pull apart when cooled. Great for nibbling, especially while playing cards.

FRUIT SLICES

3 tablespoons unflavored gelatin
¾ cup water
3 cups sugar
1 cup boiling water
Flavoring & coloring

Soften gelatin in ¾ cup water. Combine sugar and boiling water and add to gelatin. Bring to boil to 222 degrees. Remove from heat and add orange, lemon or lime flavoring to taste. Add coloring as desired. Pour in 8x8-inch wet pan and let stand 12 hours in a cool place (not refrigerated). Loosen around edges with a sharp knife, turn out on wax paper. Dredge in granulated sugar.

FABULOUS HOLIDAY FUDGE

1 (13½ ounce) can evaporated milk
1⅓ cubes butter
4½ cups sugar
Pinch of salt
2 (7-ounce) jars marshmallow cream
1 (12½ ounce) chocolate almond candy bar, broken in pieces
1 (12-ounce) package chocolate chips
1 pound walnuts, chopped
2 teaspoons vanilla

Combine milk, butter, sugar and salt in a large heavy saucepan. Cook, stirring constantly, for 6 minutes. Combine marshmallow cream, candy bar and chocolate chips in a large bowl. Pour hot syrup over mixture, stir until chocolate is melted. Stir in walnuts and vanilla. Pour into a lightly buttered 9x13-inch baking dish.

If there's a better tasting fudge, I've yet to taste it.

MAGIC FRENCH FUDGE

3 cups semi-sweet chocolate morsels
1 (14-ounce) can sweetened condensed milk
Dash salt
1½ teaspoons vanilla extract
½ cup nuts, chopped (optional)

In top of double boiler, melt chocolate over boiling water, stirring occasionally. Remove from heat, stir in milk, salt, vanilla and nuts. Spread mixture evenly into a wax paper-lined 8x8-inch baking pan. Chill 2 hours or until firm. Turn fudge onto cutting board, peel off paper and cut into squares. Tightly cover any leftovers.

Makes about 1¾ pounds

MEXICAN FUDGE

2 cups sugar
⅔ cup milk
1 teaspoon vanilla
3 tablespoons butter
1 cup nuts, chopped

Place 1½ cups sugar and the milk in a heavy saucepan. Bring to a boil. Meanwhile, carmelize the ½ cup sugar in a small pan. Add sugar mixture to milk, stirring constantly, until sugar dissolves. Boil until mixture reaches soft-ball stage or until candy thermometer reaches 236 degrees. Remove from heat. Add butter and vanilla. Beat until thick. Fold in nuts. Pour into buttered 8-inch pan. When firm, cut into squares.

Makes about 1 pound

CHRISTMAS PEANUT BUTTER FUDGE

2 cups sugar
1 cup milk
1 (7-ounce) jar marshmallow creme
1 (12-ounce) jar crunchy peanut butter
1 teaspoon vanilla

Combine sugar and milk in a large heavy saucepan. Slowly bring to a boil. Cook, stirring to soft-ball stage (238 degrees). Remove from heat and add remaining ingredients. Beat until well-blended. Pour into a buttered 9-inch pan and cool. When fudge has set, cut into squares.

PEANUT BUTTER FUDGE

⅔ cup milk
2 cups granulated sugar
1 cup marshmallow fluff
1 cup crunchy peanut butter
1 teaspoon vanilla
½ cup dates, chopped

Combine milk and sugar in a saucepan. Boil without stirring to 240 degrees. Soft-ball forms when a little is dropped in cold water. Remove from heat. Add marshmallow fluff, peanut butter, vanilla and dates. Stir only until combined. Pour into greased pan 8-inches square. Place in refrigerator at least 20 minutes before cutting. Cut into 1-inch squares.

Makes 5 dozen

GOLDBRICKS

1 large package chocolate chips
4 cups pecans
1 (7-ounce) jar marshmallow creme
1 large can evaporated milk
3½ cups sugar
2 sticks butter

Place chocolate chips, pecans and marshmallow creme in a large bowl. Butter the sides and the bottom of a large pan. Place milk, sugar and butter in a pan over medium heat and let come to a boil. Boil for 10 minutes. Remove from heat and pour over mixture in bowl. Stir vigorously until well-blended. Pour into buttered pan. Refrigerate until completely cooled.

Makes 5 pounds

HALVA

¾ cup butter (1½ sticks)
2 cups flour
¾ cup sugar
2 tablespoons water
½ cup walnuts or almonds, coarsely chopped (optional)

Melt butter, add flour and stir until mixture is a thick paste. Continue cooking over a low heat for 25 to 35 minutes, stirring frequently to keep the mass browning slowly and evenly. The use of an asbestos pad under the saucepan will reduce the amount of stirring needed. When the mixture is a light caramel color, bring sugar and water to boil in a separate saucepan. Boil until the syrup will form a thin thread at the end of a spoon dipped in the pot and held vertically over it. Pour the syrup into the cooked flour mixture and add the chopped nuts. Stir to blend thoroughly and immediately pour the mass onto a large plate or marble slab. Press it into a thick rectangle with a knife and cut it into bars before it cools.

Makes 6 to 8 bars

MARZIPAN

Rose water is the traditional flavoring. Buy it at a drugstore.

1 cup almond paste
1 cup powdered sugar
Few drops rose water or orange extract

Mix ingredients thoroughly and put on a marble slab or a chilled platter. Knead 20 minutes. Shape with your fingers into tiny fruits and vegetables. Paint with food coloring or dip in a small bowl of coloring. Tuck in cloves for stems and bits of angelica as leaves. Set on a cake rack to dry. For a Christmas glitter, crystallize. To crystallize: Cook 5 pounds sugar with 2½ cups water to 223 degrees. Do not stir after the sugar is dissolved. Remove from the heat very gently and let stand undisturbed until perfectly cold. Place shaped and painted marzipan in a pan in a single layer. Cover completely with the syrup, pouring it with as little agitation as possible. Let stand at least 8 hours. Drain in a sieve. Dry on a wire rack.

ORANGE BALLS

1 (12-ounce) package vanilla wafers
1 pound powdered sugar
1 (6-ounce) can frozen orange juice, thawed
1 stick margarine, chopped
1 cup pecans, chopped
1 small can angel flake coconut

Crush wafers finely. Mix with sugar, orange juice, margarine and nuts. Roll into small balls, then roll in coconut. Refrigerate.

Makes 4 dozen

PEANUT BUTTER MORSEL BARS

2 cups sugar
2 cups light corn syrup
1 pound jar peanut butter
8 cups Special 'K' cereal
1 (6-ounce) package butterscotch morsels
1 (6-ounce) package chocolate chips

Bring sugar and syrup to a boil. Add peanut butter and cook, stirring until well-blended. It will appear like thick brown gravy. Remove from the heat and pour hot mixture over the cereal, mix quickly. Spread in a greased 9x13-inch pan. Sprinkle butterscotch morsels and chocolate chips over top. Press morsels into bar mixture lightly with a spoon. When cool, cut into bars and store at room temperature.

Makes 5 dozen bars

PEANUT HEALTH CANDY

1 cup non-fat dry milk crystals
1 cup peanut butter
1 cup honey
½ cup sesame seeds, toasted
½ cup wheat germ
1 egg white, slightly beaten
1½ cups peanuts, finely chopped

Combine the milk crystals, peanut butter, honey, sesame seeds and wheat germ. Knead with hands until a smooth ball is formed. Cut into 36 pieces. Roll each piece into a ball. Dip balls into the beaten egg white. Drain excess and roll balls in chopped peanuts. Let dry at room temperature. Store in an airtight container in a cool, dry place.

Makes 3 dozen

CANDIED PINEAPPLE

2 cups sugar
1 cup water
1 (20-ounce) can pineapple, sliced
Granulated sugar

Boil sugar in water until a thread forms when syrup is poured from a spoon. Cut pineapple into pieces and drop into boiling syrup. Cook 10 minutes. Lift pineapple out of the syrup, drain and lay on oiled paper. After 24 hours, roll in granulated sugar. Repeat each day until fruit is dry.

CANDIED POPCORN

6 cups popped corn
⅔ cup sugar
½ cup water
2½ tablespoons white corn syrup
⅛ teaspoon salt
⅓ teaspoon vinegar

Combine last five ingredients and stir until the sugar is dissolved. Bring to a boil and cover. Cook, covered, for about 3 minutes (the steam from the cooking will wash down the sides of the pan). Remove cover and without stirring bring to the hard-crack stage (290 degrees). Be sure the heat is not to hot. Add coloring (if more than one color is desired, divide the sugar syrup and color as desired). Use plenty of coloring dye. Pour the syrup over the popped corn, stir with a wooden spoon until well-coated. When it is cool enough to handle and still somewhat sticky, mold with the hands which have been lightly buttered. This can be forced into molds. Be sure you ram the corn tightly into the nooks and crannies of the mold.

POTATO CANDY

¾ cup mashed potatoes
1½ cups sugar
1 teaspoon lemon juice
1 cup cornflakes, crushed
1 cup walnuts, chopped

Stir sugar into potatoes, mixing well. Add remaining ingredients and mix again. Press mixture into a buttered 9x9-inch baking pan and let stand 24 hours (no cooking). Cut into squares and serve sprinkled with powdered sugar if desired.

Makes 2 dozen

MY FAMILY PRALINES

In a heavy saucepan, combine 2 cups light brown sugar, firmly packed. Do not use the dark brown sugar. Add ¼ cup water and ⅓ cup butter. Heat gently to melt the butter and dissolve sugar, then bring to a good boil and add 2 cups whole pecans. Boil until a small sample cracks when tested in cold water. Remove from heat, and when the boiling stops, drop from a large spoon onto wax paper which has been placed on several thicknesses of cloth or terry towel. Remove pralines from paper as soon as firm.

This has been shared by my family for so many years and I hope your family will enjoy this as much as we have. As time goes on as time always does, I have found out what every woman knows . . . that a secret kept isn't any fun. It must be shared with every one.

Makes 18 large ones

CREAMY PRALINES

1 cup buttermilk
2 tablespoons corn syrup
2 cups sugar
¼ teaspoon salt
1 teaspoon soda
1 teaspoon vanilla
2 tablespoons butter
1 cup pecan halves

Stir together buttermilk, corn syrup, sugar, salt and soda. Cook, stirring constantly, over low heat until mixture comes to a boil. Cook, without stirring, to 236 degrees. Remove from heat, add vanilla and butter. Let cool to 120 degrees. Beat until creamy and candy loses its gloss. Stir in nuts and quickly drop by spoonfuls onto wax paper.

Makes about 2 pounds

SPONGE CANDY

1 cup sugar
1 cup dark corn syrup
1 tablespoon vinegar
1 tablespoon baking soda

Combine sugar, corn syrup and vinegar in heavy saucepan. Cook and stir over medium heat until sugar is dissolved. Continue cooking without stirring until candy thermometer reads 300 degrees. Remove from heat and quickly stir in baking soda (it will foam up). Mix well. Pour into buttered 9x9x2-inch pan. Do not spread. Cool. Break into bite-sized pieces.

TERRIFIC TAFFY

3 tablespoons butter
⅓ cup vinegar
1 cup cold water
3 cups sugar
1 teaspoon vanilla
Red food coloring

Melt the butter in a 4-quart saucepan. Add the vinegar, water and sugar. Stir until dissolved. Wash down the sides of the pan by putting the lid on the pan and boiling for 3 minutes. Continue to cook, without stirring, to soft-crack stage (about 270 degrees). Pour into a buttered baking pan that has straight sides. Turn in the edges as it cools. Add vanilla and a drop or two of red food coloring to make a delicate shade of pink. Begin stretching as soon as you can handle the candy (it will still be very hot). Stretch with the finger tips until it cools and is hard to pull. Stretch into ropes approximately ½ to ¾-inch thick. Cut or break into pieces. Wrap in wax paper.

GLAZED NUTS

2 tablespoons cold water
1 egg white, slightly beaten
½ cup sugar
½ teaspoon salt
¼ teaspoon cinnamon
¼ teaspoon cloves
¼ teaspoon allspice
2 cups whole pecans

Add water to egg white. Stir in sugar, salt and spices. Mix well. Add nuts and stir until coated. Place nuts flat side down on a greased cookie sheet. Bake at 250 degrees for 1 hour. Remove from pan immediately. Terrific!!!

Makes 2 cups

TRICK OR TREAT NUTS

2 cups sugar
½ cup orange juice
1 tablespoon white vinegar
¼ cup orange peel, grated (takes about 3 large oranges)
½ pound whole blanched almonds
½ pound walnut or pecan halves

Butter a jelly roll pan and set aside. Place the sugar and the orange juice in a large saucepan and bring the mixture to a boil. Insert your candy thermometer, add the vinegar and boil syrup until it reaches 300 degrees, or the hard-crack stage when put into cold water. Remove the syrup from the heat and add the orange peel and the nuts. Stir to coat the nuts evenly. Press mixture into the prepared pan, flattening with spatula. Cool. Separate the nuts by breaking into pieces. Store in an air-tight container.

Makes 4 cups

canning & misc.

ZUCCHINI CHOW CHOW

10 cups zucchini, ground
4 cups onions, ground
2 bell peppers, ground
5 tablespoons salt
1 quart vinegar
7 cups sugar
1 teaspoon nutmeg
1 teaspoon turmeric
1 teaspoon dry mustard
1 teaspoon cornstarch
2 teaspoons celery seed

Combine zucchini, onions, peppers and salt. Let stand overnight covered. Rinse well with cold water and drain extremely well. Press firmly to remove all the water. This is important. The next day, add vinegar, sugar , nutmeg, turmeric, dry mustard, cornstarch and celery seed. Bring to a boil. Simmer 30 minutes. Place in sterilized jars and seal.

Makes about 14 pints

DRIED FRUIT CHUTNEY

1 pound dried peaches
1 pound dried apricots
1 pound pitted dates
1 pound golden raisins, seeded
1 pound seedless raisins
½ pound currants
3 cups sugar
¾ pint vinegar
2 tablespoons salt
2 tablespoons red pepper
1 tablespoon cloves, powdered
4 tablespoons garlic, shredded

Cut peaches, apricots and dates into small pieces. Add small amount of water and cook until soft. Add remaining ingredients and cook gently for 20 minutes, stirring occasionally. Remove from heat. Ladle into hot, sterilized jars to within ¼-inch from top. Seal at once.

MANGO CHUTNEY

2 pounds half-ripe mangos
4 cups good cider vinegar
5 pounds white sugar
½ pounds golden raisins, seeded
2 tablespoons whole cloves
4 small, dried red chilies
½ pound preserved gingerroot
1 tablespoon salt

Pare the mangos and cut into pieces about ½-inch thick and 1-inch long. Use a heavy iron kettle for the cooking. Bring the vinegar to a boil. Add the sugar and stir well. Bring to a boil again, then simmer for 5 minutes. Add the other ingredients and simmer till the fruit is transparent. Arrange the fruit, spices and peppers in an attractive manner in hot sterilized jar. Pour the hot syrup over them and seal. Let stand for several days or even weeks before using, as this chutney improves with age.

EASY APRICOT JAM

You can put up any size batch of jam you like with this simple recipe. Wash thoroughly ripe apricots, remove pits but do not peel. Cut the fruit into fairly small pieces. Measure fruit and add with equal measure of sugar. Let stand for several hours or overnight for the juices to form. Cook, stirring, until the jam reaches the desired consistency, considering that it will firm just a little when it is cool. Pour hot jam into sterilized jars and seal.

This is a great way to start making jams because it is so foolproof. Makes a nice gift for the holiday season.

FIG JAM

4 cups (2 pounds) ripe figs
Juice of 2 lemons
8 cups sugar
1 bottle liquid pectin

Remove stems and ends from figs and chop thoroughly. Place figs in a large kettle and stir in lemon juice and sugar. Crush figs further with a spoon while stirring. Bring mixture to a full boil over high heat, stirring constantly. Boil 1 minute and remove from heat. Stir in pectin and skim. Pour quickly into sterilized jars and cover with lids of paraffin. Store in a cool place.

Makes 12 (8-ounce) jars

Variations: Substitute 1 cup fresh strawberries, apricots, peaches or rhubarb for 1 cup of figs. Season with cinnamon.

PEACH FIG JAM

3 pounds peaches (about 7 medium-sized)
5 pounds figs (about 3 dozen small)
⅓ cup water
5 pounds sugar
⅛ teaspoon cinnamon

Peel the peaches and the figs. Cut into small pieces. In a large pan combine the fruit with a potato masher, add sugar and cinnamon. Cook slowly, stirring often and cook until almost as thick as you like. The jam will tighten a little when cooled. Pour into hot sterilized jars and seal.

Makes about 10 cups

PINEAPPLE-STRAWBERRY JAM

4 cups prepared fruit (1 medium fully ripe pineapple and about 1 quart fully ripe strawberries)
7 cups sugar
1 package pectin

First, pare the pineapple then grind or finely chop. Thoroughly crush one layer at a time about 1 quart strawberries. Combine fruit and measure 4 cups into a 6 or 8-quart saucepot. To make the jam, thoroughly mix sugar into fruit in the pan. Place over high heat and bring to a full rolling boil and boil hard for 1 minute stirring constantly . Remove from heat and at once stir in fruit pectin. Ladle quickly into hot jars, filling within ¼-inch of top. Cover and process in water bath for 5 minutes.

Easy and Wonderful!

Makes about 8 cups of simply fabulous jam

BUTTERMILK OR YOGURT JELLY

⅓ box vegetable gelatin (¼ ounce)
1½ cups buttermilk or yogurt
½ cup heavy cream
Juice and grated rind of 2 lemons
1 cup boiling water

Prepare the vegetable gelatin according to directions for the use of vegetable gelatin.* Add the cream, lemon and the cooked vegetable gelatin to the buttermilk and turn into molds. When set serve with mayonnaise dressing.

* Soak the vegetable gelatin in warm water for 20 to 30 minutes. Remove from this water and put in boiling water, 3 cups to the box, keeping covered while cooking. Let boil 8 to 10 minutes or until it is perfectly clear. Strain through a wire sieve or strainer.

Makes approximately 3 cups

PICKLED LIMES

Boil 1½ cups salt water with 20 cups water. Wash fully ripe plump limes and pack in screw top gallon jar. Pour salted boiling water to cover and screw cap tightly. Place in dark area for at least 6 to 7 weeks. Once a week, turn jar upside down to distribute salt. When limes are fully cured, they will be a lovely yellow color (not before). Adjust recipe for the amount of limes you wish to make.

GOLDEN LEMON MARMALADE

1 pound carrots
2 medium lemons
3¾ cups sugar
½ teaspoon salt
½ cup water
⅓ cup Maraschino cherries, sliced

Clean carrots and quarter and seed the lemons. Put through the fine blade of grinder. You need 3 cups of chopped carrots to ¾ cup chopped lemon. In a large kettle place the carrots and lemon, sugar, salt and water. Bring to a rolling boil. Cook over medium heat 10 to 15 minutes. Add cherries, cook 5 minutes more or until thickened. Pour into hot sterilized jelly glasses and seal at once.

This is a great way to use lots of carrots.

Makes about 4½ pints

PICKLED PEPPERS

4 quarts long red or yellow peppers
(Hungarian banana or other varieties)
1½ cups salt
2 cloves garlic
2 tablespoons prepared horseradish
10 cups vinegar
2 cups water
¼ cup sugar

Cut 2 small slits in each pepper. Wear rubber gloves to prevent burning hands. Dissolve salt in 4 quarts of water. Pour over peppers and let stand 12 to 18 hours in a cool place. Drain, rinse and drain thoroughly. Combine remaining ingredients and simmer 15 minutes. Remove garlic. Pack peppers into hot jars, leaving ¼-inch head space. Pour boiling pickling liquid over peppers leaving ¼-inch head space. Adjust caps. Process half and pints 10 minutes in boiling water bath.

Yield about 8 pints

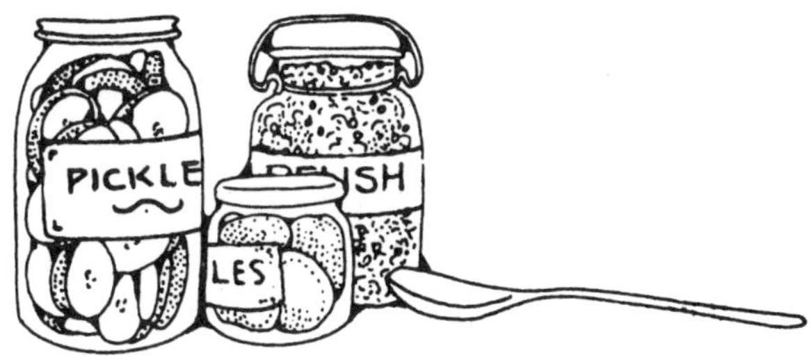

MUSTARD PICKLE

Wash and prepare:

1 quart small pickling cucumbers
1 quart cubed cucumbers (3 large)
1 quart green tomatoes, cut small
1 quart button onions, peeled
4 sweet green peppers, finely sliced
1 large cauliflower, cut into small pieces

Mix:

2 cups salt
4 quarts water

Pour over the vegetables. Let stand overnight. Bring to the boiling point and drain in a colander.

Mix:

1 cup flour
6 tablespoons dry mustard
1 tablespoon tumeric

Stir in:

Enough vinegar to make a smooth paste

Add:

2 cups sugar
Vinegar (2 quarts in all)

Boil until thick and smooth, stirring constantly. Add the vegetables and cook until they are just heated through. Overcooking makes them soft instead of crisp. Pour into jars and seal immediately.

Makes 8 pints

WATERMELON PICKLE

Lime water makes crisper pickles than salt water. Buy lime (calcium oxide) at the drug store.

Cut watermelon rind in 5 or 6-inch pieces. Cover with boiling water. Boil 5 minutes, drain and cool. Cut off the rind in small squares or wedges or in fancy shapes with a tiny cookie cutter. Weigh or measure. Cover with salted water (½ cup to each quart of water) or lime water (2 tablespoons to each quart of water). Let stand 6 hours in salted water or 3 in lime water. Drain, rinse and cover with fresh water. Simmer until tender. Drain. Add to Pickling Syrup. Simmer until the rind is clear and the syrup thick, adding water if necessary. Remove the spice bag. Pack in jars and seal.

PICKLING SYRUP

For a spicier syrup, add a tablespoon allspice and/or a piece of ginger root.

Put in a deep saucepan:

1 quart vinegar
1 cup water
2 pounds sugar (or more)

Tie in a piece of cheese cloth:

1 tablespoon whole cloves
1 stick cinnamon (1-ounce), broken into pieces

Add to the syrup. Simmer until the sugar dissolves. Enough for about 2 pounds (or 1½ to 2-quarts) of fruit.

CRACKER RELISH

1 (4½-ounce) can chopped ripe olives
1 small onion, minced
2 small tomatoes, peeled and finely chopped
Seasoned salt and pepper to taste
1 small green pepper, finely chopped
3 to 4 Italian peperoncini, finely chopped
Juice of 2 lemons

Combine all ingredients and chill several hours. Drain well before serving with crackers or melba toast. Or use rounds of zucchini, turnips or jicama.

Serves 6 to 8

CRANBERRY GRAPEFRUIT RELISH

2 large grapefruit
1 (16-ounce) can whole cranberry sauce
1 teaspoon sherry
¼ teaspoon allspice

Cut grapefruit in half and carefully cut out fruit. Reserve shells. Remove all white membrane and cut fruit sections into small pieces. Stir grapefruit into cranberry sauce along with sherry and allspice. Spoon mixture into grapefruit shells, mounding it up in the center. Serve as relish for poultry or pork.

Serves 4

ORANGE CRANBERRY WALNUT RELISH

2 cups fresh cranberries
1 navel orange
½ cup seedless raisins
¾ cup sugar
1 cup walnuts, chopped

Put orange, cranberries and raisins through a food chopper. Add sugar and walnuts and mix thoroughly. Chill and serve.

ORANGE CRANBERRY MOLD

1 recipe Orange Cranberry Walnut Relish
1 package strawberry jello
1 (#303) can jellied cranberries

Prepare jello according to directions. Melt cranberry jelly and add to jello. Chill in refrigerator until mixture is just starting to set. Fold in relish mixture and turn into a 2-quart mold. Allow to set. Unmold and garnish with fresh mint sprigs and watercress.

Serves 8

KUMQUAT-GINGER RELISH

4 cups kumquats (about 1 pound)
2 cups sugar
1 cup water
½ to 1 teaspoon ground ginger, depending on taste

Remove all stems and leaves from the kumquats. Wash fruit thoroughly. Combine sugar, water and ginger. Boil for 5 minutes. Add kumquats. Simmer, covered, over low heat for 45 minutes or until tender. Serve as a relish with roast chicken, duck or pork or as a sauce for ice cream.

Makes about 1 quart preserves

APPETIZERS

BEVERAGES

BREADS

CAKES

CANDY & NUTS

CANNING & MISC.

CASSEROLES

COOKIES

DESSERTS & FRUITS

EGGS, CHEESE AND PANCAKES

MEATS

PASTA, DRESSINGS, DUMPLINS & RICE

PIES

POULTRY

SALADS AND DRESSINGS

SAUCES

SEAFOOD

SOUPS & SANDWICHES

VEGETABLES